MW01090107

Advance Praise for *Serenade to the Blue Lady*

"Serenade to the Blue Lady is an inspiring tale of one of America's fallen heroes, a story rescued from the dusty archives of history that might help us all remember how much of the poetry of life—and the life of poetry—is lost in the hell of war."

—Phil Cousineau, author of *The Hero's Journey:*
Joseph Campbell on his Life and Work; Deadlines;
and *The Soul of the World* (with Eric Lawton)

"A bittersweet glimpse of a might-have-been Hemingway who had time for only one book—perhaps the single best memoir to come out of the war. This novel reminds us that war touches all of us, all these years later. What a life! What a loss!"

—Joe Hamelin, author of *To Fly and Fight*

"…A beautifully written account of the life of Bert Stiles. Anyone interested in World War II aviation will enjoy Cooper's excellent tribute to the life of Bert Stiles."

—Dan Bauer, author of *Great American Fighter Aces*

"Serenade to the Blue Lady is a masterful biography of Bert Stiles, the dramatic story of what it was like to fly and fight in the great aerial battles over the Continent—the exhilaration, the fear, the blood and death and, yes, the doubts. This is as real as it gets."

—Orr Kelly, author of *Hornet* and *Brave Men, Dark Waters:*
The Untold Story of the Navy Seals

SERENADE TO THE BLUE LADY

The Story of Bert Stiles

Robert Floyd Cooper

Cypress House

Fort Bragg, California

1993

Cypress House
155 Cypress Street
Fort Bragg, CA 95437
707-964-9520

Library of Congress Cataloging-in-Publication Data
Cooper, Robert Floyd, 1923–
    Serenade to the blue lady : the biography of Bert Stiles / Robert Floyd Cooper.
        p.   cm.
    Includes bibliographical references.
    ISBN 1-879384-21-3 :
    1. Stiles, Bert, 1920–1944—Biography. 2. Authors, American—20th century—Biography. 3. World War, 1939–1945—United States—Literature and the war.   I. Title.
    PS3537.T535Z63   1993
    813'.52—dc20   92-82993
    [B]   CIP
Printed on recycled paper in the United States of America

Excerpts from *Serenade to the Big Bird* by Bert Stiles reprinted by permission of W.W. Norton & Co., Inc. Copyright © 1947, 1975 by Mrs. Bert W. Stiles.

"A Fallen Friend" by kind permission of Richard Pressey.

"He Was Young" by kind permission of the Charles Leaming Tutt Library Special Collections, Colorado College, Colorado Springs, CO.

Photo on back cover by David Cooper.

Photo on page 211 by Universal Studios, Denver Colorado, courtesy of Special Collections, The Colorado College Library.

10 9 8 7 6 5 4 3 2 1

Dedication

To Mary, Kristen, Steven, and David

—

With Love and Gratitude

and...

To the memory of Bert Stiles

Contents

Preface

What we see modelled for us by everyone from our parents and friends to national and world figures can stand as a beacon for guidance or a matter for avoidance in the way we behave. How people live and grow, struggle with conflict, love and nurture, move against dark forces in themselves and others, discover zest and joy, and fulfill their destinies offer a rich source of knowledge for us in shaping our own lives. This fact is so omnipresent that we often don't see it and aren't aware of how much we are influenced.

In my early graduate school training in psychology, I was always curious about the assignment of White's *The Study of Lives*. Cast against the empirical, dry, hard science approach of the particular school in which I was studying, biography seemed too subjective and narrow. My professional experience has led me to a completely opposite view—that we learn much from the way other people live their lives.

Floyd Cooper offers us the story of an extraordinary young man whose life is the very best of models. Bert Stiles lived the kind of life that we admire and he demonstrated what it was like to be an open, zestful, inquiring human being. We have much to learn from knowing and immersing ourselves in his short, young life. We may even find in his story some of ourselves—the human qualities and experience that we have manifested, honored, and lived out—or that are prominent in our aspirations and dreams.

Bert lived with feeling—openly and deeply. Nothing in the human drama to which he was exposed was lost; he integrated it all. He constantly affirmed his love of life and the world, and the irony of the circumstance of his death blares loudly—his very lust for life and experience led him to a prolonged and fatal exposure.

In coming to know him we are caught up in the excitement and enthusiasm with which he lived. Bert's first love was writing and he reflected a remarkable creative process in the way he lived his life. Openness to feelings, awareness and contact with his inner self, a willingness to explore new forms of living and expression, an honoring of his intuition, and heightened powers of observation characterized him. These traits served him well in his writing endeavors.

When Bert lost his life in World War II, America lost a young man who seemed destined to join the ranks of Steinbeck and Hemingway. An extrapolation of his writing up to the fateful day in November, 1944, sustains this view. His published stories in such national magazines as *Saturday Evening Post* and *American Magazine*, written when he was barely 21 years old, are in themselves sufficient evidence for such a projection.

Bert joined a very select company of writers and poets when he wrote *Serenade to the Big Bird*, a book about his experiences flying missions as a B-17 co-pilot in the Eighth Air Force. Images are invoked of Rupert Brooke, Stephen Crane, Norman Mailer, and others who captured in words the horror and essence of war. Bert would take a writing pad with him on missions and make notes about his observations. On days off he would write his book, short stories, or a column for the *London Daily Mail*. While joining other crews in feeling the unspeakable relief of returning safely to England after a mission, he could also express his feelings by writing a poignant column about how beautiful the English landscape seemed to the fatigued returning airmen.

With his life in mortal danger, Bert would not give in to panic. His inner quest compelled him to observe the phenomena of war—clouds, the landscape below, flak, noise, bomber formation patterns, the planes of the fighter escort, his own inner terror, and the tragedies inflicted by the enemy on this comrades. Deeply courageous and loyal to his country's needs, Bert's writing during these times revealed his love of life and the world. His thrust to constantly expand the boundaries of his experience may have led to his downfall. Admiring the sleek, lightning-fast, P-51 fighter planes that escorted the big bombers to their targets, he volunteered for duty as a fighter pilot after he had completed his bomber missions. He died over Germany in late 1944.

One of the problems of describing the life of people who die young is that they may not leave much behind. Bert left a magnificent record of published and unpublished writings, essays, letters to family and friends, plus the reminiscences of his friends and others who knew him. Through these and the skill of his biographer we can come to know him as well as an old family friend. We see his hopes and dreams, the things he anguished over, his uncertainties, his search for his own identity, and, above all, his lust and enthusiasm for life.

In my own life and career as a university counseling psychologist, I have never witnessed the kind of spirituality in a young person that Bert Stiles manifested. In his writing he revealed a deep sense of openness and connectedness to the infinite—to his vision of God. He once wrote his mother:

> My God...is so wonderful, and beautiful, I can only sense Him. He is always there, whenever I want Him. He is just there...and I believe in Him. Maybe God is beauty itself, just beauty. Many times, when the stars and the moon are set in the deep blue, I sort of tighten up and wonder how anything could be so beautiful. Then I just look up and laugh at Him, or smile at Him, or give Him something of me. I guess I am really only giving something of me to me....

In reading his story, we get to know a young man who had the courage to look within himself and to trust his growing, changing processes. That such a fine young man was lost to the world so early, when he had so much to give it, is a point of sadness—but his overall work enables us to see his life as a matter of celebration.

Bert lived most of his life in the 1930s and 40s, a time that was every bit as complex and difficult for a young, growing person as today—although the content of problems and challenges facing today's youth have shifted somewhat.

Bert's story will remind some readers of the sweet days of their own youth—and fill them with the wonder and appreciation of their own youthful questing. For other, younger readers, his life underscores the sense of adventure and the hopes, dreams and struggles of being young. It will give all readers an appreciation of the beauty and sanctity of life.

Sumner Morris, Ed.D.
Counseling Psychologist
Director of Counseling Center (Retired)
University of California at Davis
September 1992

Foreword

In 1975, when I first read Bert Stiles' *Serenade to the Big Bird*—loaned to me by Dick Jones, a long-time Air Force friend—I was deeply moved by this young author's short autobiographical novel of flying bombers in combat in World War II. Having finished it and savored it, I felt I needed to know more about the man behind the book. A dozen or so years later, I began the quest to learn his life story—and write about it.

Richard H. Tyre, in his foreword to the first softcover printing of Stiles' book (Ballantine Books, 1947) writes: "If Bert Stiles loved every minute of his life, he also hated what he was doing. He thought war was 'ugly' and that people he was trained to bomb were just like us. His fervent wish was for a world…that will function…as one world."

If Bert Stiles had survived the war, I believe he would have contributed to a better world—whether by writing (his natural medium) or through entry into politics, teaching, activism, or other means of getting his strongly-felt message to the public—to the world. For he would have become a citizen of the world; he felt strongly about the need to "pull together" as one world.

Writing the story of Bert Stiles has been a special experience. In describing Bert's growing up in the western United States, adjusting to college, and becoming part of the Army Air Corps, I was writing about myself—I did all those things as well. Like Bert, I was a co-pilot on a B-17 in the Eighth Air Force. Unlike him, I did not transfer to a combat fighter group after completing bombing missions. If Bert had not done so he may have lived to fulfill his post-war destiny.

But the completion of bomber flying did not satisfy Bert Stiles' urge to experience life, to experience war, to live life to the fullest—even unto death.

Just who the "Blue Lady" was is speculative; Bert's friends, relatives, and biographers can only wonder. We do know he both respected and adored *his* Blue Lady. Whether She was Mother Mary or Lady Luck or some other presence, She was a constant, loving infinite being. That She lived in the sky made Her special—Bert loved the sky with its "mystical, mythical" qualities.

"Serenade" was a favorite word of his—he used it in letters, stories, in conversations with friends. It was probably synonymous to "farewell" to him—or perhaps the more romantic "I'll be seeing you." And I believe there is a tinge of fatalism in the term.

While my *Serenade* is biographical, it differs from a formal biography in its use of scenes and dialogue. There is evidence most of my "scenes" took place in one form or another. Words imputed to Bert (and even in some cases to his fellow conversationaiists) are taken from his journals, stories, or from *Serenade to the Big Bird*. Few thoughts herein did *not* originate with Bert Stiles.

Bert's letters and thoughts form an important part of this biography. Letters quoted were written by him with only a few minor changes for clarity. The chapter titles, subtitles, and opening paragraphs are Bert's own words—taken from his *Serenade* as well as from his essays and stories. Thus, this biography can be said to have been written as much by Bert as by myself.

The viability of a biography is only as strong as the sources available to the author. Sources were many, and the cooperation and interest shown by those relatives and friends interviewed was remarkable. It was almost as if Bert lived today: people remembered him, wanted to talk about him, and were still interested in his ideas, thoughts, and philosophies. It became clear to me that Bert Stiles is not a forgotten man.

The interest and cooperation shown to the writer by Bert's two sisters, May Stiles Hostetter and Elizabeth Stiles Lefsingwell, is much appreciated. May spent hours recalling her brother and other family members for my benefit. On the three or four occasions I met with her she couldn't have been more gracious or helpful. I corresponded with his younger sister, Beth; she spent many hours reading drafts and making constructive suggestions. She also furnished several photographs.

I met with Sam Newton, Bert's pilot and friend, and he recalled many anecdotes which appear in this biography. He was always willing to read a new draft or answer questions. Another fine experience was meeting with Jack Green, Bert's pilot during the latter stages of his bomber tour. He also read drafts and offered comments and suggestions.

The assistance of Dan Bauer, a writer and educator from Wisconsin, was of considerable importance. He had written a well-researched article on Bert for a flying magazine *(Air Classics,* May, 1987). As a result of his research, he knew more about Bert Stiles than anyone outside the family. He willingly shared information with me in person and by telephone, and was a significant member of my support team.

Rosemary Harley Prindle and Kay Bisenious Beimford were of inestimable help in sharing memories of their great friend, as well as ideas, criticism, and letters. Roland Dickison, Bert's "best friend," showed consistent interest and shared his memories and ideas from college days. Katherine Regan, who only knew Bert for one week during his time in England, delighted in sharing her ideas and reconstructed some of her conversations with Bert. Dr. Frank Krutzke, Bert's English instructor at Colorado College, showed a remarkable memory of those long-ago days and a sincere interest in this biography.

Strong interest and helpfulness were shown by fellow crew members of Bert's and other wartime friends: Jim Fletcher, who lived in the co-pilot's house with Bert; Gil Bradley, top turret-gun operator; Richard Pressey, who wrote a poem dedicated to Bert; Jim Starnes, Bert's flight leader in P-51s; and Gabriel Cutri, Bert's P-51 crew-chief.

Mrs. Ruth Aley, one half of Bert's well-loved literary agent team from New York, was helpful in looking over drafts. Bert's friends from college and high school contributed with their viewpoints: Dr. Robert Hermann, Jack Laws, Nancy Aitken, Dr. Melvin Johnson, Joel Husted, Steve Lowell, and others. Finally, an important acknowledgement is made to the Special Collections section of Colorado College for their cooperation in visits by the author to their stacks at Charles Leaming Tutt Library on that campus. The cooperation and interest of John Sheridan, Head Librarian, is gratefully acknowledged.

The author would also like to especially recognize with thanks a writer of the early 1950s, who first conceived the idea of writing about Bert Stiles. Hugh McGovern of Denver, with the help and cooperation of Elizabeth Stiles, Bert's mother, gathered under one cover most of Bert's letters, and, with some editing, was ready to publish them. For an unknown reason, it never happened. Mr. McGovern's thoroughness and dedication in the task was of considerable help and inspiration to me.

Grateful thanks to Cypress House President, Cynthia Frank, and Senior Editor, John Fremont, for their unfailing patience and professionalism in preparing this book for publication. And many thanks, as well, to Sumner Morris, who was enthralled by the mystique of Bert Stiles, for his encouragement and support. My nephew, Bob Cooper, an editor and writer, was helpful in editing and publicity. Several people who read drafts along the way were helpful—Mary Cooper, Dick Patrick, Jim Fletcher, Jerry Cooper, Marge Stein, and Dean Bailey. Thanks to Rick Patrick, who produced the original cover design. And finally, grateful acknowledgment to four established writers—Dan Bauer, Phil Cousineau, Joe Hamelin, and Orr Kelly—who gave of their time, knowledge, and critical skills.

Certain people at certain times make an indelible impression upon their contemporaries. Such a man was Bert Stiles, who in his 24 years left behind so much of himself in his writings, and so much in the memories of his relatives and friends. I hope *Serenade to the Blue Lady* will introduce him to new generations of readers who, perhaps unconsciously, are looking for someone to admire—for a hero, if you will, from another time.

R.F.C.

He Was Young

He was young and he dared to sing
Of freedom, love and eternal spring;
He was akin to the stars and the trees,
And claimed full brotherhood with these;
With eagle thoughts he braved the skies,
And looked on God with fearless eyes.
His straight young body and his unborn song
He hurled with a shout at evil and wrong;
And we who waited with sobbing breath
Can almost envy his rich young death.

—Anonymous

1

ONE MAN GONE,
A MILLION MORE TO GO

"Killing is in my mind, but not in my blood...."

On the run to Metz they carried a maximum load of fragmentation bombs and went after a Luftwaffe field. For the first time, Bert Stiles flew the bomb run; pride and fear fought for dominance among a multitude of emotions.

As Stiles steered the bomber to an England-bound course, black puffs suddenly appeared. The plane lurched and gagged as steel sliced into the wings. Little slivers of glass splintered around the cockpit. The right wing bucked and smoke curled out of the oil cooler.

"Number Four's on fire," Bird shouted over the interphone.

But Gil Spaugh said coolly from the nose, "Just smoke, sir."

"Smoke means flame," Ross said distinctly.

"Flame means you blow up," Sharpe said.

"All right, all of you," Sam Newton said, his voice husky, "stay off the interphone. Our Number Four is hit but we're not on fire." He glared at his co-pilot and snapped, "Feather Number Four."

Bert Stiles hit the feathering button and the fuel shut-off switch in one swift motion. He killed the mixture control, chopped the throttle and shut down the propeller control. Then he and Sam just sat there and watched while the propeller windmilled and finally feathered into a clean, upright "Y."

Behind them, twenty-year-old Bill Lewis had watched every move his co-pilot made, concentrating fiercely. Now he nodded.

The smoke had stopped before they left Germany. And then the interphone became a sounding board.

"I thought we'd had it," Ross said.

"I was halfway through the door," Spaugh added.

"Shut up on interphone," Sam said. "Anybody hurt?"

No answer.

"Take oxygen check, Bird," Sam said. "Get on the ball."

Still no answer.

Bert had a swift mental shot of the whole lower half of the plexiglass up front shot away. Benson and Bird gone, simply *vanished.*

Then Grant Benson came through cool and easy. "We're all okay here. Everything under control."

With the first flak burst Don Bird had put his feet up on the plexiglass, hiding under his flak suit. A piece of metal came through the bottom and went out the top. A jagged piece of plexiglass clipped him on the forehead and he fell over backward.

"I thought I was already dead," he said later. "I could hear the reaper, I could see the big sickle."

There wasn't much blood, but a little blood went a long way. Above them, Lewis kept looking at the feathered propeller.

"That's real honest-to-God battle damage," he said.

A jagged hole in the bullet-proof glass behind Sam Newton was also the subject of Lewis' intense interest. Flak had ripped off the metal on the lower edge of the upper turret.

Looking it over later, Bert and Lewis decided the gunner hadn't missed death by more than a long inch.

Bert could see at least three wings of B-17 Fortresses, all heading home now, their job for the day done. *Think on this, Stiles: 100 or so American bombers out there, each with ten men aboard, most of them too young to vote.* With Sam flying, he had time to look out his right window:

> I don't know a thing about killing Germans. I've never been shot at, or
> bombed. The only way I know about this war is through books and

movies and magazine articles, and listening to a few guys who came back. Killing is in my mind, but not in my blood.

The whole idea is to blow just as much hell out of Germany, and kill just as many healthy German workers as possible, and if any women or little kids get in the way, and have their legs torn off, or their faces caved in, tough. T.S.

From way up high, it doesn't mean much to me. But the more I think of it the uglier it seems.

We would be up here again tomorrow—or the next day or the next. What I wanted to do tomorrow was ski down the Canyon Run on Baldy up at Sun Valley, or wade out into the surf at Rosarita, and get all knocked out in the waves, and come in and lie in the sun all afternoon, and maybe make love in the moonlight.

Instead I was going back to war.

Bert was flying when the urgent calls started coming in. "I'm going down," a hoarse voice said. Bert looked wildly around for a plane in trouble. "Our oxygen's gone," the voice went on. "Can you get us some escort?" The heavy breathing, like a horse, was clearly evident over the radio. "My navigator is shot to hell. I got to go down." There was terror in the voice now.

Bert looked up into the soft blue sky. Somewhere up there a navigator was dying. It was pretty hard to believe.

Benson called on interphone. "Now we're over Belgium," he said.

"That big town down there is Brussels." Benson could have been a guide for a Rotary tour.

With too little to do and no flak in sight, Bert took his flak suit off. His neck ached and his shoulder was sending him sympathy pains. He dumped the thing down in the catwalk between the pilots' seats. Belgium was still enemy territory. The co-pilot found it hard to believe that somewhere down in the crazy patchwork of farms and towns and beaches there were some hard-eyed killers still hoping to knock off a bomber.

Sam was monitoring VHF radio and yelled at Bert, "That navigator is still dying. This pilot keeps calling that his navigator is dying. What the hell good does that do?"

Bert just stared at Sam; he had no answer.

They crossed the European coast and everyone relaxed. Sam eased the big plane into a gentle glide and the formation loosened a little at 16,000 feet. Bert took his oxygen mask off; when he rubbed his face it felt like a piece of fish: clammy, cold, alien, wet.

Abruptly, he put his mask back on—16,000 feet was still high. He wondered whether other crew members had taken off their masks. Wait a minute—he was the oxygen officer: he'd better make damn sure they still wore them.

"Co-pilot to crew," he said, "let's have a final oxygen check. Start with Tail Gunner. How you doin', Ed?"

"I'm doin' fine, thank you, co-pilot, sir," Ed Sharpe retorted. Bert visualized Sergeant Sharpe in his narrow funnel of a home, behind the soaring upswept tail. Ed was twenty-one years old, off a farm near Hot Springs, Arkansas. He had told the crew he expected to return to the farm after the war and simply lie under a shady tree. In the meantime, he was inclined to be something of a joker. Bert winced when he thought of Ed's position in the tail—just enough space to sit or crouch on his knees while he manned his two 50-caliber machine guns. There were windows on either side of his head, and another in front of him as he sat facing to the rear of the airplane ready to fire on fighters coming in at six o'clock.

"Right waist gunner okay," Gil Spaugh's deep voice reported. Sergeant Spaugh, also twenty-one, was a good-looking red head from Winston-Salem, North Carolina. Slow-talking and deliberate, he had told Bert once that he hadn't done much of anything before the war but go to the beach. His gunner's position was about mid-ships in the B-17's long tube of a fuselage. Gil stood beside his machine guns, which were mounted on brackets and pointing out the large open window. His line of fire covered the right side of the airplane, but not much above or below it.

There was a moment's silence before a voice boomed over interphone. "Left waist gunner still breathing pure oxygen." Basil Crone manned the left side of the Fortress, his back to Spaugh when in firing position. When out of any danger area, the two waist gunners chatted, sat on the metal floor, even tried a kind of sleeping. Crone tickled Bert; he had his kind of humor, he supposed, whatever that was. Bert sensed a kindred soul in Crone; he had lived all over Middle America and done most everything—oil fields, ranch hand, sheet-metal worker. On the crew, he was also the armorer and the only one on Keystone Mama who knew much about bombs or bomb racks. Crone was a round little guy, a sort of young caricature of Churchill.

"Ball-turret gunner okay," Beach said. Beach, the quiet man, was the oldest on the crew by far. At thirty-four, he had *really* been around, Bert supposed. Sergeant Gordon Beach was from Denver and Bert felt an affinity for him for that reason. Beach had been a mechanic, at least during the week. On weekends he was usually fishing for cutthroat in the Rockies. He was a quiet, sleepy-headed guy and the only married man on the crew.

What a place to fight a war, Bert thought—cramped as tight as a knuckle in a socket in a revolving turret. And locked in at that. He controlled his position by power as he aimed his 50s at incoming fighters from below. Beach was small, slim, dark-haired and balding. Bert didn't know him well yet, but he wanted to—he wanted to know what kind of man accepted a ball-gunner's unique position with such trust and stoicism.

"Radio doing fine, Lieutenant," Ed Ross said, and Bert realized that the choice of words probably meant that Ed was letting them know again of his exploits in London during their last leave. Ross, who was twenty-three, was from Buffalo, New York, and had also been around. He had been a clerk in civilian life and had jumped at the chance of life in the Army Air Force as a flying sergeant. Ross was a handsome devil, Bert thought—dark hair, good build, nice smile.

His radio operator's post was in a kind of cabin just forward of the bomb bays and aft of the pilot's compartment. At his table on the left side of the plane he operated VHF and liaison radio sets, marker-beacon, the homing set, and radio altimeter. He could be a very busy man—or have nothing to do at all. During fighter attacks, his 50-caliber guns pointed to the rear from a slot at the top of the cabin.

"Engineer okay, sir," Lewis said from immediately behind Bert. The co-pilot had a good feeling about Lewis; although the kid was only twenty years old, he gave off an aura of confidence, particularly about engines. Bert admired anyone who knew about engines; *he* sure as hell didn't. Lewis hadn't done much after high school except drive a cab in his native Grand Island, Nebraska, and take his girl out whenever he could.

Lewis manned the upper turret when he wasn't watching the engine readings or advising the pilots about the workings of the B-17. The Engineer customarily stood behind the pilots, watching over their shoulders for any sign of trouble. When fighters attacked, he became an instant gunner and Sam and Bert had to fend for themselves.

15

"Bombardier station okay," Don Bird said from the nose. As a fellow officer, Bert had seen more of Bird than he had of the enlisted men. They had bunked together, eaten together, gone on liberty together. Don was twenty-four, from Oswego, New York, and, before the war had worked in a bank. As a bombardier instructor, he could probably have avoided combat altogether; but he had talked about his ambitions with Sam and Bert one night at the Officers Club in Alexandria, Louisiana. "I guess I want to see what a war is all about," he said. "I want to wear the ETO ribbon with a star on it."

Bird was smallish, wiry, and careful in his actions and thoughts. He and Bert were not particularly close. His work station was in the very front of the airplane, directly behind a conical plexiglass bubble from which all the world stretched before him. To his left were his instrument panel and bomb controls, including a switch operating the bomb bay doors and a release switch for toggling the bombs. The Norden bombsight itself was kept in the navigator's space.

"Navigator okay, Bert," Grant Benson said. Bert felt drawn to the slim, blond, twenty-two-year-old Benson. The navigator was not easily ruffled and fit in well with the crew. From Stambaugh, Michigan, he had attended a year or so at Michigan State, then knocked around the country before joining the Army as an infantryman. Later, he had eagerly transferred to the Air Corps.

Benson's area was directly behind Bird's in the nose cone. Above his head was the navigator's astrodome. His desk extended across the back of the bombardier's seat and had a radio compass recessed in its right side. On Grant's sidewall were such accouterments as a driftmeter, an aperiodic compass, a map case, and oxygen, interphone and suit heater outlets.

"Pilot okay," San Newton said at Bert's side. It might be considered unnecessary for the pilot to tell his co-pilot that he was okay and still breathing oxygen, but Sam believed in crew discipline and so completed the ten-man oxygen check. Sam was twenty-three years old and had left his home in Sioux City, Iowa, to attend Colorado College. He had first met Bert when both pledged the Phi Gamma Delta fraternity there. They had been friends but not particularly close. He had joined the Air Force in May 1943 and had gone through most of his training on the West Coast. Having been selected for first pilot training, he had gone through intensive B-17 training in Hobbs, New Mexico.

The two pilots had met again by accident at the Second Air Force combat pool depot in Salt Lake City and had talked a WAC into putting them on the same crew.

Bert considered himself lucky to have a friend and a first-class pilot as his head man. Sam was tallish and stocky, with dark hair and a casual manner most of the time. When flying, though, Bert had noted that Sam was all business, and inclined, in fact, to be something of a disciplinarian.

They began a gradual letdown over the Channel, their formation loosening a bit more. Bert knew he was over-controlling the throttles again, but he was hot, his oxygen mask was trying to gag him, and he was tired almost beyond measure.

He didn't even see the black, twin-engine fighter flying parallel to them, high on the port side. But Sam Newton did.

"Pilot to crew," Sam called on interphone. "The plane at ten o'clock high is a Mosquito. One of ours. Do not shoot. Repeat—do not shoot!" Sam figured it was their base C.O., flying out to check his returning warriors.

The Mosquito resembled the German JU-88; a few Mosquitoes had accidentally been shot down by U.S. bomber aircrews.

But Colonel Terry was not out just to observe his troops. Sam, still on interphone, didn't hear the colonel's transmission. But Bert Stiles did.

"Commander to all Red Swordfish aircraft," the colonel said. "We have reports that General Eisenhower is due at our base this afternoon. So tighten up that formation. You're flying like a bunch of drunken cadets. Let's show the General what a sharp outfit we have. Come on, *tighten up that formation.*"

Bert, flying his airplane as best he could, took the orders personally. God, he thought, we've been four hours in formation over enemy territory, getting shot at by everyone and his niece, and the Colonel wants to put on an air show for the General. He lost control momentarily.

"Oh, blow it out your ass, Colonel," he said on VHF.

There was a moment of stunned silence from the Mosquito. Then the Colonel angrily replied: "Who said that?"

Once again, Bert spoke into his mike: "You will never know."

The C.O. came on again, and Bert could sense his anger and frustration. "Aircraft who just transmitted, identify yourself. Repeat, who made that crack?"

There was complete radio silence from more than thirty airplanes.

"Transmitting aircraft, state your number and pilot's name."

Silence once again. "This is a direct order. You are already guilty of insubordination. Don't make it worse. Who are you? Who the hell is transmitting?"

Still silence all around.

Sam Newton had not become privy to the exchanges. Bert decided not to enlighten him.

Less than an hour later Sam brought the B-17 in gently in a full stall landing. As they were unloading equipment, they watched planes from another squadron land. Red flares arched skyward in the traffic pattern; someone had been hurt—or was dead.

The equipment hut was jammed with people and it smelled like a stable.

"How was it?" someone asked.

Bert turned and saw that it was the Catholic chaplain. He forced a smile and said, "Milk run. A joy ride."

The chaplain's return smile was just as forced. He was not fooled. "They shot down two," he said. "The whole crews are gone."

Bert heard the details later. The two Fortresses had been in the high composite, and had made a 360-degree turn at the target when they ran smack into a group of ME 109s there in the clouds. The Germans had come out of the sun and made only one pass. One Fort blew up and one went down burning. Bert knew both co-pilots; one he had called La French because he couldn't pronounce his French-sounding name.

Bert felt his skin tingle and his eyes mist as he stood in the crowded equipment room thinking of his late acquaintance:

> La French was a good guy, the kind of guy you want to be around. He was all alive the last time I saw him. He rode that bike of his like it was Seabiscuit. And now he was just blood and little chunks of bones and meat, blown all over the sky. Or he was cooked, burned into nothing.

After debriefing, Colonel Terry called a brief meeting of all officers on the mission to Metz.

"All right, gentlemen," he said. "One of you transmitted a personal insult to me, your commanding officer. Now, who was it? This is a direct order: speak up *now.*"

There were lots of exchanged glances, some guffaws, and various puzzled looks from those who hadn't heard of the incident. Sam Newton looked at Stiles, Bird, and Benson, in order.

"Know anything about this?" he asked, sotto voce.

All three looked surprised, puzzled, and slightly insulted. Bert grandly rolled his eyeballs.

A few minutes later, the Colonel, frustrated, decided not to push the issue further. He barked, "Dismiss," and strode angrily out the door.

General Eisenhower never did show up at their base.

Bert Stiles walked to his quarters alone, begging off from a ride in a jeep with Sam and some of the others. Bassingbourn, home of the 91st Bomb Group, spread out on all sides—runways, taxi strips, hangars, buildings of all shapes and sizes. It had been an RAF airfield and its accommodations were superior to most newer bases built hurriedly by the U.S. Army.

He and Sam lived in a two-story square building called the co-pilot's house—the name originally given it by the RAF. It was just the two of them in one large room at the front of the building. Compared to combat officers in other Eighth Air Force stations, it was heaven. Bassingbourn was widely known as the "Country Club of the Eighth" and the co-pilot's house was an example of its special facilities. It was like Colorado College all over again—the quarters were even better than the Phi Gam house in the Springs. And the co-pilot's house had something extra: an orderly named Tommy. It was a fine feeling, like in a Jeeves novel, having your own man around to make you feel special.

Bert entered their room; it was empty. Throwing his cap and jacket on his bed under the window, he stared out through the thick glass, thinking again of La French:

> One man gone, a million more to go. Maybe everyone in the world will get it this time. There are shells enough to go around. If some efficiency expert could just figure a way, there would never have to be another war. The senselessness of it, the ugliness, is overwhelming.
>
> In an endless procession, wars have swept the world, growing from stupid little brawls with clubs and rocks to the mechanical perfection of a city flattened, so many bombs to the acre, so many planes per square mile. Fill up the bomb bays and send the planes over; send in the ground troops to bayonet the ones who were only stunned.

Soon his despair faded, leaving only doubt and a deep sadness. Forbidding himself such morbid thoughts on a fine sunny afternoon, he strode out the door to look for his bicycle. Billy Behrend, a co-pilot who lived across the hall, was behind the building inspecting his own bike. Bert didn't know him well. Billy was smiling now; Bert had never seen him without a smile.

"It's early," Billy said. "Let's go for a ride."

They rode out into the countryside following a twisting dirt road. There was a church with old gray walls, and houses with thatched roofs, and a pub in a village too small to justify one. Breathing deeply of the country air, Bert's mood lightened. It was good to be where he was. Just to be moving, just to be riding down a road on a bicycle, laughing once in a while, not knowing where the road led and not caring. The world was endlessly big—so big and soft and magical.

He and Billy were crowded off the road for a moment by some little kids pulling a wagon full of milk bottles. A bit farther on, they came across a muddy pond with some dirty ducks reveling there. They marveled at the symmetry of the hedgerows and saw woods blanketed in bluebells.

He knew he could have died that day; he already felt he was on intimate terms with death. To be on *any* terms with death was sobering enough. Combat is a frame of mind, he concluded: it requires commitment and temporary abandonment of the soul. It demands sacrifice of self.

And what is truly horrible, he thought as he steered his bike around a pothole, is that the presence of death demands a sort of zest for life—an unnatural, shameful zest. Ergo, war is most shameful when it is most glorious. Theory of mine.

> There are all kinds of people, senators and whores and barristers, and bankers and dishwashers. There are Cockneys and Gypsies and Fascists. There are strip teasers and Lesbians and cornhuskers and longshoremen. And there are writers and lieutenants and shortstops and liars. There are prime ministers and thieves and presidents and drunks. There are forest rangers and Germans and beggars and holy rollers.
>
> And some day we are going to catch on that no matter where they were born, or how their eyes slant, or what their skin color is, they are just people. They have legs and arms and eyes, if they are lucky. Some have breasts and some have testicles.
>
> But they are people. They are not masses. They are not slaves. They are people, partly good, partly bad, mostly balancing out. And until we call them people, all of them, we are going to have a sick world.

Enough of this somber philosophy, he thought. Look at the lowering sunlight on the willow trees, listen to the whisper of the wind through the aspens. There is still a little hope there, and love, and perhaps compassion. There are still little kids, and mudpies, and hollows deep in the timber where the rabbits roam.

Billy, who had been at Bassingbourn for nearly a month and knew the countryside, swung wide into a narrow lane.

"Hey, Stiles," he said, "I think this is Cambridge Road. Yeah, it is. There's a place up here where they sell fresh strawberries."

Fresh strawberries were sort of an impossible dream, like milkshakes and Sun Valley and riding the waves on the beach below La Jolla. They found the place, a wide green field swarming with the luscious fruit. The farmer's wife would only sell them four pounds each. Cradling their purchases, and anxious now to return to their base to start a royal feast, they turned their bicycles around and headed back the way they had come.

A little way down the road they came to a tree-lined dirt lane that led to a huge castle of a country house.

"Let's stop and eat these," Billy said.

They left their bikes outside the fence, went through an unlocked gate and found a wide tree to flop under.

The sun filtered through the leaves and the grass had a cool, sweet smell to it. For a moment Bert felt a sense of peace, a quiet wave of relief. It didn't last long; in the far distance, he could hear planes. Intuitively, he knew they were fighters, probably coming home from shooting up Paris.

"Think they're P-51's?" Billy asked, his mouth flush with strawberries.

Bert looked at him with quick interest. "I'm sure of it. Hey, are you another frustrated fighter pilot?"

"Yeah, I guess I am. I sort of like these Forts; well, I respect them anyway. Eleven missions out of the way. Brought us back every time. But I would personally much rather fly a fast, sweet ship like the Mustang any day."

Bert's interest had sharpened. "Hey, let's work together on this thing. I've got a long way to go—twenty more of these buggers. But then—God, I'd just love to get in the seat of a '51, take off with tail up, roam the skies. Think of the speed and independence! God."

The two new friends talked for a while about their mutual interest, popping strawberries into their mouths between thoughts. Later, stretching out in the still-warm sunshine, his stomach full, a friend by his side, Bert let his mind wander. He was in high school; he was in Denver; and he was in love with the world.

2

A MERRY LIFE
IN THE BEST OF COMPANY

"When I was 10 I told my mother that
I never wanted to get any older...."

A Fort lives in the sky, from three to six miles up, and the only real things up there are the throttles and the feathering buttons, the engine gauges and the rudder pedals, an oxygen mask full of drool, and a relief can half full of relief. The flak is real when it clanks on the wings. The rest of the time it is only a nightmare of soft black puffs and yellow flashes right outside your window.

"Listen, I can get my dad's car tomorrow," Paul McClung said to his closest friend. "Let's buzz up to Estes Park."

They were walking down the broad front steps of South High School, through for the day. Paul had turned sixteen and had his driver's license. Bert Stiles was a reluctant fifteen; his birthday wasn't for another three months.

Bert pummeled his friend on the back. "Great idea, buddy," he said, a grin spreading over his face. Bert, slimly built, with black hair and a slightly dusty complexion, was instantly enthusiastic. If there was anything he liked more than lake fishing, it was skiing in the Rockies. But now, on this sparkling day in May 1936, the season was for fishing.

"I have to clear the way with the parents, though, Paul," he went on. "There's something on with church this weekend. Can't remember exactly what. Call you after dinner."

Washington Park Methodist Church, in their South Denver neighborhood, was an important outlet for Elizabeth and Bert W. Stiles, Bert's parents. They expected their three children to attend church regularly.

Bert had recently crystallized his thoughts about God and church: he was *for* God, but not necessarily for the organized church. But he had realized no success whatsoever in securing the acceptance of this doctrine by his parents.

Bert used every step of the four-block walk from South High School to his house at 1245 South York Street to compose his speech to his parents. He picked time and place carefully—after dinner, in the comfortable dark-panelled living room, with his sisters May and Beth present for support.

"It isn't *that* often I get a ride to the mountains," he began, "and already Paul is a good driver."

His parents looked up curiously, his mother from clearing the table in the adjacent dining room, his father from reading the *Denver Post.* May and Beth were both studying; neither looked up. Elizabeth and Bert W. Stiles exchanged glances.

Bert told them about his longing to try the lakes above Estes Park that weekend. It was the right time: the water level had receded a bit, the weather was clear, and Paul had wheels. Bert added he would pack his own lunch, get to bed early, and not disturb them in the morning.

"Bert, have you forgotten the Epworth League picnic tomorrow?" his mother asked. "Don't you *want* to go?"

It was the kind of question Bert hated. "I'd *normally* want to go, Mom," he said, carefully. "But this is the first chance I've had to go fishing since last October."

"Seems you have a pretty clear choice, Bert. Church picnic as planned, or taking your pleasure."

Bert looked at his father for support; Bert W. loved fishing as much as his son did.

"Lake fishing is good for the soul, Elizabeth," he said.

"But—but—you've known about the church picnic for weeks."

Both May, two years younger than Bert, and Beth, nearly four years younger, had become interested observers. May, who was nearly as enthusiastic about most sports as Bert was, aimed a surreptitious wink at him to show support.

"You know, Mom, Dad," he went on, quickly, "I can find God up there, too. It doesn't have to be in church. I feel closer to Him in the mountains than anywhere else. In fact," he added, "God is *there*. I'll be talking with him tomorrow—if I get to go."

Elizabeth Stiles hesitated. Was her family *willing* her to allow Bert to miss the church picnic? In the end, she relented, somewhat sadly, but with grace.

As the oldest of the three children, and the only boy, Bert often felt he was the guinea pig for his siblings. But far from resenting it, he relished it.

Bert's father had graduated from Colorado College in 1910, and worked for a few years as an English teacher. Then, due to lack of pay in that profession, he had decided to work for himself. He formed his own electrical company in Denver after World War I.

Elizabeth Huddleston Stiles had moved West from Jackson, Mississippi, to marry Bert W. Her father, George Washington Rufus Huddleston, was a Methodist minister and president of Millsap University in Jackson. After graduating from Millsap, she earned a Masters Degree from Columbus University in Psychology and English.

Bert's parents had met when Bert W. visited Jackson while stationed at an Army base near there. They were married in Jackson in 1919, with her father officiating. Their first home was in Loveland, Colorado. They later moved to Pueblo, and finally Denver, where they settled for a lifetime.

Bert Stiles was born on August 30, 1920, at St. Luke's Hospital in Denver. When she first held her baby, his mother called him a Japanese doll because he was small-boned and cute and had jet black ringlets of hair.

In later years, Bert remembered his third-grade teacher, Miss Chrysinger, who smacked him on the behind because he laughed at a little girl when her dress flew up and showed her drawers. And how could he forget Miss Myers, who ordered her entire class to build birdhouses? Or Miss Brierly, who stood watch in the shower room to keep them from sliding on their stomachs across the floor? And there was Mrs. Pascal, who made her class stand and recite a poem each day.

Bert later wrote a theme he called *Dear Mother:*

> I had the kind of childhood a child ought to. I was the happiest little
> boy who ever lived. When I was 10 I told my mother that I never

wanted to get any older. It was too much fun being little, playing kick-the-can in the alley on long spring nights, going on hikes in Cherry Creek Forest, swimming in the park late at night and getting chased by the cops, riding my bike all over everywhere. And going fishing with my dad, and kissing Jane at a sixth grade party.

There was never much money. Competition from larger electrical firms kept B. W. Stiles working long hours to support his family of five. Through a labor of love, Elizabeth Stiles contributed to the family income by teaching piano in her home nearly every day. She also taught her own children to play. Beth was a natural musician; she was to inherit her mother's ability and love for music. May and Bert took piano with less skill and more complaints. There were other lessons, too: Bert on the clarinet, May on violin, and Beth on cello.

Often, they formed a family trio, playing at church or family gatherings.

To such neighborhood friends as Ralph and Eleanor Knight, Travis Railey, and David McWilliams, Bert was free-spirited and friendly. In the mid 1930s, after he entered junior high, Bert wrote:

> Byers was a bad time in a lot of ways. There was always something about sex to worry about, and to try to look up in dictionaries. The girls all started to get cagey and fill out, and the boys mostly had pimples, and I had to learn how to dance.

"Bert," his father said one spring day in 1933, "I don't think you've always enjoyed yourself going to my fraternity with me. But you might this time—next Friday night."

Bert looked up from his book. "Why is that, Dad?"

"Dutch Clark will be there."

Bert leaped to his feet. "Really? You're not kidding, are you, Dad? My gosh!"

Bert had kept a football scrapbook since he was about seven years old, and Dutch Clark filled several pages. Clark was a halfback from Colorado College in the late 1920s. A few years later, Bert wrote: "When he came along and swivel-hipped his way to football immortality, he became my idol. I lived and dreamed Dutch for three years; he was my hero of heroes."

Late Friday afternoon, B.W. and his twelve-year-old son drove the sixty-odd miles South on Highway 75 to Colorado Springs. It was one of the highlights of Bert's life to meet Dutch at the famous "Bull Pen" of the

Phi Gamma Delta fraternity at Colorado College. Bert followed Colorado College closely, along with other schools in the Rocky Mountain Conference.

The young Colorado native loved sports. He had learned tennis from his father, a good player, and he, in turn, taught his sister May to play. Beth was not particularly interested. Bert became a proficient tennis player, strong on quickness and agility, less so on the skills of the game.

But Bert learned to ski on his own, and fell headlong in love with the excitement, the speed, the sheer romanticism of downhill skiing. Later, he wrote about sports:

> I could have made it in at least three: basketball, tennis, baseball, perhaps swimming. Then there is fishing, so lovely a sport. And there are others I have chased after: football, golf, mountain climbing.
>
> There is only one sport which is completely satisfying for me—skiing. It is a *joyful* sport. I love the freedom, the speed, the exhilaration, the *joy.* Skiing folk are carefree and get a kick out of things. The best cracks and the fastest comebacks flow glibly from the mouths of skiers. Skiers lead a merry life in the best of company.

The family journeyed to the mountains often despite the cost of gasoline and lack of discretionary money. Bert fished with his father, with friends, alone. These were halcyon days for him, in the mountains fishing or skiing.

A few years later, Bert wrote to his friend Kermit Livingston about his feelings for sports:

> What I've got—athletically—are two things: fine coordination and competitive spirit. I learn how to play fast and I love to play. I'm not big and I'm not overpoweringly strong. What I want most is to look good at a sport, to have good form, to play gracefully. I want to win, too, but I don't care much if I lose.

Bert developed other interests while growing up in Denver. He rose like a meteor in Boy Scouts; merit badges in camping, trail-marking, compass, fire-starting, and identification of stars clearly showed his interest in the outdoors. At a Court of Honor on December 16, 1935, he was awarded the Star Scout award by Charles Stavely, the scoutmaster, with his parents, sisters, and cousin Frank Stiles in the audience.

But he dropped out within a month: there were just too many other things to look into. And scouting had become too structured for his free-spirited thinking.

By age fifteen he questioned rather than reacted; dreamed instead of analyzed; developed his imagination rather than his conformity. Much of the time he pleased his parents; he *liked* to—when he could. Other times, he rebelled. Did he *have* to follow their guidelines all the time?

Other interests—strong, long-standing ones—were reading and writing. He read everything he could lay hands on. He told Kermit Livingston that he first read *Robin Hood* when he was six years old, and figured he had read it five or six more times before high school. His usual method of selecting a book in the library at Washington Park was to seek out those that were the most thumbed. Favorites were Thomas Wolfe's *Look Homeward Angel* and the adventure books of Nordhoff and Hall. He subscribed to *Boys Life* and read each issue straight through.

At Byers Junior High and, later, South High School, there would be an occasional writing assignment. Bert's friends would moan and groan at the pesky composition. How to begin? What words to use? How to put those words into cogent sentences? But Bert loved the task. He would begin with hardly a thought, and the words would flow, and flow pleasurably.

He soon knew the deep joy writing gave him—feelings of completeness, intense satisfaction, creativity. He was hooked for life, never happier than when he was creating sentences from words, paragraphs from sentences, a story from an accumulation of paragraphs. He was amazed at the way words flowed. He decided they must come from deep within his secret self.

Until 1932, the Stiles family had been living in a one bedroom-with-sleeping-porch house on South Race Street. With a family of five, and children ranging from eight to twelve, B.W. Stiles concluded the family needed more room. They liked their neighborhood in South Denver just off University Avenue. Friends and relatives were nearby. So they waited until a neighborhood house became available, settling on a two bedroom, one bath house on South York Street. They were still close to church, shopping, and schools. South High School, where they planned to send all three children, was four blocks away.

Their new home boasted such refinements as a music room and a separate dining room. There was also a partially-finished basement. For the first time in his life, Bert had his own room, carved out of the front part of the basement. He moved all of his books downstairs, borrowed an old radio from his friend Jack Scott, and had all he needed, the significant ingredient being privacy.

The three Stiles siblings were close enough in age to be good friends, but far enough apart to have their own sets of friends. May was strong and wiry, with blue eyes and light brown hair. She joined Bert in sports activities—particularly tennis and mountain climbing. Beth, younger than May by about twenty months, was much like her mother, with a dominant interest in music and the arts. In looks, with her brown eyes and dark brown hair, she was more like her brother.

Bert didn't date until high school, although he had been well aware of girls since grammar school. Later, while overseas, he wrote: "I have spent most of my life in love with some doll or other. It began with a gal named Jacquie I kissed at a party in the sixth grade and ever after there was always someone."

By the time he entered high school in the fall of 1935, Bert was ready for the challenge. Realizing it wasn't all fun and games, that he would be developing character traits which would deeply influence his life, he determined to make the most of it. Some teachers made a lasting impression upon him. In memoirs written several years later, he wrote:

> I remember Miss Morrison, a tiny, white-haired woman, who made her classes memorize theorems word for word, and every proof step by step, just for the good of the mind. She thought the world was going to hell because the people in it were lazy and undisciplined thinkers. She said math was good for me because it made me think coherently and logically and reasonably.

It was an easy five minute walk—or three-minute bicycle ride—from his home to South High School. The brick school building, at the corner of East Louisiana and South Franklin street, was composed of several connecting wings, with vast athletic fields behind it. The high school served most of the South area of Denver. There were about 2,500 students enrolled when Bert Stiles attended.

A tower stood atop the administration building which was famous for its four-faced clock. Bert noted later in a letter to a friend: "None of the four faces ever agreed because the pigeons used to sit on the hands."

Soon after he entered high school, Elizabeth Stiles, a perceptive woman, noted in her journal: "Bert already has a life of his own. His contemporaries know more about his thoughts than his parents do." Her acknowledgment of this showed respect for him as a separate and distinct individual, and added to his security and self-esteem.

"I want to thank you, Mom," Bert said one day in his mother's kitchen. He had just trudged upstairs from his room in the basement to join his mother as she prepared dinner.

She turned and smiled at him. "Whatever for, Bert?"

He returned her smile. "Well, actually, for a lot of things. What I had in mind was for your special genes—your *English* genes. You were a college grad in English, and you taught English. Well, some of it has come down to me."

"You've always done well in English, Bert."

"Sometimes it's embarrassing. Almost always A's. I do best on themes. And I've been writing more short stories. Sometime I'm going to have to see if anyone wants to read them. Oh, I don't mean family," he added, quickly. "You'd read them just out of loyalty, wouldn't you? I mean *paying* readers."

Bert was a joiner. Within his first two semesters in high school, he reported for the football, baseball, basketball, and ski teams. He also joined the Rebel Club and news staff. His best friends included Bob Hermann and Mel Johnson, both of whom he had topped for school president at Byers Junior High. Other friends, many of whom he fished or skied with, were Paul McClung, Jack Scott, Charles Vivian, Jack Shannon, and Phil Bissell. He also had a number of girl friends, although none were "steadies" for more than a month or two.

He became senior class vice president and was also in charge of school assemblies. As president of the ski club he was particularly active in planning winter trips. One of his favorite involvements was the Rebel Club, South High's booster organization.

In the spring semester of his junior year, he wrote a letter on his newly-acquired Corona typewriter to the Denver office of the National Park Service:

> I am an 11th grade student at South High and will be 17 late this summer. I am doing well here, getting good grades, going out for sports, and work part-time after school.
>
> I love the mountains—fish, ski, hike, I do them all. I think I would like to make the mountains my life work. I've talked to many rangers during visits to Estes and Boulder and what I'd like to do is be a junior forest ranger this summer. I'd clean campgrounds, work on trails, wash

pots and pans—anything! And I wouldn't want any pay—just board and room. I'd be good at this. So may I come in and discuss it with you?

Sincerely, Bert Stiles.

It wasn't easy getting the attention of the large Federal office. But he was persistent; he telephoned, wrote two more letters, and finally secured an interview with a supervisor.

Surprisingly, he was given a job—as the first, albeit unofficial, junior forest ranger in the service.

On Sunday, June 12, 1937, B. W. Stiles drove his son to his first assignment, at Glacier Basin Station. Bert kept a log that summer and wrote for that date: "We jammed the car to the roof with our camping stuff, including seventy pounds of food." Later journal entries were of friends and fishing and the working life:

> The first day we picked up every paper in the campground. We work twice as hard and get paid four times less than the rangers.... My bunkies are noted night owls—Ernie Field and Bob Erie. We went fishing one night and I fell in Beaver Pond.

> Howard Viney and Jim Barrie and I packed to the top of the ridge and over to Odessa Lake and I glissaded down a long snowy slope. I caught a nice rainbow at Odessa; but we had to head back. So we went down to Brinwood and thence home, went we, the tired three. I slept like a brick.

It was Bert's first extended period away from home—and most of the time he reveled in it. However, after his parents and sisters had to cancel a visit one weekend in early July, he wrote to them: "I am being left in this godforsaken place without a ray of light from the sophisticated outside." He penned a cute note to his sister May on her fifteenth birthday on July 18 and a postcard to his father imploring him: "Dad, come fishing with me. Lots of fish here!"

His journal listed seventy-three lakes he visited that summer, lakes with names like Finch, Ouzel, Chickadee, Pool of Jade, and Ratcliffs Puddle.

His best friends in the high country that summer of 1937 were Annie and Ernie Field, a temporary ranger and his wife. To him they embodied the spirit of a happy marriage: fun-loving, talkative, athletic, dedicated to the outdoors. The Fields were in their mid-twenties; they were drawn to the sixteen-year-old who suddenly appeared in their lives. Bert stayed with them several times at their small place in Estes Park. He proudly introduced them to his parents. Two years later he wrote about them:

> I guess I was in love with Annie, she was so keen, so sweet, so dark and lovely. I used to wash dishes for her and we would laugh and talk for hours. And Ernie was just about the swellest guy I ever knew. But Annie was my buddy.

> I loved that summer. I visited the high lakes and walked the trails with my little tyrolean pack and fishing rod and dreamed my dreams of the world to come. For six weeks I was stationed in the Wild Basin country South of Longs Peak. Those last weeks were the happiest I have ever spent. My whole earlier life seemed to recede into a hazy background....

Even while working in the mountains, Bert began writing stories about ranger life. Before he left Denver, he had written to *Saturday Evening Post* for a list of literary agents. In the summer of 1937 he wrote several stories and noted in his journal: "I decided then and there I was going into the story-writing business. So I wrote to Curtis Brown and sent them four stories. I was darn sure that by the middle of September I would be rolling in dough."

To his intense disappointment, Bert Stiles found his athletic ability not up to his enthusiasm. He always seemed to be second string. At 5'10" and 140 pounds dripping wet, he was small for football. And lack of height relegated him to a permanent role as sixth man in basketball. While playing a strong enough second base on the diamond squad, there were bigger, harder-hitting infielders who got the starting nod.

But he was the best skier in high school and played tennis among the best, although basketball practice kept him from going out for the net team.

The "solo" sports of fishing and skiing captivated him. He joined the South High Mountain Club, the ski club, and the Junior Colorado Mountain Club. His sister May also joined this latter group and both climbed Longs Peak and several other mountains— Gray, Elbert, James, Rosalie. All were above 14,000 feet.

"Bert, did you get your application in to Colorado College?"
Bert looked at his father sheepishly. "Not yet, Dad."
"Still waiting for a miracle?" his father asked gently.

They were on the front porch after dinner, just the two of them. Bert had just graduated from high school.

"Not exactly, Dad. I like C.C. *You* were there; *you* liked it. It's just that—well, I like Lewis and Clark, too. Or Washington State. Or Stanford—if I could get in."

His father smiled slightly. "I'll bet you just want to get out of the area, out of the state, away from mother and me. I don't blame you, but out-of-state tuition is high."

"I know that. What *is* important is to be near fishing and skiing and the mountains. And that's Colorado. But that's also Oregon and Montana and California. Dad, I'm going to C.C., all right. I guess it's ordained. But—sometime—I want to travel, roam the world, live on the beach, hike the trails of the Cascades, float the Snake River, ski Sun Valley again. And I haven't even mentioned the South Seas, have I?"

His father said nothing for a moment. "It'll be a long life, Bert, but college first. Colorado College is a good liberal arts school—just right for your literary interests. And your mother and I have worked out what we can afford to send you each month."

"Thanks, Dad," his son said, unexcitedly. "I'll try not to let you and Mom down."

3

ONE YEAR, ONE LIFETIME

"I wanted to get out and travel
and go to hell in my own way."

We went to Dessau, over by Leipzig, and the fighters were snarled up all day long. There were brawls all over the sky. A couple of Focke-Wulfs strayed around our tail. Every time they have time to queue up and come slow-rolling through, plenty of people get killed. The most hopeless feeling in the world is when you just have to sit there and wait for it, knowing you're either going to be dead in a couple of seconds, or you're going to be one of the still breathing ones....

Hey, Bert thought as he sat beside his father on the trip to Colorado Springs, I'm off to college. He had been eighteen years old for less than a week, he was through forever with Denver's South High School, and a number of friends had made the same college choice.

He knew his parents had really made the decision for him. He liked Colorado College, but it was his dad's school, he was headed for his dad's fraternity, and here he was in his dad's Willys, rattling along at forty-five miles per hour. And now his father was actually giving him advice: get organized, study hard, and, most important, stay away from intoxicating drinks.

The prospect of four years of college was not appealing. He wanted to see things, to feel things. "I wanted to get out and travel and go to hell in my own way," he wrote in a theme the following year. "It wasn't a new feeling—every kid in the world has it. I just didn't get over it. I thought if I dug hard enough, dreamed hard enough, and gave everything I had, I could get at the world of my dreams."

He was proud of the fact that he had talked his way into working two summers for the National Park Service. He had considered taking a permanent job with the federal agency, but without a college education he knew he'd end up as foreman of a labor crew or chief clerk in some office. Better to try college; it was what his parents wanted, and probably what he did as well.

Now, as they approached the northern border of the small college town, Bert turned for a final look at his beloved Rocky Mountains. Just a week ago, he remembered, he had walked the trail one last time, deep into his thoughts. A light mist had made the tall pine trees ghostly, magical. Standing with his hands on hips, eyes skyward, his thoughts had been mystical:

> Longs Peak is out there, up there, in the misty distance. I can see the purple of the evening creep magically over the whole range. Part of my soul is here in the Wild Basin country, dreaming, hiking, fishing. God, I love it here.

Bert was glad several good friends were making the trek to Colorado College with him. It would be like an extension of high school. He had known Mel Johnson and Bob Hermann since Byers Junior High, and the others—Bob Schwartz, George Winters, and Jack Scott—since that first year at South High.

He knew he would be "rushed" by, and probably be expected to join, Phi Gamma Delta. It was his father's fraternity. The rush chairman had driven to Denver twice during the summer to recruit him. He'd been promised a job at the fraternity, a necessity given the family's meager finances.

But he wished he weren't walking right down his father's footprints. He wrote about it later:

> My folks are keen eggs. I used to cry sometimes when I hurt them; but our ideas are miles apart. They want me to grow up to be a useful, worthwhile citizen, a pillar of the community, just like they are. They want me to live up to their standards. And my standards aren't the same as theirs; our ideas are crosswise.

> Those times at home were hell. I couldn't tell them what I wanted. They let me know that they were for me. But I wish they didn't care. I wanted to be on my own—taking off for the moon.

Bert liked Colorado Springs, a quiet, residential city of 30,000 nestled in the foothills of the Rockies. The city was just large enough to support a college, and the college fit the town: friendly, comfortable, and rich. Known as "The Springs" to most intimates, the city had wide, tree-lined streets, a fairly small commercial section near the South end of town, and a reputation as a healthy place to live. The Garden of the Gods, West of town, was a natural wonder of huge red and white sandstone rock masses in numerous strange shapes.

Later, Bert wrote about his new home city:

> The Springs is a lovely city in September. Pikes Peak towers up almost hanging over the town. The streets are wide and the houses are castles—a rich man's town. Here come the tired millionaires from the East to drink in the dry air and live in quiet. Visitors come to check it out and wind up living there forever. There is little business going on, just a city of pleasure, big houses, and a charming college.

B. W. Stiles pulled the Willys, wheezing and coughing, directly up to the Phi Gamma Delta house at 1122 North Cascade Street. The car noises caused various half-smothered comments from his future fraternity brothers and Bert blushed deeply. He began to feel the omens stacking against him.

Later, Bert and his father walked South on Cascade Street, toward the center of Colorado Springs, past Murray's Drug Store, the Art Center, and stately old homes. At Shadburn's Restaurant, they feasted on shrimp and fries for lunch, Bert's favorites.

Bert wrote in his journal about his father:

> It would be swell if you would leave this to me, Dad. We both feel like heels. This is new to you to have a kid act like I do. You can't figure me out; I can't figure you out. We're both good guys—but we're so different. Please, Dad, don't let me hurt you. If I do things you don't understand, just remember we *are* different.

Rush week was a whirl: beer with the Kappa Sigs, spiked punch with the Sigma Chis, ping pong with the Phi Gams. He wasn't about to worry about his parent's prohibitionist views. Then he was standing for congratulations with twenty-one other pledges, most of them half-gassed after the obligatory beer session. "It's done," he thought, "I'm a Phi Gam pledge, I guess it was ordained—in the stars."

As a freshman and a pledge, he had to wear cords, sweater, and a dink's cap, spending a large chunk of limited cash for them. But what the hell, he thought, I have to look the part: a naive, eighteen-year-old freshman who hasn't learned to drink.

Colorado College was the classic campus to Bert—a small, serene Liberal Arts school. Founded in 1882, it had grown to 795 students by 1938, 40% of them from Colorado Springs.

Palmer Hall stood prominently in campus center. Bert was to spend a large part of his freshman year in Palmer basement, studying biology. Perkins Hall (music and dance) was close by; the library was West of Perkins Hall. The most impressive looking building on campus was Shove Memorial Chapel. Bert described it in a letter home as looking like a medieval castle. Lennox Hall, the student union, was just off campus, across Nevada Avenue to the East.

He described the student union in a letter to a friend:

> Lennox had a grill room and magazines which were swiped after the third day. Especially *Esquire*. It also contained a large room with a radio, phonograph, and soft chairs where everything goes on from Chinese Checkers to the preliminary motions toward sexual intercourse.

The Phi Gam house had a tiger in its front yard, the emblem of Colorado College athletic teams. The three-story house faced East, with views of Pikes Peak from upper rear windows. Monument Creek, with its year round flow of water, was a block westerly; tennis courts, football field, and track flanked it. A park meandered along the creek toward downtown. "The secluded portions of the park," Bert wrote, "were much used by wandering wooers."

On the banks of the creek was the Art Center, low and modern and white. A small auditorium just off the lobby housed *Koshare,* the student drama club. Bert thought the center the best thing at the Springs.

He wrote: "There lived some of the best looking, most immoral people around."

The Phi Gam house took some getting use to—it looked like a barn in the process of falling down. Painted a sickening yellow, it had cracks in the plaster and water stains here and there. The front lawn was a drainage ditch; the wood fence had few whole boards left. Cars were parked helter-skelter in the side yard. Battered furniture filled the garage. Beer bottles, many broken, lay at random around the yard.

In the center of the living room stood a large table originally from Glen

Eyrie Castle in the Rockies. The grand piano was scarred and missing several keys. The furniture took a frightful beating from sixty brothers. Bert's journal entry read:

> In the hallway stood mail boxes for each brother, where the mail was never put after the first week. The phone booth, with numbers of every bag and queen in town, was under the stairs. The closet co-mingled balls, bottles, forgotten books, shoes, coats, newspapers—and you could never get into it. Everything that was ever lost eventually turned up there.

The Bull Pen was the heart of the fraternity. There were the bull sessions, the councils of war, the bridge games, the informal chapter chatter. There, Ethie, the one-testicled fraternity dog, slept the long nights through in front of the fireplace. On the walls and shelves were tarnished silver cups, banners, medals, all the trophies of long-lost brothers. There were faded pictures of Fijis of yore, and a framed forgotten letter from President Coolidge. The ghosts of a thousand unknown brothers haunted the Bull Pen. The soul of the fraternity resided there, nurtured by the talk, the jokes, the plots, the dreams.

The kitchen was the domain of the cook, a cantankerous, loud-mouthed woman with an oversized posterior. Bert, who soon had a dish-washing job there, hated "Cookie" with the rest, cussing her with choice adjectives, albeit under his breath.

He was assigned to a room with a senior from Denver's East High School. Steve Lowell was a husky football player with light brown, prematurely-thinning hair. The two, initially wary of each other, soon became friends.

In the second week of school, the two repaired downtown to Rusty Gilbert's Cafe, on Bijou Street. From the outside Rusty's didn't look like much, a cheap eatery where truck drivers and farmers sometimes snatched a sandwich and a bottle of beer. But in a large inner room the college crowd talked of classes and professors and dates and skiing, and soon learned the ways of the drinking set. Bert wrote about it later:

> Colorado College is a drinking school composed of prohibitionists changed to imbibers. Rusty's would be crowded with boys and girls; some came to quench a thirst, some to drink their sorrows away. It was a haven for long talk and slow sipping. Everything slips away at Rusty's—money, cares, inhibitions.

Steve and Bert sipped draft beer at a table the size of a checker board. Bert had trouble with the taste of beer, but he was willing to experiment endlessly. Smoke, loud talk, and juke box music dominated every sense.

"I have some doozies as professors," Bert yelled at his companion. "A weird bunch—topped off by old Powell."

Steve Lowell, an English major, knew about Desmond Powell, terror of the English department. "Does he intimidate you?"

Bert reflected. "Damn right. I went to his office to ask who he would recommend I take English from. Told him I wanted the best. Know what he said?"

"Ha! Bet he named *himself.*"

"Sure did. But, you know, Steve, I *believed* him. So I'm in his class. We start by reading Robert Louis Stevenson."

"Know much about him?"

"Hell, yes. He's one of my all-time favorites. I've read everything old R.L. ever wrote."

They rested briefly from the struggle to make each other heard over the din. "What else you taking?" Steve asked.

"Economic History. Professor Anderson. A Swede—and seems like a good egg. Then M and M—Medieval and Modern History. With another M for a teacher: Malone. Know him?"

"By reputation. Didn't he spend time in China?"

"That's him. Quite a character. Small guy, bright-eyed, rides a bicycle around campus. Shows lots of movies."

"Don't even *think* about sleeping through them."

Bert grimaced. "Gotta sleep *somewhere*—sure can't sleep at the fraternity. Too much noise and too damned cold." He made a face into his beer glass. "Does this stuff *always* taste this bitter?"

Steve smiled. "You'll get used to it."

"Then there's Biology," Bert went on. "Professor Gilmore is my old buddy. He thinks I'm majoring in fishing. But I like him. A little roly-poly guy, gets a big kick out of everything."

Bert paused to look around. Despite doing most of the talking, he had noted five girls he wouldn't mind meeting. Two had no boys in the party. And three had eyed *him*.

A warm glow engulfed him. Love made the world go around.

Bert's parents could barely afford $50 per month for his education, and it wasn't enough. So, Bert called upon an old friend of his father's, the dean of freshmen. Knowing Dean Rawlings was an avid skier, Bert told him of his own skill in the sport and soon had what he called a "dream job." Working on a ski tow four hours each Sunday, he was paid for eight. And he could ski when not working. The job was sponsored by the National Youth Administration, one of Roosevelt's babies.

Life as a pledge did not sit well with the free-spirited boy. Up at 6:30 every morning, clean toilets, sweep the hall, help Cookie serve breakfast. Every day. On Sunday nights Bert would lie in his narrow bed analyzing his week: living away from home...able to make some decisions on his own...friends all around. These were positives. But the negatives were piling up: Where was the money? When would he meet a girl he liked? Why were classes so stultifying? And why should he clean the boots of a boy one year older than he was? He wrote later:

> I have never been so low as I was in the morning through those first months. I wouldn't have given two tax tokens for controlling interest in the world. I hated the place with a blind, unreasoning hate—the utter lack of privacy, the doleful not-enough-sleep feeling, the gutter talk of the brothers.
>
> And when could I write? I had the imagination, the desire, the goal—everything but time.

Bert had not lost his desire—his *need*—to write. He found time to write letters or in his journal. But he had little time for his real love: short story writing. God—did he have to put it on hold until next summer?

There were laughs in class. Professor Gilmore would interrupt a serious lecture if he thought of a good story. Once a stray dog wandered into the room. "Hello, you son of a bitch," he said. Then, ignoring the snickers and gasps from students, he added, "That dog—any dog—is a natural, legal son of a bitch."

Bert's love life was a string of fiascoes. On a double date with Jack Scott, his date was a lovely girl in red. But he soon found she had run with some pretty sharp fellows in high school, and seemed far above him socially. He wasn't even sure he could kiss her.

For a fraternity party, he dated a brunette named Sally, but it just didn't work. He couldn't dance well; she was a classy dancer. He took her home early—she made no objection—then walked alone along darkened streets, thinking savagely. At the Bullpen, he downed two beers from the icebox and let his sullen thoughts surface. He was sick of bad dates, unhappy with fraternity life, tired of studying. The only good thing to come out of the evening was a better understanding of beer.

And then he met Rosemary.

There was to be a final party at the fraternity before the Christmas break. Jack Laws, a high school friend, had met a shapely brunette. He was sure Bert would like her even though she was still in high school.

"Aw, these things never work out, Jack," Bert said. "A high school girl? She's too young for me."

"She's one year younger, for Christ's sake."

"You sure she's good looking?"

"Take my word for *that.* C'mon, give it a try."

From the beginning, it was a mutually attractive affair. They spent most of the evening talking, sizing each other up. Later, with several others, they drove to a bar in Austin Bluffs which wasn't too particular about I.D.s. Before they separated, they had a date set up for the Phi Gam Shipwreck Dance. It was to be at the Silver Shield, a hideous old power plant on the outside, a lovely ballroom within.

Both wore pajamas. Bert added ski boots and gators; Rosemary wore huaraches. Jack Bohler and his date came wrapped in large bath towels. Bert's ski boots didn't fit well and he and Rosemary were soon dancing barefoot. Though drinking very little, they were soon acting tight as ticks. Mel Johnson went around in a black tie and jockey shorts, while Jack Scott was soon bare to the waist showing off a self-tatooing job.

In spite of a noise level as high as the nearby Rockies, Bert and Rosemary found much to say to each other. He marveled at this young high school lass: she had looks, class, maturity, and was she ever intelligent. He couldn't find anything wrong. He called her his "dream girl."

Christmas vacation was a time for introspection for the freshman. On Christmas Eve he begged off from his family for a few hours; he said he had to meet someone. Alone, he walked the streets of Denver. Huddled in an overcoat, with Christmas lights all around and holiday music from somewhere, his natural exuberant spirit surfaced. He began to shake off his lengthy "down" period. His thoughts were upbeat:

Look at those people hustling by, happy-hurrying, seeking last minute presents. Who are these people passing in the night? What do they dream of? This is a cleansing night: the bitterness and cynicism I've stored up is melting like magic. Oh, Christmas! Thank you, God, for the man who gave this night; I would have liked to talk to Him; maybe I'm talking to Him now. Hello there, Jesus, let me remember this night forever....

His mood held until New Year's Eve, particularly since his favorite cousin Frank Stiles and Frank's parents came for a visit. He skied and went to movies with friends, talked with his sisters May and Beth, and wrote for long hours in his bedroom. At midnight on New Year's Eve, alone, he saw *The Man in the Iron Mask*—his friend Jack Bohler had canceled out at the last moment. He found himself losing himself in the picture as he always did. He wrote later:

I left the theater and walked alone. Walking through Washington Park, I asked God, please make this year—1939—a good year, make me a good guy, don't let me get hard and bitter. I clenched my teeth, laughed at the sky, and thought, "It *will* be a good year, I *know* it will."

Stiles was one of four skiers to compete against Colorado A & M near Estes. Conditions were perfect. Finishing sixth in a field of twenty in the cross-country disappointed him. He pushed off late in the slalom, lagged at first but cut the flags close, skiing at the top of his skill and grace.

He had telephoned Annie and Ernie Field the previous night; they had come to the meet. At the finish line, they were exuberant.

"You got a place, Bert," Ernie yelled in his ear. "You were great, just great."

The three of them were a carnival in the snow, all over each other.

The head finish judge took the microphone, his deep voice crackling into the middle of their celebration.

"Number 54—Bert Stiles—missed flag Number 7—disqualified."

Stiles tore his glove off, smashing them in the snow. "Damn, damn," he said aloud, "Why couldn't I have used my brains? I went outside, Ernie, *outside,* instead of inside."

Annie gave him a hug and held him tight. "You were great, Bertie, you're here, that's all that matters. Oh, Bertie——."

And, suddenly, his impending foul mood evaporated. Here in the mountains, with his best friends, he was in heaven. What did an old ski race matter?

He lost his ski board job the next month; it was politics and Bert didn't know how to handle it. He had to have more money or his folks would be in deep trouble. He began a job at Shadburn's Restaurant as a dishwasher—but it didn't last long. He just couldn't get along with the bossy little chef. Finals week was a mad interlude of study and worry. Bert camped in the library twelve straight hours, ramming the textbook down his throat in a frenzied effort to learn a semester's worth of material in one night.

In his mail slot that night he found a letter from *Esquire Magazine.* Furiously, he tore it open. It was in answer to his letter to the editor asking the magazine's readers for a "College where dwelled a demi-God of far away who lived amid beauty, loneliness, and adventure." Now, Bert's face lit up like the sun reflecting off of Pike's Peak as he read the Editor's reply: "Your letter will appear in the *Sound and Fury Department* of our March 1939 issue. We hope you find your dream school."

Hell Week arrived with a flourish the following Saturday: a walkathon, pledges tied together in twos. Bert wrote:

> Look at the actives grinning, the sons of bitches...round and round, truck, you pledges, get hot, get in the groove, give, send, truck on down....

> Hours went by; midnight came and was swallowed up. Then fire drill: out of bed in a kick, into the second floor can, grab a mouthful of water, down on hands and knees, crawl down the stairs, spit the mouthful on the fire, then crawl back up the stairs for more....

It was like that all week: close-order heckling morning and night; no time for studying.

Bert took it, but raged inwardly. Is this what all those pledge meetings were about: So we learn the grip and the ritual and *then* what? Why, then you're a "brother," one of the great brotherhood of actives. Allah be praised, he thought, it had better be good.

As Hell Week wound down, *Esquire Magazine* appeared on the small news stand at Murray's Drugs. Snatching a copy, Bert quickly found his letter. Weariness and shame instantly fell away. He read it twice, enthralled by *his* signature: "The Call of Faraway Places." How could anyone resist his pleas for the "right school," where one could read, write, play, talk, *love—all without pressure?*

The insidious climax of Hell Week on Saturday morning was to set pledge against pledge—to tear down their one remaining possession: camaraderie. Bert and Bob Hermann were ordered to swat each other—hard. Bert broke three paddles on his high school buddy; Herm broke a couple on Bert's backside.

Then it was over; candlelight and blindfolds, handshakes and whispered congratulations. The next day, the alumni paid their respects. Bert was thrilled that his father was there. They shook hands solemnly, smiling, sharing their kinship.

Bert was on the phone with Rosemary nearly every night. No subject was taboo. His eyes glowed after a long session with her. Finally, he had found a woman he could talk to. And maybe love?

She arrived in a beautiful off-white dress; he wore skiing knickers and a lumberjack's checked shirt. With his oiled black hair parted down the middle, Rosemary told him he looked damned strange. It was the annual Spring Bowery Dance.

The punch committee mixed orange and lemon juice with grain alcohol in ten gallon milk cans. Rosemary and Bert sat on the stairs sampling it.

"You tight, Bert?" Rosemary asked.

"Not yet, Rosemary. Can't remain in this state very long, though. The only people I know would be teetotal at an event like tonight would be my parents."

"Good for them—holding to their principles. Bert, did you see Jack Bohler? He's been drinking that innocent-looking punch since the moment we arrived. That's grain alcohol."

"And on an empty stomach."

"Sally has been in hysterics, afraid Jack was going to pass out on her. She knows he has a tender stomach."

"Jack has been acting strangely," Bert said. "He was wandering around with one eye looking left, the other right. That's the opposite of cross-eyed, I guess. I wanted to talk to him—but I didn't know which side to approach him on. When I stood directly in front of him, he couldn't see me at all."

"And Jack Laws," Rosemary said, laughing, "he laps up that grain, spills his cookies out in the dark somewhere, then fills up again."

Bert perfected his newly-developed drinking habit that night, but he was far from drunk because he remembered to kiss Rosemary good night. Several times.

Bert approached the neat, one-story house a few blocks from campus with trepidation. Tucked under his arm was his prized copy of Don Blanding's *Vagabond House*. When Professor Powell had asked the freshman to come talk literature with him at his home, Bert thought he would faint.

Powell was kindness itself to his potential protege. He brought out beer—good imported beer—and immediately spoke of his friend Thomas Wolfe. Bert, who had decided Wolfe was his favorite author, was awed. The next four hours passed quickly: talk of writers, books, music, art, ambitions, travel to exotic places.

It was just midnight as Bert walked home under twinkling stars, his thoughts inflamed by love, ambition, by the need to create something special, something *great.* And he decided, then and there under the dark sky, that he wouldn't work for the National Park Service, or get into business or a profession. He would be a writer, a *writer,* and a damned good one. He began as soon as he reached the Bull Pen, putting down some thoughts about the evening with Professor Powell:

> We spent the last hour playing records and talking. He had a collection of records that would have wooed Orpheus himself...I felt the music, felt the chords strike in my soul, bend my thoughts...the mood of the music was my mood—gay with the gypsies, sad with the false clowns, proud with the soldiers...the music was a perfect counterpoint for our earlier talk of reading great literature, of *writing* great literature.

Colorado Springs was lovely in the late spring, with lawns greening rapidly, leaves magically out, late snow sparkling on Pikes Peak. Bert and his brothers trudged nightly to the library, coked at Murray's, walked briskly down campus lanes at night under stars large and luminous. Bert often walked home alone, his thoughts bouncing wildly:

> It's all sort of wonderful, this life. People try too hard to be serious— they make things gray and ugly—they take the joy and beauty from it...but I want everything—the night, the stars, lonely beaches, silent shadows, bright lights, lovely dark-eyed women, booming surf. I can have them all—by having faith, by loving.

He had gone to an Arts Center picnic at Black Canyon behind the Garden of the Gods. They had played softball until everyone got so tight they could no longer run the bases. Then, most drifted to a huge bonfire and ate roast chicken and sourdough bread and macaroni salad.

Bert had no date and soon hitched a ride back to the Arts Center. There he met his ski buddy Fred and sat in the hallway, discussing love, drinking a bit, watching people come and go. Then in through the portals walked a dark-eyed, dark-haired girl he had never seen before. She sat on the steps with them and told them people called her Margot. She would tell them nothing else. Bert's ski friend left for somewhere, and Bert and Margot sat for a long time in the busy hallway, talking and sipping beer.

Before long she put her head on his shoulder, and Bert thought she had the deepest, dreamiest eyes he could remember seeing anywhere. He kissed her gently; then again with more force. He could feel himself tightening up like a piano wire.

Soon they walked into the night. And Bert could feel, all through his body, a delicious, bubbly, fuzzy feeling. Her room was close by and the first thing he noticed was a wild-looking nude against a background of white clouds.

A few months later, in a reflective mood, Bert wrote about the evening:

> She turned out the lights and I kissed her again and both of us melted. Here I was a virgin and here she was a pretty gay girl...it was so deliriously wonderful, waves upon waves of passion, into the morning. I'll never forget the feeling of the morning, with the good hard honest sunlight. But she wasn't there. She had thrown a blanket over me. I wasn't hung over, just a little weak. I kept thinking I ought to feel degraded; but I didn't. I couldn't remember much, but it was a wonderful memory....

With finals looming ahead, Bert alternated between drowning his sorrows at Rusty's and withdrawing into a cloister of books. He ran a maze of studying, drinking, and collapsing in his room.

One night after Bert had returned to the Winter Palace, his roommate Steve Lowell chose to recall for Bert what Bert's father had told a roomful of brothers the preceding fall: "Bert is dead set against drinking; you won't have any trouble with *him.*" Was that really only eight months ago, Steve asked him, that my roomie Bert was a virgin and a teetotaler? Purest of the pure? Steve shrugged, grinned, and let Bert off the hook: it happened to everyone sooner or later.

On Friday, with three finals finished, he'd had enough. "The hell with this," he told Bob Hermann, who was studying with him in the Bull Pen. "I'm going to call 'The Fair One.'"

"Margie, Jean, Margot, or Rosemary?" Herm asked, grinning.

"The last named," Bert said, and strode downstairs to see if the phone was in use. After a ten minute wait filled with glares at a brother calling home, Bert dialed M-4354.

Rosemary's mother answered the phone and said, "She'll be back at 4:30, Bert. She's out with Bill."

"God," Bert mumbled aloud as he stumbled out of the booth. "I've just decided to be in love with Rosemary and she goes out with Bill Prindle."

After his last final he stayed over the weekend, mainly to see Rosemary one last time. He took her to dinner at the Broadmoor Hotel Sunday night, using his last few dollars. They walked home slowly, hand in hand, as the moon came up in the East. He hadn't thought that anything as cold as the moon could be so filled with promise. He pulled her gently down onto a stretch of soft grass, sloping gracefully to a moon-reflected pond.

"This is eternity," Rosemary said, softly.

He looked into her eyes. "Eternity is falling through space for endless time," he said. "Think of the incredible thrill of it. You get a taste of it in skiing. For an instant, the soul leaves the body. At the bottom of the slope you can't remember where you've been. You only know it was beautiful— and that you have to do it again...to live for an instant in eternity...falling through space with someone...with *you*...a kiss for each mile—and a chicken drumstick in the other hand. That would be eternity, wouldn't it?"

She laughed. "What a strange mind you have."

He turned serious. "Rosemary, I want you to be my girl. Will you be my girl? Tonight and forevermore?"

"I'll see you in the fall, Bert. We can talk about it all next year."

"I may not be here in the fall. That's what I've got to decide this summer. But if I come back, Rosemary, it will be because of you. And if I don't, it'll be in spite of you."

Six months later, over the Christmas holidays, Bert Stiles wrote a 200-page journal about his first year in college. The final words were mystical, a bit sad, a little crazy:

> So ended one year, one lifetime. I lived it, was happy, was sorrowful.
> I loved it, I hated it. I saw it in dawn, by day, in sunset, at starlight. I
> dreamed there, I was beaten there. I saw hopes built, some smashed,
> some realized. I laughed, I cried. One crazy mixed-up lifetime was
> crowded into one year. Now it was gone, all the fun, all the sorrow. I

had been born and had died...and now as I came away, the visions
came before my eyes; remember this, remember that. The picture, the
whole thing drifted through my brain, not as reality; but as a dream.
And so I let it lie, a dream of the past, a memory of one year, one
lifetime.

4

A RENDEZVOUS WITH THE UNIVERSE

"I felt pure beauty for the first time;
I was fiercely eager to dive out there
in that beautiful blue of the night…"

The dead body could have come from anywhere, Seattle or Wichita or the valley of the Three Forks of the Wolf. Maybe the guy was a quiet one who taught a Sunday school class, maybe a dreamer waiting for a princess to dance down a moonbeam out of the sky, maybe a drunk. But now he was dead, mangled and smashed, an ugly pulp no good to anyone. Maybe he was lucky—out in a single flash of agony. He didn't scream or grovel on the cold aluminum and slowly stiffen as the pain closed off his nerve endings. He just went away and left a useless body.

While her son was still at Colorado College in June 1939, Elizabeth Stiles had asked him to write of some of his beliefs and convictions. He gladly complied in this letter to her:

I have no idea who or what I am. I don't want to know—it is enough to wonder. There is no one me; there are so many selves. And as my personality develops the self changes. Who knows what one person is? He is a thousand persons wrapped into one.

'Take it easy'—that expression is one of the best codes to live by. Just take it easy, and take things as they come. Hope and dream, and fight when fighting is in order, and love, and dig, and life will come along. Tolerance and the ability to see both sides of things is essential for living.

The National Park Service had no opening for Bert that summer. Fidgeting, he lived with his parents, earning menial money doing odd jobs. Since his "Letter to the Editor" had appeared in *Esquire,* he had received dozens of letters, most from people who wanted to share an adventure with him. There were several suggested trips, two marriage proposals, and sympathetic comments from nearly everyone. But he couldn't move on any of the proposals—he was dead broke.

It was an unhappy early summer. Jobs were meaningless: washing dishes, painting the house of parents' friends, picking cherries at fifteen cents a box. He talked to his parents about his travel aspirations. He mother, dead set against his leaving school, was adamant; his father less so. Sometime, B. W. said, you can travel. But not yet. The first year of college can be discouraging, but go back for another year. You're still only eighteen years old; there's time. It was the familiar story he had been hearing for years.

After a boring workday, he would come alive at night: writing short stories. He would describe a young ranger, about twenty-three, single, but with admiring eyes for a pretty girl. They were classic stories of the genre, containing conflict, a pseudo resolution, new conflict, near disaster, final resolution. Forest fires, storms, a martinet as a boss, imminent layoff—the conflict ranged widely but was always resolved. But why couldn't he resolve his own conflicts?

He mailed his stories to several magazines, but with no success and little feedback. He kept at it, dauntlessly, working in his basement room at night and on weekends, if he wasn't fishing or swimming or playing tennis.

The rejection slips piled up. He papered one wall with them and was able to laugh about it, albeit hollowly.

World news fascinated the young writer; he always sat up straighter during the Fox newsreel before double features at Washington Park Theater. His face reddened as he watched 160,000 Franco troops parade in the "liberation" of Madrid. That's three Fascist dictators riding strong, he thought—Franco, Hitler, and Mussolini.

Britain, Bert noted, had finally decided Chamberlain's policy of appeasement was not working. Reserves were being called up for six months' special training—just in case Herr Hitler *did* decide to launch a war. And Charles Lindbergh stated his isolationistic views that the Atlantic and Pacific Oceans were formidable barriers. Much as he admired Lindy, Bert did not agree with him.

During the first week of August he landed a job as laborer with a federal road crew—and was immediately sent to a favorite place, the Wild Basin Region. The work was pick and shovel, oil-patching, weed hoeing, mostly back-breaking stuff. He hated it because it didn't lead anywhere.

A letter to his parents told of his unhappiness: "Most of the guys here are old boys in a rut," he wrote. He liked Sid and Chuck, the only other young men, but neither could talk worth a damn. They were from another planet, he thought—a silent one. Working near Estes, he caught a movie occasionally. In the dark theater, a good film in progress, he lost himself completely; *he* became the main character. "If I lose myself in a motion picture," he wrote, "then am I not for an instant that person on the screen, and thus no longer me?"

He labored into September, past the commencement date of classes at Colorado College. He missed his friends there, but not the college, not the fraternity. Rosemary wrote asking where he was. His parents wrote notes asking what he was going to do with his life. He wrote letters to famous people, asking their advice on how he could become a writer. He was thrilled when several responded: Don Blanding, Charles Nordhoff, Stephen Leacock, Courtney Riley Cooper.

When his job ended in late September, he returned to Denver richer in purse but with even more undefined goals and visions. First he had to deal with the unhappiness of his parents. They did not hide their feelings: you should be in college, not here at home. At least you should go for a good job, they said, perhaps as a stockboy at a grocery, until spring semester in January. And you can live at home; we won't charge rent.

At nineteen, he was old enough to be on his own, he thought. His parents, he told his friend Jack Shannon, had lost their hold on him.

At an adventure movie, *Daughters Courageous*, he heard John Garfield say, "I've got a date with the world, a rendezvous with the universe." He told Shannon, who was with him, that Garfield spoke for Bert Stiles, too.

"I've *got* to leave Denver, Jack," he said.

"Swell, Bert. No reason why you can't—is there?"

"Two things: money and parents."

"Money—well, that's a universal problem. But, if you lived with Ober up there on the border you wouldn't need much."

Ober Oberholtzer had been a pen pal of Bert's for several months—a man in his early forties who lived on an island on the Minnesota-Canada border. His free-wheeling lifestyle had appealed to Bert, and Ober had asked him to come up.

"That part's okay, but my parents are something else again. They look so hurt when I tell them how I feel."

"But—you have to do it."

Bert looked at his friend and nodded slowly.

He swam alone at the "Y" the next day to think it over. After a punishing hour in the pool, he felt ready for another "parent conference." He would wait until dinner was finished—people are more reasonable on a full stomach.

"Mom, Dad," he began, "Can we have another of our famous talks?" Although his words were light, Elizabeth and Bert W. knew intuitively that it would be a serious encounter. All three sat on separate chairs in the dark-paneled living room.

"The time has come, folks, for a decision about my future. I'm not ready for college just now. I will be *some*time. I believe in education, but I'm pretty young. I want to see some real life for a while."

His father said, "But you've been out four or five months already."

"Dad," Bert said, carefully, "when I'm ready to go back to college, I will. If I don't ever go, it'll be my decision."

It was the wrong thing to say: Bert heard again the reasons why college was a necessity. In that climate, he nearly didn't mention his hoped-for visit to Ober in upper Minnesota. When he did, his folks were incredulous.

"Do you know what that sounds like?" his dad asked. "Like— vacation, fun, the kind of thing you do a few weeks each summer. Not all year, not when there is so much else to do here."

"Yeah, I know: work, study, and be a good little boy."

His parents were silenced by the bitterness in his voice.

He met Jack Shannon at noon the following day.

"I've gotta go, Jack," he announced.

"Good for you. When?"

"Tonight—if everything goes right."

"What will your folks say about that?"

"I'm not going to tell them."

"What're you going to do—just leave in the middle of the night?"

Bert smiled suddenly. "Actually, that's about it—I'm going to leave on the midnight Greyhound."

His parents had gone to a church meeting; they would be back about 9:30. He left before nine, taking the Number 5 city bus to downtown Denver. It was Tuesday, October 17.

He had more than two hours to kill. He called Rosemary Harley in Colorado Springs, receiving sympathy, support, just what he needed. After he had hung up, he turned his jacket collar up and strode pensively along dark sidewalks, trying to visualize his future. He wrote about it later:

> So I walked out into the blue and down into the open space in the park and tried to figure things out. I was all mixed up. But I decided, right then, that I wanted to marry Rosemary some day. For now all I wanted was to be in love with her. Next, I figured, me and the stars figured, that I wanted to write—for the rest of my life. And third, I wanted to roam up there in Minnesota, and wander and seek and search, for what I did not know....

Arriving at the bus station on Glenarm Street close to midnight, he bought a postcard from a machine, found a one-cent stamp, and block-printed a note in pencil to his parents:

> Hello. I'm going to see Ober. I had to go. I'll write you. Take it easy. I'm happy now.
>
> Love, Bert Stiles

When the bus pulled out about 12:30 a.m., he was as keyed up as he had ever been in his life. He was sorry about the postcard—they wouldn't receive it until Thursday. Meantime, they'd probably feel the earth had swallowed him up.

By bus to Minneapolis, by car up Highway 65 to Duluth, then via train to Ranier, Bert wended his way North. It was 1:00 a.m. when he arrived at the small town of Ranier near the border. He felt as if he were at the edge of nowhere. Walking through the misty darkness, he stumbled across a lake at the edge of town. Across the water, the northern lights blazed and the stars seemed close. Shivering with cold and excitement, he knew he was exactly where he wanted to be.

Ernest Oberholtzer had been a diplomat in Hanover, Germany, had traveled throughout Europe by bicycle, and had once taken a six-month trip by canoe to the Baffin Islands North of Hudson Bay. Now he was a self-styled conservationist. To the nineteen-year-old college drop-out, he seemed the epitome of a successful businessman-adventurer.

Ober, as he was known to everyone, took his young charge in hand, introduced him to his two women employees and showed him his private island. They lived in two houseboats jacked out of the water—one for the kitchen, one to live in. The only other building was "The Bird House," so called because it was built vertically—three stories, with a lookout on top.

There were marvelous things on the island: an outboard kicker boat, two canoes, rowboats, fishing tackle. Inside were further treasures: two pianos, a violin, volumes of twelve-inch records, and books by the masters: Keats, Shakespeare, Kent, Shelley, Milton, Wolfe, Hemingway.

Ober, who had never married, found Bert to be everything his letters had promised. He treated the younger man as an equal; he thought of him as a son.

But there was work to do. Board and room was not free. Bert hauled rock, ferried sand from shore to island for various projects, chopped wood, cleared brush, cleaned fishing gear. He was rewarded with all the fishing he could take, unlimited use of the canoes, and time for swimming, reading, music, and talk. His rampant romanticism was touched as never before.

A letter to Rosemary from the "Bird House" bubbled over with enthusiasm, ending this way:

> Last night we paddled in the moonlight to The Frenches (a lakeside bar) and coming home it was so untouched, so remote, so clean, so *haunting*, that I felt pure beauty for the first time. I felt so peaceful that I never want it to end. I was fiercely eager to dive out there into that beautiful blue of the night.
>
> I would stay here forever—if it weren't for you.

He thought of Rosemary often. He couldn't get her out of his mind; he didn't want to. But it hurt, she being so far away, when he was doing such wonderful things she couldn't share. He remembered his last visit to the Springs, just before he had left. Mostly they had just looked at each other and laughed wistfully. Thinking of her now under bright, northern skies, he knew he had to return. Life here was an absolute joy—but it was nothing without Rosemary. He wrote of her in his journal:

> She's the kind of girl you could live with for a million years and find her just as keen every day. She's got brains—she's moody, lovely, lonely (even in a great crowd of guys thronging her house) and she's

happy. But most of all she has emotions—she feels the night, the stars, the moon, people, everything.

In Denver, he greeted his parents with trepidation. Had they forgiven him for running off? The answer came from hugs and teary eyes. Settled in at home, and with ten days left before returning to the Springs for the spring semester, he retired to his basement. And during that week and a half, he churned out a 50,000 word thinly-disguised autobiography which he named *One Year, One Lifetime.* It was the story of his first year in college; in it, he was "Bob St. Clair." Finished, he put it away on a bookshelf and promptly forgot it.

His reunion with Rosemary Harley was pleasure itself, but he found himself at the same stage as at the tearful parting the previous June. She was in college now, she still had a host of admirers, and he felt he had nothing particular to offer her. But he was delighted to be a five-cent phone call away from her as he signed up for new classes.

A shock came with the absence of his mentor Professor Powell. The English instructor had not been given the full professorship he thought he had been promised and had left for the East Coast.

God, Bert thought, walking home from Rusty's after a few beers, I've been back a week and what do I find? Rosemary and I have slipped a gear somewhere, old Powell is gone, I can't get the literature class I want, and my writing is on hold to make way for fraternity meetings.

Within a few weeks, his spirits were lifted mightily; he had met Krutzke, Dickison, and Stuart. They were people he needed then: an inspiring professor, a buddy, and a romantic girl.

Curious about why Professor Krutzke's American Literature course had filled so early, Bert decided to audit the class. Bert's first impression was strong: a slim, dark-haired man in his mid to late thirties. After he heard him lecture, he added other attributes: brains, knowledge, style.

Frank Krutzke had arrived at Colorado College the previous semester from Swarthmore College in Pennsylvania, and, even after one semester of teaching, had become a student favorite.

After the third class of non-registered attendance, the professor caught his eye as class was breaking up and asked him his name. Bert told him, then added: "You don't mind if I sit in once in a while, do you, Professor Krutzke?"

"Once in a while?" Krutzke said, smiling. "Seems like I see you every class. You would make me more comfortable if you could find a seat."

"No seats available," Bert said, smiling back, "Your classes are too popular."

With that kind of start, they soon became friends. Bert wanted to get to know Krutzke personally. He already knew where he lived on Pelham Place, near campus.

While Bert had many friends at the Fiji house, none had become special to him. Playing tennis one day at the college courts, he found himself partnered with a tall rangy freshman named Roland Dickison. He was soon glad they were partners; the guy had all the shots. With Bert's quickness and the shot-making of Dickison, they demolished their opponents.

"You in a house?" Bert asked as they walked home.

"I'm a Beta," Dickison said, "but I'm not sure why."

Bert did a double-take. "Hey, you're my buddy," he said. "I'm not sure why I'm a Fiji, either."

"I'll buy you a beer and we can talk about it."

"How can I turn that down?"

When they separated nearly two hours later, they were well on their way to a fast friendship. As they left, Bert said, "So long for now, Roland."

Dickison looked hard at him. "That 'Roland' came out a bit forced," he said. "My friends call me 'Sleepy'—and I consider you my friend."

"Great—I accept. But why 'Sleepy'?"

"I sleep a lot in class—and I guess people notice it."

Bert and Sleepy Dickison played tennis again the next week. Both had been ready for a close friendship; it occurred naturally and completely. They found they had several things in common besides tennis: a sort of irreverence for the conventions; a healthy skepticism about college life, especially fraternities; a love of books and literature; and a strong desire for stimulating feminine company. They resolved to line up a couple of pretty girls and seek the delights of the Springs together.

Many of Bert's free hours were spent at the Art Center on the corner of Cascade Avenue and Dale Street, a few blocks from the Fiji house. It wasn't necessarily the artistic attractions; he simply liked the people there. And it was a delightful venue for writing—there he found peace and inspiration. It was there, too, that he first began to write poetry, but he wasn't too happy with it.

By mid-semester, Bert felt he knew Professor Krutzke well enough to ask him to read *One Year, One Lifetime,* the story he had written over

Christmas about his first year of college.

He took the manuscript to class with him one day and waited until the other students left.

"Professor" he said, then waited until the English teacher looked up. "You remember I told you I'd done some writing? Well, here it is." He tapped a binder he was holding. "A full length story, laid right here in the Springs."

Krutzke took the proffered manuscript, careful to keep his face neutral. "Is it good writing, Bert?"

The young sophomore answered carefully. "It's my first effort at anything this length. It's probably amateurish stuff. But—I'd like to know what you think of it."

"How much rewriting have you done?"

Bert reddened. "Well, none—yet. I was hoping you would give me some pointers on where it *needed* rewriting."

Krutzke said nothing for a moment, and Bert's heart sank. Finally, the professor said, graciously, "Certainly I'll read it, Bert. Just don't count on it any time soon, though."

With effort, Bert let two weeks slip by; Krutzke said nothing further about the manuscript. He could read it in one short evening, Bert thought. What's taking him so long?

A few days later, the professor hailed Bert on the steps of Palmer Hall. He handed the manuscript back, then told him it showed style. With some work, it could be worth sending in.

Bert was elated. "Worth sending in to a *publisher?* My gosh, Professor Krutzke, you've made me a happy lad."

"But it'll take lots of work. Come over to my house later this week and we'll talk about it."

Bert couldn't stop thinking about girls; with Rosemary on temporary hold while they sorted out their feelings for each other, he looked around him for someone else special. And with Rosemary's help, he met Nancy Stuart.

He and Rosemary, with Sleepy Dickison and a few others, had gone to a hockey game at the ice rink at the Broadmoor Hotel. Colorado A & M was the opponent, and the Tigers easily defeated them. After the game, someone suggested they go into the hotel bar for a drink, but Bert declined.

"The Broad is too much class for me tonight," he said, "and there is the matter of lack of loot. I might just walk around a bit." So saying, he put his hands deep into his jacket pockets and turned up his collar; a chilly breeze had floated down from Pikes Peak. There was some chatter from the others until, suddenly, there were Rosemary and Sleepy trailing along.

The reflected lights from the hotel, dancing and twinkling, gave the black waters of Broadmoor Lake mystic qualities, Bert thought. They began a walk around the lake, each wrapped in thought. Ahead, a car had stopped and they could see two girls talking inside. As they approached, one of the girls came over to say hello.

"Hello, Rosemary," she said. It's me—Nancy Stuart."

She had met Sleepy but not Bert. Rosemary introduced them.

Bert's antenna had stiffened; he studied her closely. Her hair—what color was it? Was it blond? Reddish? Hard to tell in the pale light. He quickly took in her compact body, a well-shaped head, and a mannerism that, well, was just plain sexy. He wished he could see more of her in the half-light.

Nancy, as though reading his mind, began to lift her skirt.

"I've got this dumb bruise," she said, to all of them. "I fell down on the ice, of all the stupid things to do. I'd never make a hockey player. Want to see it?"

Without waiting for an answer, she lifted her skirt high and pointed out a brownish, bruised spot. She raised her panties several inches to show the extent of the bruise.

While Rosemary smiled in the background, Bert and Sleepy goggled at her while exchanging quick glances.

"Let me see that, Nancy," Bert said. "I'm pre-med and this is the kind of injury I should know more about."

Nancy laughed lightly. "Tell me what you think, doctor."

"I think it's very lovely," Bert said.

"What, the bruise?"

Bert began his usual slow blush. "The bruise is okay," he said, "but I was thinking about your innermost thigh." And he couldn't resist adding, "Is there more?"

"You bet there is, buster."

Later, after they had walked Rosemary home, Bert remarked to Sleepy, "That's the kind of girl I'd like to know better."

He certainly tried. He asked her for a date the following weekend, and, until the spring semester ended, he romanced her to the extent his imagination and finances would stand. When Nancy wanted to go to the Broadmoor or someplace likely to be expensive, she would pick up the check. Her parents, from an East Coast manufacturing family, had sent her West because she had demanded it.

In Bert Stiles, she found the uninhibited, romantic, western boy she had unconsciously been seeking. He was someone who could match her wit, romance her in open style, go along with her often wild schemes for having a good time. Hell, she thought, at times he embellished them to levels she had yet to experience. They were kindred spirits.

So, with his friendship with Sleepy Dickison, Professor Krutzke's interest in him, and keeping up with Nancy, Bert began to feel his life in the Springs was getting pretty classy.

One Saturday in late April, he excused himself from a Fiji beer bust in order to write. He had these characters, these plots, and he *had* to get them on paper. With the house empty, he holed up in his room all day—until after midnight—writing short stories. In sixteen hours of nearly continuous composing, he produced four complete stories and outlines for two others. What a day, he thought, yawning, as he stumbled into a shower and bed. My brothers drank too much beer, exchanged too many ribald jokes, accomplishing exactly nothing, while I—while *I,* wrote some pretty damn good stories. Even if they don't make me a cent, he concluded, I'm pretty goddamn happy about this day's work.

As time permitted, Bert polished several stories he had written during the past six months. Most were about rangers. He sent them off, one by one, to various publishers. And he wondered what had happened to *One Year, One Lifetime,* which he had sent to Simon and Schuster a month earlier.

By the spring of 1940, Bert, along with millions of other students, had begun to believe war was inevitable. The student newspaper, *Tiger,* ran editorials indicating that while students abhorred Nazi tactics, a campus pool showed they opposed involvement by 290 to 20. Bert, as an Associate Editor, wrote in a May issue of the news daily:

> You find, though you visit your professors and smile when you pass
> on campus, you scarcely listen to them in class. You find that instead

of studying, you spend time at Murray's, Rusty's, at Lennox House, or at the Hogan. You find your hangover is masked under frivolity and the gay desperation of a generation who sees perhaps one more year of the good life before plunging into the darkness....

In early May a letter finally arrived from Simon and Schuster who had been reading his autobiographical novel, *One Year, One Lifetime*. He frowned as he read the now-familiar phrases which amounted to another rejection slip. But, in the last paragraph of the letter came a surprise: although it was deemed by Simon and Schuster to be "wordy, juvenile, and certainly not new," they had sent it to a literary agent who *might* agree to read it. Please await developments.

A second surprise came a week later, this one a letter from Aley Associates, Literary Agents, New York. He tore it open; the agency acknowledged receipt of a manuscript from Simon and Schuster and stated their agency charged a $10 reading fee for unsolicited work. Did Mr. Stiles wish to remit this amount?

Infuriated, Bert wrote immediately:

Dear Mrs. Aley:
Your letter requesting a ten dollar fee is not acceptable. You may recall that I didn't send "One Year, One Lifetime" to you; it got to you through an action I knew nothing about. I don't own ten bucks. When I do—I'll think about it. But I can't pay you to read it.

Within a week, the following letter arrived:

I must apologize. Your letter was well taken. We have been in a rush here, and the wrong letter was mailed.... There is much to your book that I like; it is a fresh, unusual, bittersweet look at that first year away from home.... The Aley Agency is in business to nurture young writers like yourself to the point where they *can* publish. Do send us more of your writing.

Sincerely, Ruth Aley

Bert was ecstatic. He began to believe he *could* write something publishable. He never forgot Ruth Aley's kind letter.

He spent the rest of the summer, and well into the fall, on a lengthy trip to southern California, where he lay on the beach, supporting himself through jobs arranged by the parents of a fraternity brother. From there he hitched rides to Chicago, where he stayed with Aunt Helen, a favorite relative, and to Yellow Lake, Wisconsin, where his friend Johnny Westlund lived. Johnny had asked his fraternity brother to "come visit" sometime and Bert was merely complying. He returned to Colorado College a few days late, but still was able to register.

His parents, unhappy with their wayward son, wrote to him that in their opinion he was "mentally lazy, sponged on his friends, and lived only for himself." Bert, intensely unhappy with what he felt was an unfair letter, wrote at length to them, refuting each of their points, and ending in this way:

> I have wound up with the concept, the faith, that life is lovely, strange, fascinating, crazy, and fun. And I believe I can go through life enjoying most of it, instead of putting in eight, ten, or twelve hours a day at drudgery, then enduring life afterwards with dulled senses and dragging nerve endings.

> A parent probably sees a child as an offshoot of himself. But to the child he is the projection of some genes and chromosomes; he is not the combined characteristics of all his ancestors; he is himself alone...I don't want to be you, Mother, or you, Father, or anyone else but me. I'm not a boy with my grandfather's nose—I'm me, take it or leave it.

During the summer of 1940, world events took a tragic turn, with France falling and the Germans unleashing millions of pounds of bombs on Britain. The RAF were outnumbered, but proved its Spitfire was the world's best fighter plane as it shot down hoards of German raiders. Bert was alternately dejected and thrilled by the turns in the war. He and Sleepy agreed they were predestined to be a part of it.

He began the fall semester by moving out of the fraternity. "More than anything else I need some quiet time," he told Sleepy. "The Fijis are good people, no doubt, but I crave my own definition of time, of space, of choice. I'll still be able to visit the house when I want— which may not be too often."

He and Nancy Stuart continued their romantic twosome. A summer on the East Coast had not dimmed Nancy's desire for the company of this Rocky Mountain westerner. As for Bert, he was still smitten. "I feel so alive with her," he told Sleepy. "She keeps me off balance, exhilarated, in suspense as to what she'll do or say next. And this is exactly what I need in a girl."

One further reason Bert had moved out of his fraternity was for privacy—he *had* to have it. How could he entertain a girl with other guys around? One night, after splurging with dinner at Shadburn's, they walked

North to his room. Bert's heart was throbbing with anticipation. Would his gentle wooing result in her falling in his arms during the magical evening ahead?

Would she? Within five minutes of closing the door to his room he knew how the evening would turn out.

"Love, love, makes the world go around," he thought.

It was typical of Bert to offer somewhat mysterious, often cryptic, information to his parents. He was aware of his ability to discomfort, even shock, them. Consequently, when he wrote that he would like them to meet his dream girl, they didn't know what to expect. Especially since he described her as a "problem child of the first water. She's the sweet, gentle, gun-moll type."

They arrived at the back door on York Street one Saturday with no warning, having hitch-hiked from the Springs. They wore levis, saddle shoes, and sweaty cotton shirts. Their hair was wind-blown. But their faces were fresh and young and friendly, and Elizabeth Stiles easily invented a quick lunch.

He presented his Phi Gam pin to Nancy at a fraternity party in March 1941. In announcing this to his parents, he wrote that "I have a girl who is intelligent, beautiful, witty, and as sexy as they come."

But his romance with Nancy did not cause any change in his relationship with Rosemary. If Nancy were his true love, Rosemary was his true friend and confidante. There was deep mutual admiration between them.

When Bert became editor of *Tiger* in the spring of 1941, he churned out editorials on a variety of subjects. They appeared in nearly every issue. He wrote about going to war, the uselessness of college, local graft, and the rejection of a Jewish boy for fraternity membership. This latter hurt him deeply; the fraternity involved was his own Phi Gamma Delta, and he nearly resigned as a result.

After reading several more stories from Bert, Ruth Aley decided he had definite promise. Although his intellectual interests ranged widely beyond fiction, he wrote short stories exclusively, feeling this would lead more quickly to publication. Ruth Aley and her husband Maxwell agreed. His stories concerned forest rangers, sports, romance, adventure—the things he loved.

As the spring semester wound down, he took stock of his future. He was finishing his fifth college semester, he had received his Associate of Arts Degree, he could gain a full degree in a year and a half. Did he want to finish, graduate, look for a satisfying job?

His answer was a resounding NO.

As usual, he preferred putting his thoughts into writing when addressing a serious subject:

> This letter will tell you without any doubt, my folks, what I think. I've written a lot of letters like this but somehow you never seem to think that the "me" who writes them is the same "me" who can't talk to you— when you are there looking so sad. On a typewriter, I can be ruthless and I can't see your frozen faces.
>
> I'm through with college for a while. Many times this semester I've figured the fake and sham I'm making of college wasn't worth the cost. I don't care for what they make you work at in college; it just doesn't seem important. Colorado College is a playhouse. It's here for the getting, but almost no one gets it.

Everyone said America would be in the war: it was just a matter of time. Bert felt that during the war the system was going to take a terrific rocking. He knew he would need to take control of his life, to work at something he could do tolerably well and that he loved. He described his feelings in a letter home:

> And so I'm going to be a writer, and a good one. I've evolved into a competent craftsman, a guy who can build things with words. To be a success, I need understanding, compassion, and skill. I think I have compassion now, and understanding and skill are coming.

In mid-June, with still no definite plan on how to spend the summer of 1941, he received another letter from Ruth Aley:

> You really should come back here, Bert...it's time we met. We can do your career so much good, Maxwell and I. Do you suppose you could break away from school, girls, family, and job to come East?

Could he? He was through with school, had no jobs or prospects, and was feeling independent of his family. As for his girl, she had departed for—of all places—the East Coast.

There was nothing to hinder his going, except money, of course. Always money. Well, he'd sell his reserve skis, borrow from Sleepy, and hitchhike rather than take a bus. He'd manage. On June 24, he wrote to the Aley Literary agency:

I'm checking out tomorrow. And I'll wend my way by thumb across
the continent. It will be a hell of a trip and I'll be so damn tired when
I get there I won't know quite what to do...but I'm coming.

With Maxwell and Ruth Aley in New York ready to guide him on a
writing career, and with Nancy Stuart in New Jersey ready to continue a
torrid romance, there was nothing in the world he would rather do than
"wend his way" East.

5

WENDING HIS WAY EASTERLY

"I was born with stars in my eyes. I
was born lucky, and if I keep true,
then the luck will stay forever...."

*From the day you start out in a B-17 they tell you that formation flying
is the secret of coming back. When the Luftwaffe lies low for a few
days, the formations begin to loosen up and string out and take it easy.
Then one day the 190s come moaning down out of the clouds and the
whole wing blows up and three or four ships out of each squadron
straggle home. After that some pretty fair formation is flown for a
while.*

New York: a writer's Utopia, a place of excitement, of destiny, perhaps of
eventual acclaim. Bert's thoughts bounced like a rubber ball from wonder
to desire to anticipation. What a world he had been born into. He had a level
chance to become an acknowledged writer here on the East coast. And
Nancy was here, too. Both were romantic dreams: the romance of loving
and the romance of writing. He was the luckiest guy in the world.

Wending his was East had not been routine. He had sold his skis for
$15, borrowed money from his parents and a few friends, and accumulated
more than $100, just enough to begin the trek. His parents had wanted him
to take a bus, until he reminded them that he simply didn't have the money.

Hitchhiking through Omaha, he was picked up by the state police, and sent home by bus. Furious and frustrated, he refused to let his parents talk him out of trying again. He used his thumb when we could, using funds for bus fare only occasionally.

The bus station in Orange, New Jersey, was nearly deserted. Bag in hand, heart in mouth, he telephoned Nancy; she borrowed her father's Packard to pick him up. She clung to him tightly while he plastered her face with kisses. It was worth the wait; he was delirious with happiness.

Nancy's folks were wonderful to him. The four of them dined in an elegant room overlooking a spacious, forested yard. Servants were at beck and call. Wine flowed; lights were dim. Bert, wearing a blue sports coat—his only one—was adequately if not ostentatiously dressed.

He and Nancy swam at the Orange Lawn Tennis Club pool, drove the Packard to New York City and Long Island, meeting Nancy's friends along the way. Bert was thrilled by it all: elegant surroundings, the free flow of money, Nancy at his side.

Nancy Stuart wondered how much she loved this black-haired boy from Colorado. She was used to boys gawking over her; she had money, charm, and sex appeal. But this Stiles was a special breed, an intense yet laughing boy from the mountains, a sensual and caring—but still somehow irreverent—boy from another part of the world. Could she be happy married to him? Would he easily submit to living in the East? To having her father or uncle start him in banking, investments, a big city profession?

She decided that, while she might talk him into living on the East coast, she could never change his oft-stated lifetime goal. That damn writing was too important to him. Make a weekend scribbler out of him? Never.

Fairfield, in coastal southwest Connecticut, was the home of two people Bert had yet to meet—but already admired. They had a New York office, but did much of their work at home; hence, their suggestion that he come to Fairfield.

Walking from the bus station to their home on Burr Street, he found the house set well back amidst dense trees and shrubs. There was no answer to his ring, and he walked around the side of the house to see four people seated on lawn chairs, enjoying late-afternoon cocktails.

"Hi, there," he said, approaching them without hesitation. "I'm Bert Stiles. Do the Aleys live here?"

The first week at the Aley home was filled with excitement. Writers dropped in, agents called, the telephone was busy. Bert wrote home that Mrs. Aley was "beautiful and wonderful." Ruth Aley took him in hand, introduced him to their friends, began handing out advice immediately. In a nice way.

After the guests had left on that first day, she took him out to the rear of the house and indicated a disreputable barn, chicken pens, corrals, and various sheds.

"This will be both your home and your livelihood," she said, pointing at the barn. "Live in the top half, paint the lower. Then paint the upper part—if you can find a ladder."

"Mrs. Aley," he said, "you're not creating a painting job because you're sorry for me?"

She turned to face him. "As it happens, I'm not," she said, her tone indicating she didn't like the question. "The barn *does* need painting. You need a place to sleep and eat. But, more important, you wouldn't be sleeping or eating or painting if Maxwell and I didn't think you had talent.

"You'll be working for a friend of ours, too, Bellamy Partridge. We wrote you about him. Lives close by, writes good stuff, and says he needs typing, proof-reading, and listening."

At the door of the barn loft, where he was to stay off and on for three months, she turned back to him. "Come up to the house for refreshments when you've settled in. We'll talk about you—and writing."

Bert was thrilled by her words.

And so Bert Stiles became a writer. He was no longer a student, a skier, a lover, a happy-go-lucky kid with stars in his eyes. He was still a son and brother, he supposed, but that wasn't so important, now. He was a writer. For the first time he was among people he could talk to, plan plots with, use literary language on, and discuss the most important thing in his life. No longer was he among friends who had only a casual interest in writing, if any; no matter girls who thought he was some kind of nut; no concern now with parents who didn't understand his grand passion. No one in Colorado did, except perhaps Professor Krutzke. But he had to come to Fairfield, Connecticut, to the home of Maxwell and Ruth Aley, and *by God,* he had *arrived.*

Bert found Maxwell Aley somewhat less sympathetic than Ruth, perhaps more businesslike—but equally demanding. Both of them demanded the best from any writer in their charge, and from Stiles in particular. They saw latent talent in this raw-boned westerner. No, not really latent; it had already arrived, but it needed polishing, like a fine stone. It needed stroking, like their Siamese cat. And above all it needed understanding.

During the second week he rode in to New York with Maxwell Aley, to the agent's office at 342 Madison Avenue. Maxwell took him to lunch at a little French restaurant— and introduced him there to Max Wilkinson, an editor with *Colliers.* Bert was amazed—and deeply pleased—when Wilkinson told him he had read his story, "The Wildcatter."

On the street again, walking back to Madison Avenue, Maxwell leaned close to Bert to be heard over the street noises, and said, "Listen closely to everything you are told, Bert. You will learn something from everyone. If an editor suggests more plot, less plot, longer scenes, more love interest— do it. At least consider it. Learn discipline, and hard work. This is not an easy business."

In Fairfield, Mrs. Aley told everyone on the phone that Bert was on the verge of publishing, not caring whether Bert overhead her. He began to believe it, and work harder toward the goal, which was Mrs. Aley's plan from the beginning. He wrote ten hours a day in his loft, painting perhaps one hour in return. The painting was finally finished; the writing was not. The Aleys were nice people, he thought—patient, understanding, like parents—but God were they ever demanding! Ruth or Max would read over his daytime production every evening, always with a red pencil close by. Then would come the talks: correcting, deleting, changing.

The young aspiring writer endured alternating periods of high and low. Would he really make it—or was he just another hacker wasting everyone's time?

The Aleys were perceptive people; they didn't work their charge constantly. Their son, Maxwell, Jr., known as Bunny, came home from college and became a good friend of the visitor. The two boys would swim in the Sound, play tennis, double-date. During the last weeks of July and into August, Bert alternated between writing, trips to see Nancy, and calls upon editors, the latter in the company of his agent and mentor, Maxwell Aley.

Bert wrote to his parents in late August:

> There is a lot I could say tonight but I don't have the imagination or energy to say it. The social life is gay and I have a good tan. But after

I beat away at this all day I don't want to read or listen to music or go to the movies. I'm learning a lot and if the pressure would ever ease I could do a lot better. But it's wait and stew and one more rewrite, and talk it over, and maybe *Colliers* will take this but *Satevepost* turned this down and we'll have *Redbook* look this over. All very fascinating, and very maddening, and very wearying.

The Aley residence was called the Dower House. It was built in the 1790s, its white clapboard siding an imposing structure on Burr Street. On occasion parties would be held in the lower half of the barn while Bert banged on his typewriter above. A large English setter named Barry had the run of the yard and became Bert's special friend; a new Ford stood at the curb out front. It was a comfortable place to spend the summer.

In late August, anxious to escape the tedium and enervating heat of his writing abode—and more importantly to see Nancy—he hitched a ride to Orange with a neighbor. He settled in with the Stuart family for the weekend. Nancy's parents had decided they liked him.

All day Saturday Nancy and Bert admired each other's bodies at the swimming pool of the Orange Lawn Tennis Club, sipping cool drinks, talking animatedly.

"What clothes did you bring, Bertie?" she asked, looking up from kneading his taut brown stomach with long fingernails.

"Clothes? Well, I have the trusty old blue sports—."

"The dance is semi-formal. You'll need a suit, Bert."

"Oh, come on, Nance. No one will even notice."

"Come on yourself. They're tight on this. The club has a bouncer the size of Man Mountain Dean."

"For Pete's sake, Nancy."

"Don't be dense, Bertie. All the boys wear formal. You want to be out of place? This *is* a pickle. Too late to buy a suit today—well, maybe Daddy has one you can borrow."

He sat up and faced her directly. "I don't want to borrow a suit from your father."

"You'll have to—if you want to go to the dance with me. Come on, Bert—you'll meet Susy, Ralph, Bob. Great fun."

Bert's voice took on a slightly ominous timbre. "Let's do something else. Alone. Let's just be alone tonight, Nancy. Forget your friends."

"You'll see me all evening. God, it must be close to five. We'd better get home and find you a suit that halfway fits."

They left the Stuart home about eight o'clock, Bert driving the Packard. It hadn't been easy to find a dark suit at the last minute. Nancy's brother-in-law had finally come through. Bert was unusually quiet on the way to the club.

Dinner was superbly served under soft lights on the terrace overlooking the swimming pool. There were eight of them, and Bert never did learn all their names. Not that he tried.

Nancy spent most of her time talking to her neighbor on the other side, a tall, blond chap named Ralph something. The young girl on Bert's left was a diminutive girl with dimples, who was incapable of uttering anything intelligible; he soon gave up trying to make conversation and sat mute most of the time.

The company was so far out of his league he didn't even want to try to know them. I should just grab Nancy by the wrist, he thought, like a caveman. Then take off somewhere. After ten more minutes of silent hell, the idea even seemed feasible

Then Ralph asked Nancy to dance. But Bert forestalled him. "She's with me, buddy," he said, not remembering his name. He had the grace to smile to lighten the words.

As Ralph stalked angrily off, Nancy turned a flushed face to her escort. "Bert, for God's sake," she began.

"Let's go, honey. "Let's just blow out of here right now."

"Come *on,* buster," she snapped. "This is my party, my friends. Sure we'll go—later. But, for now, we stick around—we've only begun to have fun."

"Do you really call this fun?"

Her patience disappeared in an instant. "Damn well know it is, Stiles. You've never taken *me* to any place *this* nice."

Bert fought off an acid rejoinder, one eye on Ralph, who had decided to return. "Hey," he said to the tall young man, "this is still a private conversation."

Ralph came up close, towering over Bert. But he addressed Nancy. "You want me to leave, Nance?" he asked.

"Oh, stick around, Ralph. Maybe you and my wild western date here can have a decent conversation." She ambled off.

"How you doing, chum?" Ralph asked. "Enjoying yourself?"

Bert just glared at him.

"So you're from out West," Ralph went right on. "I've been to L.A. several times, and to 'Frisco a couple times, too. Good open cities. You're from—where?"

Bert took a deep breath. "Colorado," he muttered.

"Nice country, I hear."

"Yeah."

"What college you go to?"

"Colorado College."

"Oh. What's your degree in?"

"I didn't graduate."

"You drop out—or what?"

Bert unconsciously stood on tiptoes as he faced the much taller man. "I'm just not going there now."

"Well, I'm Harvard myself. Bob, he's Yale. Jack already graduated from Harvard Business School. Do you types from the West have any college worth a damn?"

"Just a minute, goddamn it——."

"Nancy told us you hitched a ride back here. What's the matter, don't you know how to buy a train ticket?"

Bert knew his face was flushed. "I didn't happen to have the money," he said. "I wasn't born with a silver spoon in my mouth like you types."

Ralph clenched his fists, obviously angry. "Hey, listen, cowboy. We put up with you because Nancy brought you. But, do you think we like having a hick like you around? By the way, your suit is so big it would fit a cow. Don't you know how to buy clothes, either?"

Bert cocked his arm to lash out at the other's jaw. But he felt his arm grabbed—tightly—by someone behind him. It was Bob, another of the party, who had been around his friend Ralph often enough to anticipate trouble.

"Hey, none of this," he said. "This is a *nice* place."

"Meet me outside, you asshole," Bert breathed into his tormenter's face.

"With pleasure."

Again Bob broke them up, steering them away from each other. When Nancy returned, Bob told her she had better get her date out of there before they *all* lost their club privileges.

For the first five minutes driving home in the Packard, there was an ominous silence. Then all hell broke loose.

They mixed insults the rest of the ride. He was acting like a caveman. Couldn't he even be nice to her friends for one evening? Why was he such a boor?

And he asked what had changed her from the carefree give-'em-hell girl he loved in Colorado? Had she reverted to type now that she was back in the country club set?

Bert wrote to Rosemary the next night from the Aley's house:

> It looks like that beautiful little love affair has gone down the drain. I'm still the one who's out...and she's inside. Something just faded away. I guess I kind of ask for it—and I usually get it. But I'm going to stay in love until it's all over...though it seems pretty much that way already...one fragile chance in a million that it will bloom again.

He also wrote to his mother that week, describing first a cleaned-up version of the scene at the swim club. He added: "You don't know how close you came to having a new daughter."

As he was fond of doing, he also added a few lines of personal philosophy:

> One of the troubles about being parents after one of the offspring has checked out—is that when you hear from them they are usually down, and you get a one-sided picture. Because, when I am up on the moon, I usually don't write letters....

Maxwell Aley returned home one evening the following week in a euphoric mood.

"Let me tell you, kid," he began, "I talked to Erv Brandt today—you remember him: head fiction editor of the *Post*—and he started talking about 'Shining Armor.' Bottom line is, he's passed on the thing, Bert. Wesley Winans Stout, *Post* editor, will do it if Erv recommends it strongly. What do you think of *that*, kid?"

Later, at dinner, the agent said, "You and I are going to do a serial soon. When you go into the Big Town after you've sold a few stories, we'll start meeting the big people—and you may be headed for Hollywood."

Ruth Aley put up her hand. "Max, let's not start talking Hollywood to this impressionable young guy."

"The talk I hear," Bert said, "is what a rathole Hollywood is, and what it can do to writers—serious writers, that is."

"Hollywood or not," Max said, "you're going to get *hot.*"

On August 28, he received a special letter from his mother:

Twenty-one years ago a little Japanese doll of a baby with long black hair came along. You had dark eyes and exquisite little hands already reaching and grasping for the things life was holding for you. So you may know, on this birthday that makes you an independent citizen, you have brought only pride and joy to B.W. and me.

Bert told the Aleys he supposed it was the best letter he had ever received.

A return letter flowed from his typewriter that night, thanking them for their thoughts, and adding:

So now I am 21. And a lot of things have to be different now. I don't have to worry about being a child prodigy. If I had clicked at 20, that would have been something wonderful. If I don't click at 21, that will be something rather sad. This is one game I'm going to beat...because I was born with stars in my eyes. When they came to me they said, "Look at this little dark-haired boy. He's one of the odd-numbered ones; he's set for the big ride." I was born lucky, the deep kind of lucky, and if I keep true, then the luck will stay forever....

War often intruded upon Bert's thoughts. Sons of some of the Aley's friends were being drafted, and Max told him he could get him into the Merchant Marine school; Bert dismissed this as not the real war. He wrote to Rosemary: "I figure this is a war America should be in, and the sooner we are the better—and with everything we've got: money and ships and planes."

Ned Brown, a Hollywood agent, called upon Bert one day when he was alone in Dower House and asked him to write a 7,000 word serial about rangers for the movies. Bert became so excited about it that he began as soon as Brown had left. By midnight, still alone, he had written nearly 5,000 words, then took a long look at it and tore it to pieces.

My career is standing still, he thought.

On September 8, deep into an article in *Writer's Digest*, Bert half-heard Ruth Aley conduct one of her many telephone conversations. "If you're not ready to buy," she said, "just send it back. We're not going to embarrass you by selling you something you don't want. We'll ship it to someone else."

There was a pause for a moment, then Ruth added: "I don't know, I'll have to ask Bert."

Bert Stiles leaped to his feet, heart throbbing wildly. Ruth Aley hung up the phone, then put her hand on his shoulder.

"This is it, Bert," she said. *"Post* has offered $500 for 'Ranger Takes a Wife.' We're there, Bert."

"But you didn't accept. You put him off."

"Trust me, Bert. We have a sale. We'll just wait for Maxwell."

Later that evening, the second telephone call came through. Maxwell Aley casually took the call—and the deal was made. Late that evening, the young writer wrote to his parents:

> So this is the day I've dreamed of, and knew would come—and didn't know would come— and prayed for. This is a lovely day. There are clouds and a faint breeze—but mostly there is music—sky music— and it is coming straight my way. This is *my* day up here all alone in Connecticut.

Within a few days *American Magazine* purchased "Sun Valley Susan," also for $500. He was on his way.

His life became a merry-go-round of flattery, excitement, and meetings with the big names of publishing. "A young literary sensation, when he is discovered by the critics, will be Mr. Bert Stiles, who came to town last summer from Colorado Springs with something like two dimes in his pocket. Stiles has just celebrated his twenty-first birthday by receiving two fat checks," wrote Charles Driscoll in his newspaper column, "New York by Day."

Another literary columnist described the newcomer as one who "writes easily and has the light touch that is so welcome in stories these days." Erv Brandt of the *Post* told Stiles, "You write 'em, we'll buy 'em, and we can write checks pretty fast."

After two weeks of this, Bert wrote to his parents:

> And this is only the beginning, for little Roderigo is on his way up and over, and he is going to be plenty good, and the world is going to know his name. This kid in the Connecticut farm-commuter country knows now it is possible—and he is glad and proud and very, very happy. So thanks to my mother and father, and my school teachers and Krutzke and Maxwell and Ruth—and most of all thanks to the guy who dreamed up this world.

Hollywood's interest in the young writer was not a dream. Dick Mehland of the New York office of Paramount invited Maxwell and Bert to his office. Bert wrote: "We rode an elevator to the classiest inner sanctum I've ever seen, with paneled wood office, fireplace, everything. We talked turkey to Mr. Mehland. He said, 'We'd like you to go to Hollywood right now.' Then he showed us the contract: $150 per week."

With Hollywood agent Ned Brown as a traveling companion, Bert drove to the tinsel city in late October. He found Hollywood a "slick place," but one where, intuitively, he knew he didn't belong. Even so, he gloried in the offer and enjoyed tremendously writing this kind of letter to his parents:

> I may have a house on the beach, and a sailboat and an English setter like the Aley's dog Barry and a beautiful wife, and a daughter named April with long blonde hair and brown dreamy eyes, and she is going to be nuts about me. And you guys can come swim in my ocean, and fish and lie in the sun....

Hollywood was not for him, and he told them so. Maybe next year. Once out West, he stayed there, asking the Aleys to send his meager belongings. The call of the West was great; Colorado was a balm after the frenetic life of the East Coast.

Colorado Springs, with the first snow glistening on Pikes Peak, was as different from New York as one of his Ranger stories was from *Look Homeward, Angel.* Rosemary Harley, Sleepy Dickison, and Jack Mohler were still in school and his original class of 1942 was in its final year. In November he saw Colorado College down Colorado State 21 to 7 at Washburn Field to win the Rocky Mountain Conference. One of his friends, Bill Singen, had secured a delay-en-route from his air base to play for the Tigers. Singen responded in style by scoring two touchdowns.

Bert talked to Singen, and began to think about the air service. They didn't draft you into that service—it sounded like an elite organization. Was it time for him to take some such decisive step? Hold on, he told himself: I'm a hot writer, I just got back to Colorado, I still have some living to do before I leave the civie ranks.

Besides, he wanted to get to know Kay Bisenius better.

Kay was a small, dark-eyed senior from Boise, Idaho. He was attracted by her bright, breezy personality. Only thing was, she always seemed to be with someone else. Most recently, she had been dating Sam Newton, a fraternity friend. Kay was president of her sorority, Kappa Alpha Theta. He tried for a date often.

Without school as a distraction, and living in a small room a few blocks from downtown, Bert wrote "The Ranger Meets the Family." It was immediately purchased by *Saturday Evening Post*. It was his sixth sale in three months. He still kept in touch with New York and made arrangements to have dinner with Erv Brandt of the *Post*, who was coming through on December 7.

On that Sunday morning, he was banging away on his typewriter when he heard a commotion outside his front window. People were yelling about something and it didn't appear they would quit anytime soon. Irritated, he leaned out the window.

"What's going on?" he asked of several men students talking excitedly in the middle of the street.

"The Japs bombed Pearl," one of them said, and Bert sensed the excitement and outrage in his voice.

Hurriedly, he put on shoes and sweater and scampered outside. There he learned all the students knew of the attack.

Bert walked slowly back upstairs, his face grim. There would be all-out war now, he knew. Turning on his small bedside radio, he listened to the same news over and over. He puttered around his desk for a while, not even attempting to write. My God, he thought, how can I do anything as mundane as rewriting a short story? He knew, without a doubt, that he would soon be in the middle of this war.

In late afternoon, he met Mr. Brandt as planned and they spent the remainder of the day together, dining at the Broadmoor Hotel. Their talk was mostly of the attack on Pearl Harbor; writing and publishing was nearly put aside for the night. Even so, Bert came away from the dinner with the strong feeling that *Satevepost* liked his work—and wanted more.

At Christmas, with his parents and sisters, he was cool and upbeat, sanguine, almost brash at times. Hell, he was twenty-one years old, he had made good in his chosen profession, and he was about to enlist in the service and have the adventure of a lifetime.

In his old basement room, he started his second novel, which he tentatively named *Call It a Lifetime*.

He also had time for thinking. The Marine Corps was still a possibility, but what about this flying business? He had read so many stories and books about flying: the Driggs books about World War I combat; and, more recently, *Wind, Sand, and Stars,* by the French pilot-writer Antoine de Saint Exupery. What an exciting union, he thought—piloting by day, writing about it by night. He wanted to explore what the author meant by "The witchery of flying." And he shivered with excitement at the hidden potential in such phrases as "meditation in the vast temples of night" and "the wonder of nightfall in the air."

Bert Stiles had not flown at night (he had only been in an airplane twice in his life) so he had never experienced what Saint Exupery meant, but his love and awe for the hours of darkness fired his imagination. He could easily understand the mystique of flying in the black of night. And his own special force—the Blue Lady—would be there, watching over him.

Yes, he would have to try for one of the air services. And why not for Aviation Cadet training in the Army Air Corps? In fact, why not enlist tomorrow morning?

"I want to get up in the air, Mom," he said at breakfast. "Have some adventures I can write about someday—see what it's like in a war—put up with a little discipline. Bet you think I need *that,* don't you, Mom? So I'm going to check it out, and if my luck holds, I'll have a new career in the sky."

But the Air Corps recruitment center on Broadway Street in Denver did not immediately agree. They found a slightly damaged retina in his left eye. He might be accepted for non-piloting positions on an air crew. Or he could take another physical in a few months. Meantime, he shouldn't forget to check with his draft board.

He moped around his parents' house, hardly talking to them. Then he made two decisions—he would return to Colorado Springs, his emotional home, and he would try other services where there *was* a chance for flying. His thoughts crystallized in a letter to Maxwell and Ruth Aley:

> I kind of hate the idea of being a soldier, but I'd rather have a little head start by joining the Air Corps than be a flatfoot on the ground. I suppose I'm almost a pacifist at heart; but I'm not clear enough on my ideas to take a stand. So I'll just go along, and try to see if I can understand a little better....

The next several months he contacted several services. The RCAF thought it could use him and tentatively assigned him to a class beginning in June 1942. He reported for a physical in Chicago for the Navy Air Corps. The eye doctor there advised him to forget about flying. He took the Army

Air Corps physical again—with the same result. And the draft loomed larger.

 Even with his service unsettled, he was having a good spring and summer in the Springs: writing, dating Kay Bisenius, meeting with Frank Krutzke to talk about writing, and contacts—though infrequent—with his mentors the Aleys.

The charm and openness of Kay enthralled him. He sent her "telegrams," hand-written messages on blank forms he had appropriated from the Western Union office. One such message, delivered to her doorstep personally on March 16, 1942, read: "Deep Fog Banks of Lurid Devotion—acres of dusty desire," and it was signed by "Reynard O'the Willow."

More serious, he wrote to his parents in early May:

> So I am going. Down deep I'm a pretty peaceable guy. I don't want to kill anyone, but one of these days perhaps I will. I'm going over there because it seems to me the English are fighting for what I believe is worth fighting for....

> I guess I want to see what war is like. I've read all the books, and I went to Sunday School, and I've got all the mental sets against it. But it must be something like falling in love—you have to go through it to know what it's like. Despite my belief that we aren't solving anything by this war, there is a time when every man must fight.

In the May 1942 issue of *Phi Gamma Delta,* the quarterly issue of his fraternity's house organ, Bert wrote in the third person summarizing his life. He concluded it this way:

> At this point the luckiest-guy-in-the-world, Bert Stiles, taps his typewriter by day and chases a dark Kappa Alpha Theta by night. His world is mostly in suspension waiting to see whether he's going to get into this war in a Kittyhawk or as a draftee hauling a Gerand.

Bert Stiles was enduring the uncertainty so common with millions of young Americans. The service was there, beckoning, just out of reach, but coming as certain as death and taxes. The fact seriously inhibited the pursuit of other goals. Later in the month, in a troubled mood, he wrote again to his parents:

> Up until last summer the things I've wanted to do were wandering the world, the seeing, the looking, the wondering. The Vale of Kashmir was more important than any person; catching a big swordfish at Acapulco was an end in itself. The lonely chasing of rainbows was my

life. But it's not that way anymore.

People are my thing now—it just isn't any good without someone else.
Now my life is built around people—only it isn't built, it just hangs.
And a good part of the time it isn't much good.

It was the summer of 1942 and here he was, six months after Pearl Harbor, still in civies, waiting for the damn flying services to beckon. God in heaven, didn't they want willing pilots? Nothing from the Army, the Navy wasn't interested, even the draft board was silent.

B. W. and Elizabeth Stiles, with May and Beth, drove to Colorado Springs in late June. It was a fine family reunion; they drove up the Pikes Peak road, well past Manitou, into the high country. The sky was a brilliant blue, a breeze kept the temperature down, a few gray-white clouds billowed frivolously in the western sky. Bert felt refreshed in spirit as he bid his family goodbye early Sunday evening. They all knew it might be the last time the five of them were together for a long time.

The Springs was dead in summer; Kay Bisenius was in Boise, and he missed her terribly. In July, he sent her a telegram:

Dawn is slow STOP lawns are mowed STOP and you are quite sweet framed in mushrooms and alfalfa STOP I'm coming up there.
Love, Bert

Kay worked at the Ration Board and could not get time off on short notice. Her mother was at work, too, so Bert sat at home with Kay's younger sister, Carolyn. After talk was exhausted, he took to his typewriter again, completing the first draft of a love story. Reading it to the three ladies after supper one evening, he secured a preview of how it might be received by the magazines. One face showed rapture, one strong interest, one forced attention. Oh, well, two out of three.

On Saturday afternoon, Kay and Bert, with three of her friends, pooled their gasoline coupons and drove to Payette Lake, where the movie *North-west Passage* had just been filmed.

Bert invented a reason to leave the others off somewhere. He and Kay drove to Charlie's Garden on Sylvan Beach, an area of fountains and bird baths and stone walkways leading to flowered grottoes.

Kay, attempting to forestall the moment of truth she knew was at hand, was rambling away about the beauty of the place, when Bert suddenly reached for her.

"Shut up, Kay," he said. "I don't want to talk about arbors or birdbaths or flowers. I want to talk about *us*.

"Kay, I loff you madly," he went on, keeping it light, "and I'm about to fly away in the wild blue yonder—and I might not come back—and you're here and I'm here—and so tell me you loff me, too. And if so, let's go off in a merry daze and get down to shacking up."

"And if I said I didn't love you, Bert?"

"That'd be regrettable. But we could still shack up."

"You writer-fellows are all alike," Kay shot back, "one-track dirty minds."

They both dissolved in laughter and Kay felt she had escaped the commitment she wasn't ready to make.

Back in Colorado Springs, Kay still in Boise, Bert wrote to her of his personal philosophy, continuing an aborted talk:

> Kay, I believe each person is a dual thing— he is a part of humanity and he is part of himself. And the perfect life is when he coordinates the two just right...it's queer: when you're sad everything comes in more intensely and more acutely. I used to think it would be great to live without sadness, but you shouldn't. If you do, you aren't any good. As long as anyone is sad, then you've got to be sad, too. Because you're part of the world and it's part of you.

In October the war finally caught up with Bert Stiles; he was ordered to service with the Army Air Corps. They apparently had forgotten about his left eye.

There was no argument from Bert Stiles. If any man was ready to enter military service, it was he. Hell, he rhymed, there's a war on, Hitler's on the loose, I'm over twenty-one and as healthy as a goose.

He was leaving Rosemary and Kay, and a few other girls strewn around the country. But, hell, it would be over soon, he thought. And I won't be giving up my writing: I'll write in barracks, on leave, even in the damn airplane. Just let me experience life, he concluded, and I'll come out of this war a better writer.

Goodbyes were not difficult; most of his friends were in service. His parting from Rosemary was sweet and sad, but not prolonged. They vowed to exchange letters, and he asked her to keep his manuscripts until after the war. As for Kay, they exchanged a few more sad letters, but theirparting, restricted to the mails, was upbeat.

One of his last calls was at Frank Krutzke's house on Pelham Place. On his last day at the Springs, he had coffee with the professor, talking quietly. Then he stood up, shook hands, and said, "Goodbye, Prof, I'm off to war."

In Denver, he hugged his mother tightly, told her not to worry, shook hands with his father, then said: "Don't worry, folks, I'm in the hands of the Blue Lady. Now and forevermore."

1. Bert, about 8 years old, at home in Denver.

2. Bert's parents, Elizabeth and Bert W. Stiles.

3. Bert with his sisters, Beth and May, circa 1929.

4. Bert was a Boy Scout, attaining the rank of Star Scout.

5. Graduation photograph from South High School.

6. The Stiles family home on South York Street in Denver.

7. Bert in the Rockies in the summer of 1937.

*8. The family orchestra, circa 1936. Bert on clarinet, Beth on cello and
May on violin.*

9. Palmer Hall on the Colorado College campus.

10. Shove Chapel, Colorado College.

11. Rosemary Harley, about 1940.

12. Roland (Sleepy) Dickison, Bert's close friend in college.

13. Aerial view of Denver, circa 1940.

14. Seated on the steps of his fraternity, Bert Stiles contemplates his career as a college student.

15. *Colorado College skiers in 1939 (l to r): John Pleasant
'40, Bob Talmadge '42, George Peck '40, Captain of the
ski team; Bert Stiles '42, George Harmston '40, and John
Button '40.*

16. *Bert Stiles and Kay Bisenius, Colorado Springs, 1942.*

pressure and in a moment the airplane settled in with a slight bounce.

He thought he could discern a slight nod from the goggled head four feet in front of him. Mr. Heinrich spoke for the first time in five minutes: "Touch and go; let's try it again."

There was no lack of comment by Heinrich after the next takeoff. "On the last pattern," he said, "you lost 100 feet on downwind, you didn't appear to see another plane over your right shoulder on base leg, and you began your turn too soon on final. And your crab was too pronounced."

Bert's spirits collapsed. He flew the second pattern in a daze as he tried to absorb all that Mr. Heinrich had said.

Four more times Bert repeated the same landing routines. Not all were smooth: he lost 100 feet of altitude a time or two, bounced the plane in twice, pulled the Fairchild off the ground a bit too soon another time.

After the sixth landing, Heinrich lifted a gloved hand and pointed towards the hangar. "Let's go in," he said.

Parking the plane beside another trainer, Bert waited for instructions. Should he cut the engine? Was his flight over? Hell, was his flying *career* over?

The instructor said nothing; he carefully alighted from the front seat, hopping nimbly to the tarmac. Looking back up at his student, he kept his tone and face deadpan. "Go ahead, Mr. Stiles, take her around the pattern. Three times."

Bert, experiencing ambivalent waves of excitement, pride, and terror, lifted a hand, then grinned and nodded.

Mr. Heinrich stepped away, then looked back one more time. "Keep her straight and true," he said. "And good luck."

Everything went right: traffic was not heavy, the wind didn't change, the engine didn't fail. Bert felt he was riding a live animal, was *controlling* a live animal, one that did his every bidding, was eager, sensitive, powerful. He was ecstatic.

As he banked onto the base leg, it came to him that there wasn't that familiar and dependable head in front of him. God, he was alone up here! Nothing but open sky. What a feeling.

He let such thoughts evaporate; he needed to concentrate as he never had before. He had to do this right for three landings. Hell, he thought, he could kill himself tomorrow, but now he had to complete three safe landings, step away from the airplane—then hear what old Heinrich had to say. And it didn't have to be all good either. He would be—finally—a member of the flying fraternity.

Four days later, May 17, was the day before his father's birthday. Still in an expansive mood from his mastery of the primary trainer, he wrote to B. W. Stiles:

> Dear Dad: Tomorrow is the anniversary of your being born. Which was a very good thing for practically everyone. Especially for me and my sisters. So I hope it is a good day—and that you are happy. Maybe by your next one we can go fishing in the Gulf Stream: just fishing.
>
> When a pilot solos, he is entitled to wear these wings. How would you like to wear these on your fishing hat? I would like to think of you wearing them there....

A gamut of emotions had engulfed Cadet Stiles during the five months of Air Corps training leading up to his first solo flight. He had felt frustration, boredom, fear, hate, ennui. But there had been just enough positive points along the way to enable him to keep his sanity: the joy of flying, comradeship, mastery of a machine, a feeling that he was doing something worthwhile for his country, if not necessarily for Bert Stiles.

It had begun on January 7, 1943, at a dusty, sprawling classification center in San Antonio, Texas. Whether standing naked in line awaiting a physical exam or being issued dog tags or being fitted with clothes, he found it impersonal, tiresome, often degrading. He was assigned to Cadet Squadron 103 and issued Serial No. 234655.

He knew both physical and psychological testing would help determine his assignment—pilot, navigator, or bombardier. He passionately wanted pilot training, and he did all he could to slant his responses in that direction.

He had been assigned a bunk midway through the second story of a large wooden barracks building. The shrill siren screamed during a ten minute free period before lunch.

Reaching the door ahead of most of the others, Bert wheeled around and faced his comrades: "Take cover," he screamed. "The ME-109s are strafing us! Under the mattresses, ye buckos."

He turned back to the door, feeling fulfilled if a bit foolish, to come face-to-face with Lt. Ingallis. He popped to attention in front of the glaring squadron lieutenant.

"*Stiles*, eh?" he said, "Private Stiles. I'll remember that name. Now you listen to me, and you listen hard!" And there followed what Bert later described in a letter home as a "private air raid all of my own."

He saw himself as caught up in a giant and unseeing military machine without mercy, care, or intelligence. He knew this was a short period of his life; it would be over soon. But why did it have to be nearly unbearable? Did that make them better soldiers, better flyers?

Always appreciating humor, Bert looked hard for it in his fellow soldiers, and found some—most of it raw, hard-hitting, basic humor. Not too subtle. But in the officers, and even most non-commissioned officers, he found little humor. They took things so seriously—he couldn't buy a smile very often.

After two weeks at San Antonio without mail, he wrote home:

> They are trying to make this a big time prison. Schedule: up at 5:30, eat at 6, clean barracks 'til 8, physical training 'til 9:30, drill until 10:30, lunch at 11, PT and drill and retreat and gas attacks in the afternoon. You should see my Kelly Klip—worst haircut ever seen on man. Little bertstiles doesn't feel anything like a soldier. None of the stuff here is really bad, just pretty bogus. Four weeks today. In some ways it seems like four years, in some like it hasn't happened yet.

He borrowed a typewriter from Squadron First Sergeant Binson to write to Ruth and Maxwell Aley. He didn't want them forgetting him and picking up another aspiring young writer off the streets. After all, he was only twenty-two. Not over the hill *yet*.

The young private found several fellow soldiers to like: one guy had the build of Sleepy; another reminded him of Bob Hermann; a third looked a lot like Steve Lowell, and even had his voice. Pete Langer didn't remind him of anyone, but he sure could play ping-pong. They played every night for five nights, trading wins and losses. Langer was tall, baldish, slightly older. Their friendship really took off when Bert found out he was a Harvard graduate in English Literature.

Assignment orders were posted one cold morning. With immense satisfaction, Bert found he was slated for pilot training. His ego deflated somewhat when he learned that over 90 percent of his class were to be pilots; it would have made a better story if he had been more exclusive. Well, he reasoned, that's where the need is. Pilots were apparently dying faster than bombardiers or navigators.

Carrying the morbid analogy further, he wrote home that night: "I've got new dog tags on now—two copies—one for the loved ones at home, one for the corpse." Elizabeth Stiles, reading this message in the house on South York Street, paled, gritted her teeth, but didn't shed tears. She was used to fatalistic comments from her son.

Gaining new friends meant losing old ones. Some of his best buddies were off to other bases, probably gone forever. He wrote home that friends lost in this first of many separations were "Langer the bald-headed Ph.D.; Zitis, the New Yorker; and Wiener, the washed-out pilot."

Pre-flight was intensive: classes in code, math, physical training, drill, organization of the Army. And cold water shaving, mess hall duty, demerits, parades, sarcastic first sergeants. It never seemed to end.

But he always had time for writing: letters, short stories, articles for *The Tailspinner,* the base newspaper. At times he wondered what he was doing as a pilot trainee. He might have swung a writing job—with Maxwell Aley's help. But would he want to miss out on flying a fighter plane? Hell, no—he would have experiences he could write about forever.

On March 12, a week before his underclass stint was to end, he wrote home, his mood jubilant:

> I'm in the clear now—if I don't get off the ball. The idea is you have to be tough and cool, and so sharp that when you finally get in a plane you can look four directions at once, check 179 flight instruments, shoot your two outboard cannon, wave goodbye to the control tower, and sing Dixie at the top of your voice.

Graduation was low key: merely another formation at which the Base Commanding Officer, Colonel Davis, congratulated them; briefings (warnings?) on what to expect at Primary Training; and the posting of orders. Bert was assigned to Sikeston, Missouri.

Their troop train rambled on through the night, across the mid-southern part of the country. Arriving on base at Sikeston in time for breakfast Easter morning, they were allowed the remainder of the day to get settled. Bert wrote a long letter to his mother that Sunday night:

> Thinking of Easter reminds me of a letter you wrote long ago, Mother. Do you remember it? So perhaps tonight is a good night to tell you a few things about the way I work inside.
>
> I'll be holding hands with death each day. I'll have to be as good and cool and smooth as I can. But beyond that, the Blue Lady will have to

hold my hand. Which is a light way of saying that whoever has handled my case through the years will have to keep on doing the job. I remember your letter had a part about never being alone. This is a wonderful, comforting thought now.

She lives high in the sky...above the sun and back of the stars. She's as far as the end of time and as close as the wave length of a whisper. She's always there...to laugh with, to talk to, to walk with. Why it's a She I couldn't say...maybe because of you...maybe anything. But she's my Lady of the sky...my Lady of Luck...my Blue Lady...and my life is in her hands.

Tonight I'm on the edge of something big. And as long as I play my hand as clean and hard and straight as I know how—then it will work out. So it seems to me your son was born under the right stars, and so far everything has been going along. How far it will go or to where, is out of *my* hands. It's in *hers.*

His first ride in an Army plane was on April 28 at Sikeston, Missouri. Among the horror stories told in Pre Flight was that one's instructor could "make or break" you, that most of them were has-been pilots who were either reckless or uncaring or worse.

Bert found the opposite to be true. Mr. Heinrich was a quiet little guy, a civilian under contract to the army to give new Aviation Cadets their first flying experience. They were to fly Fairchilds, a single-engine, single-wing airplane. They were painted blue and yellow and appeared somewhat ungainly.

Although Mr. Heinrich had a mild voice and seemed willing to repeat everything twice—or more often—Bert almost immediately felt pressure. His romantic soul *demanded* that he fly well; his masculinity *insisted* that he master this machine; his ego instructed him to forgo *everything* else— and concentrate as he never had in his life.

So—first, the horizon: make sure it doesn't maneuver too much. Mr. Heinrich said it should be just above the nose of the airplane. Simple, really—if it's higher you're in a dive; if lower, you're climbing. So move that stick forward or back—and automatically. But keep those movements of the stick under control; overcorrection is a danger, too.

Meantime, watch that airspeed, keep your eyes roving, watch out for other airplanes. After a vertical correction, check that airspeed—it will fall off or increase as altitude changes. And never forget (for more than a moment) the direction you're heading. Hey, stay on the assigned 200-degree course. You're wandering, Mr. Stiles. You're climbing, too. Notice your airspeed fall off? You can do something about it, you know. Anytime now. Fine, fine. Now let's learn a coordinated turn.

For a ride or two it seemed impossibly complex to Bert. How could he watch everything at once? On the ground after the first ride, Mr. Heinrich asked him if he could ride a bicycle.

"Of course," Bert answered.

"How old were you when you learned?"

"Oh, I guess about five or six."

"So at five or six you learned to steer and pedal and retain your balance all at the same time. Not an easy group of skills if you think about it. In flying, Mr. Stiles, you have another group of skills—involving heading, altitude, power and a few other things. No harder to learn than bike riding, given your present age and maturity. Don't worry about it—it will come. I won't rush you; you can practice all you like."

But Bert knew he had to make reasonable progress or, no matter how nice a guy Heinrich was, the cadet would become the latest victim of the "washing machine."

He flew every morning that first week, between one and two hours each time aloft. And—slowly—he began to feel the sky was part of him, that he *belonged* there. He wrote home: "The sky is mad and lovely, and everyone is going nuts—what with discipline, weather, and worry about washing out. And the wind is terrible—they send pilots from here to the Aleutians for a rest."

For cadets with no previous flying experience, a minimum of ten dual hours were required before soloing. When Bert reported to Mr. Heinrich on May 13, he had nine hours, fifteen minutes. He suspected he would be shooting landings for an hour or more. As he fell into step beside his instructor, he asked himself: could this be my last ride? Will I thrash around in the washing machine—and then go under forever?

Looking back on it, Bert decided the solo flight had been pretty routine. He had just followed his training, and he and the Blue Lady had brought in his little Fairchild together.

He piled up flying hours, both dual and solos, though more of the latter. He no longer doubted his ability to get the plane off and land it safely. It was like taking his parent's car out of the driveway on South York Street and driving a girl or a gang of boys all over Denver. It became automatic.

He loved aerobatics—snap rolls, slow rolls, loops, spins, even such tame maneuvers as lazy eights. His reasoning was that the better he could perform aerobatics the more likely he would be assigned to fighters, a goal he cherished.

Flying never became routine; it was a constant challenge to survive. He wrote to his parents about a check ride:

> I got a 30 hour check yesterday—and I have to do it over again. Because I gave that ugly horrible Lieutenant the worse ride of all time. I didn't do one thing right. On a simulated forced landing I would have crashed into a hay loft if it had been the real thing.

He felt so high after passing that particular check ride that he spent all day Sunday writing a short story entitled "Check Ride," then sent it off to the Aleys with high hopes.

Graduation from Primary Flying training meant he was halfway through aviation cadets. On June 29, with little time for celebrating or even reflecting upon his career progress, Bert boarded still another train, this one to the base in Independence, Kansas, in the southeast part of the state—in country as flat as a dance floor.

They had heard the usual latrine scuttlebutt about how tough it was, how they would still wash you out for little reason, how BTs were tricky machines to fly. The toughest flying was ahead, he figured. Meanwhile, was he ever tired.

The round-nosed Basic Trainer 13-A—no-nonsense, heavy, and ugly—was as different from the Fairchild as the Kansas plains from the Rocky Mountains. If the Fairchild was a Chevrolet, the BT was a high-powered Chrysler. Even so, it was considered just the right transitional tool for teaching cadets: a half-step toward the even more high-powered AT-6, the plane waiting for them at Advanced Training.

The BT gave Bert the feeling he was finally flying a warplane—of one sort of another.

His apprehension about Basic Training was quickly realized. After only a few days, he wrote to Rosemary:

> This place is worse than Sikeston—a 14-hour day running from 5:45 to 7:30—and then night classes. My instructor just graduated and he's never flown a BT-13, either; so that makes two of us learning to fly it. These instructors hate their jobs so much some of them go quite mad. The military life has palled so badly that I fear I will try drinking iodine before long. What a wretched place this is....

On a flight the following week, a solo cross-country, Bert became hopelessly lost. Where the hell was he? The flat plain in this part of Kansas looked like a flatter one in the next state. The map wasn't any help; he had no checkpoint, no reference. Finally, he did what his instructor had wryly suggested he do as a last resort; he buzzed a town and read the name on a water tower. Well, what do you know? He was in Locust Grove, Oklahoma. Just fifty or sixty miles off course.

He learned formation flying and wrote to his parents: "You have never heard such words as my instructor used to describe the way I fly formation. I soloed because he got too scared to go up with me anymore."

After his friend Al Schulenberger washed out, Bert became even more wary of the "washing machine." Al had been a good pilot. He knew it was never too late to be eliminated from the program. He noted the class seemed to crack up a plane nearly every day. Most were groundloops.

As his birthday approached in late August, he wrote home:

> One more week here. So say, "Let him be good for five more days—let him stay lucky." By the time one is 23, he ought to be a little way along the line—but I'm as deep in the fog as ever. I'd like to end up in a P-51 but it seems a million miles away. If I can stay out of trouble, I might swing it....

Stiles celebrated his twenty-third birthday on still another train, this one en route to Eagle Pass, Texas. Once on the base, he dumped his barracks bag by his new bunk and hiked down to the flight line with some of his fellow cadets. A fierce wind, kicking up dust on the dirt street, kept their heads down.

The AT-6 was slick looking after the planes he had been flying. In fact, he thought, if he put his imagination into high gear, it looked *something* like a P-51. He could hardly wait to give it a try.

But after soloing on September 11, he decided it was just a bigger Basic Trainer with more power and retractable wheels. He wrote to his parents: "I soloed the AT-6 and got my wheels up and down okay on my check ride; so maybe my instructor will let me stay awhile."

Maxwell Aley wrote that he had sold "So Long" to *Liberty Magazine* for $250, and "Check Ride" to *Yank Magazine*. Bert was ecstatic. He could still write, he could still sell.

A week later, with several hours of solo flight time, Bert returned from his sixth training flight. He noticed another trainer just settling onto the apron. No problem, he was far enough ahead of him. His own landing was adequate, even good considering the sun was directly in his eyes and a crosswind slanted in from the left. He relaxed on his landing roll. What would he do tonight? There were no formations; he could read, take in a movie, perhaps write to Rosemary—

Another plane swam suddenly into his sights—directly ahead of him. Pulling the stick sharply into his stomach and jamming right rudder, he watched horrified as his trainer began to turn—but much too slowly. With a wrenching sound, his propeller jammed the tail of the other AT-6.

A moment later both planes stood still on the landing strip with their two cadet pilots sitting immobilized in shock. As if in a dream, Bert noted a red flare billowing from the control tower. Then came an ambulance, a fire truck, and a jeep, red lights rotating on its fender. The emergency vehicles surrounded both planes, people hopped out shouting things—and Bert Stiles felt as low as he had in his life.

They were critiqued separately in the Squadron C.O.'s office; the other pilot was taken first. Bert knew his fellow pilot vaguely. When he came out of the C.O.'s office, Bert thought he was looking at a ghost.

The Squadron Commander, a captain in his late twenties, had flown fighters in combat in the 15th Air Force. As Bert strode sharply into his office, he noted the Captain's leathery, weary face now contained only one emotion: fury. Bert, who felt like crawling under the nearest desk, instead drew himself to stiff attention. His salute was one of his best ever.

"Sir, I'm sorry…"

"Shut up, Stiles. Wait until you're spoken to."

He remained at attention while the Captain sized him up.

"Mr. Stiles," he said, his voice vibrating with disgust, "you've just cost the Air Corps thousands of dollars, you've helped write off two Sixes, and by God, you've helped Hitler win the goddamn war! Now what in fuck happened?"

"Sir, I have no excuse."

"Come on, Stiles, try. Tell me *something* about it."

"Well, sir, since you ask specifically, the sun was in my eyes, there was oil on the windshield, I had just finished a crab from a crosswind, and —"

"All right, Stiles, that's enough excuses. You could no doubt go on all day. Just tell me what the hell happened."

Standing at crisp attention, Bert took five minutes to go through his every action and thought from the final approach on. While he was talking, he made a conscious decision *not* to blame the other pilot. He would play it straight all the way.

As he was talking, the C.O. never let up on eye contact.

Even after he finished, the Captain didn't waver his glare.

"You haven't commented on the other plane, Stiles," he said finally. "He was parked right in the middle of the strip. Are you implying he had a right to be there?"

Play it straight and clean. "I accept full blame, sir. I shouldn't land without knowing I had a clear path."

"That's hard to disagree with, Stiles. If you were the C.O. here, would you wash out a cadet who chewed a tail?"

That's a helluva unfair question, Bert thought. Damned if I do, damned if I don't. "Sir, I can't make that decision. That's the responsibility of higher authority. I'm sure you'll be talking with my instructor—and others."

"Damn it, Stiles, don't tell me who I should talk with." Another long pause, as the Captain continued his steady glare. "As you so coyly say, I *do* want to talk to your instructor. Also to the Squadron Ops Officer, also your ground school instructors, also to your *mother* if I choose to."

"Yes, sir."

"You're dismissed, Mister. You're confined to barracks until we send for you. If you hit the washing machine, you'll be out of here tomorrow. If you survive the machine, I want you in the air tomorrow. Now, get the hell out of here."

Cadet Stiles stayed on his bunk the rest of the afternoon and into the evening. His bunkmate brought sandwiches from the mess hall. Someone else brought a bottle of beer, but Bert refused. Beer on his breath? Not a chance.

About nine o'clock in the evening, he was called into the Base C.O.'s office. Besides the commanding officer, the Operations Officer and his flight instructor were also present—along with the still glaring Squadron C.O. The base C.O. nodded to the Squadron C.O. to proceed.

The Captain made it short: "Cadet Stiles, you're still in Aviation Cadets. At least until tomorrow. You fly at 1300 hours with Lieutenant Johnson here. Two hours of the toughest dual you'll ever have." He stopped for breath. "Now—dismissed!"

In a daze, Bert headed for the tap room on the way back from the flight line after a successful check ride. He ordered two beers, downing the first in a series of quick gulps. He thought about the events of the past twenty-four hours. Elated that he had come out of a bad situation, he was glad he had played things straight and true. But, he thought, he had seen his brother officers use rank, position, and situation to beat down on him. The lover of fun and spirit and elan had seen a slice of the real world—and it wasn't pretty. Could combat be worse?

He wrote a note to his parents before he piled into bed:

> So—sun in my eyes—oil on the windshield—crosswind—plane stopped on the strip (illegal)—and I rammed him. My instructor was very sad. I am so off the ball it scares me. The old washing machine chewed me around for a while, then spit me out in one piece. I can't understand why I'm still around.

Bert worried continually that his accident would result in an assignment from the bottom of the barrel. In the meantime, he was authorized to buy officer's uniforms: tropical slacks and shirt, black shoes, Class A dress of green blouse, gray wool slacks. He also picked up three pairs of gold bars—those worn by second lieutenants. He was beginning to believe it would actually happen.

Graduation Day was November 6, 1943; he had been in cadets one day shy of ten months. The base Commanding Officer, the same light colonel who had made the final decision not to wash him out of Cadets, presented him his silver wings in front of a small crowd of local friends. There were few parents or relatives present.

It was a cold, dreary day, but Bert felt his spirits soar to new heights. After his wings were mounted on his left breast he fingered them often the rest of the day. That night, snug in his narrow bed, he offered a silent prayer to his patron:

> O Blue Lady in the sky: I'm coming up to fly with you. Teach me the secrets of living gloriously in the wild blue yonder, take me by the hand and keep me safe in your warm embrace. I am one with you, a sky bird now, and I'll never be the same earth-bound being ever. O help me, Blue Lady, my lady of luck, to meld with your kingdom in the sky, and to fly safely with you forever....

7

CREWS ARE BORN, NOT MADE

"I'm doing what I want to do—
flying birds around the sky—and
I guess I've gotten tolerably good
at it...."

The day we went to Paris the sun had a clean sweep all the way out. We came in from the West, and after I jacked the RPM up and got my flak suit set, I started looking for Maxim's and the Champs Elysees. I could see the Eiffel Tower and the river, and I could probably see almost everything else, because I got a good long look. I can say I've been to Paris, but travel by Flying Fortress is a hell of a way to go anywhere. No matter how bright the sun is, or how clear the air, no place is very satisfactory from four miles straight up.

Sand and salt were the order of the day at Salt Lake City, seeping under eyelids and putting a furry coating on tongues. Lieutenant Bert Stiles arrived there on November 20 by way of Colorado Springs and Denver. The two-week graduation leave had gone fast, as leaves do.

Wearing his uniform a bit self-consciously, he had spent the first few days at the Springs seeking out old friends. There were few. The men were in service; the women married. Mrs. Harley told him Rosemary was in California; Sleepy had gone into the Merchant Marine; other friends had disappeared somewhere. He spent two days skiing behind Pikes Peak with a casual friend, poked around the campus and fraternity, talked most of one day with Frank Krutzke. But where were the laughs, the wine, the women, the song?

In Denver, his mother hugged him tightly, not wanting to let him go. His father shook his hand, eyes moist. B. W. couldn't seem to take his eyes from Bert's silver wings.

Bert didn't see his sisters—both were in college out of Denver. He did run across a few high school friends still not in the service, accompanied his parents to Washington Park Church, swam at the "Y" for old times sake, and simply walked around his old South Denver neighborhood.

But four days of home led to itchy feet. He had a week to go before reporting to Salt Lake City and he had not had enough of his "emotional" home—Colorado Springs.

"Guess I'll take off tomorrow," he said, as they sat at the dinner table, the three of them.

"Can't you stay a few days more?" his mother asked, her voice quavering slightly. "There are lots of people you haven't seen yet."

"You said you didn't have to report to Salt Lake until a week from today," his father added.

Bert lay his spoon down by his chocolate pudding and sat up straighter. "Listen, folks, there are things I want to do—places I want to see—people I want to touch bases with. At the Springs."

"You've *been* there," his mother said.

"I didn't *see* anyone," Bert said. "That was just a teaser. You see, I—" He stopped, noting their frozen faces. Were all parents this way, wanting to hold on to their offspring? Oh hell, he decided, I'll allow a day at the end to stop through one more time. They *are* my only parents.

On the bus to Colorado Springs (as an Air Corps officer he had decided he'd give up hitchhiking) he settled back deeply into his seat, staring at the snow-covered Rockies out his window. He was pretty lucky, he knew: loving parents, two clever sisters, lots of friends, a published writer, a flyer now—and with the Blue Lady out there waiting for him. His thoughts roamed widely:

> I've been Lady Luck's favorite son—I've had a wonderful time in life and met some swell people. I know there are ways to get what you dream about and love, if you get in there and dig and fight. But now I'm caught up in something pretty damn big—bigger than I can fathom, much bigger than my little dreams and problems. But—I'm

doing what I want to do—flying birds around the sky—and I guess I've gotten tolerably good at it.

It was a lonely week. Rosemary hadn't returned, there were few students he still knew, and everyone seemed to be about eighteen years old. He sat in on one of Krutzke's classes but the professor was busy and he hated to take his free time. On his last day there, it came to him that he didn't need human relationships. He hiked up to the Garden of the Gods, well scarfed and gloved, seeking solitude, physical activity, pure mountain air.

He strode up the gradual incline with ease—God, he was in superb physical condition. That was one thing the Air Corps did for you. His thoughts came tumbling out:

> One big puzzling thing is who am I—this Bert Stiles? I am a million selves in one— and often one soul living aloof from all the others. I've been many things—student, conformist, lover, dreamer, wanderer, yes, writer, too. I've worked on a road crew, been a Junior Forester, fisherman, student, skier, second baseman.
>
> And so now I am a flyer...and a warrior...and a potential Goddamn killer....
>
> Above all else I am a dreamer, a wistful seeker. And at these times I am supremely thankful. My existence would be intolerable without these moments when I can sense eternity. I can be in hell, but for an instant another self emerges and a bit of blue sky comes and I look into everlasting beauty.

He walked upslope fast, stretching his legs forward to pump blood faster through his body, deliberately punishing himself. He needed, he *demanded,* to feel his very existence in sore muscles, shortened breath, in heightened awareness of being alive in God's world. There was Pikes Peak, a wondrous mountain, a place he would always remember in any part of the world they might send him. He'd always come back, he decided, whenever his soul needed refreshment, whenever his spirit needed a lift.

Glancing over his shoulder, he could see lights flick on in various sections of the Springs. A corner room at the Antlers Hotel popped into light—perhaps some poor boob home from a day of work or on his way to dinner and a love match later, who knows? To the South, he could see the distant lights of the Broadmoor Hotel. Ah, such lovely times he'd spent at the Broad. Perhaps he would have been better off to sack out there for the entire leave— preferably with a lovely lass who idolized him.

Facing West, toward the darkening sky, his thoughts turned mystical:

My God is my very own. He lives where there is beauty. I find Him most out in the night sky—the deep starlit blue, where it is so painfully beautiful I sometimes can't even think straight. I tell him everything— my dreams, my hopes, my all. He is the power, the one I turn to. Every time I sense beauty, I turn my eyes to the blue and we meet in spirit for an instant.

When I think of immortality I cannot see how these thousand selves that are me could possibly end. With death I will gather all the particles that have become me—and will ease me out into the blue finally—per- haps—to meet my God. I see no reason why a man cannot conceive his very own eternity; and mine, I dream and hope and pray, will be out in the blue. I will be in motion—millions of miles in a long dive—then float— adrift. Eternity will be the gaining of the realm of beauty—the capturing of the thrill of that beauty, that I find up there in the sky....

Salt Lake City was somber and military when Bert arrived in late 1943. It seemed a place of destiny—here he would learn of his future with the Air Corps. He knew his orders were for co-pilot on a bomber, but he had no other information.

His orders were to report to the Commanding General, Second Air Force Combat Pool. Of course, this meant overseas: combat. This is what it's all about, he thought. He would never find his Blue lady in a Link trainer stateside.

With thousands of other flying officers, most of them second lieuten- ants like himself, he wandered around, getting his bearings, staking out a BOQ, instinctively looking for someone he might know. And, amazingly, he did find a friend.

He was in the officer's club lounge seeking a cup of coffee when a tall officer tapped him on the shoulder.

"Well, for Christ sake, Bert Stiles."

Bert whirled around, a grin already on his face. "Hey, Sam, is that really you?"

Sam Newton gripped him by the shoulder. "So you made it through, Bert."

"I see you did, too, Sam."

"Piece of cake."

They quickly decided the reunion was worth a beer or two. They never stopped talking during the next half hour, comparing notes on training fields, airplanes, love life, where all their friends had gotten to. Bert gave his friend a brief rundown of his route through four bases in three states. "And," he added casually, "they pinned these wings on me down in Eagle Pass. I told them I wasn't a hot pilot like you, but they insisted."

Newton told him of his six-month run through Rankin Field ("I flew Stearmans there—great little plane to learn on") to Merced, California, for Basic and Fort Sumner, New Mexico, for Advanced. "I flew the 'Bamboo Bomber' in New Mex," he said, "and I guess I was already slated by that time for bombers.

"So what do you think you're headed for, Bert?"

"I'll tell you a little story, Sam."

So Bert told his college friend of his experience chewing the tail of another AT-6 in Advanced Training.

"I ended up near the bottom of the barrel, I think. Looks like co-pilot for me on a four-engine bomber."

"I'll be on the big ones, too."

"Sure, Sam—but as first pilot."

"Yeah."

"*Co*-pilot, damn it! I wanted fighters so badly I'd of given my left nut—freely—for a P-51 or a P-38."

Bert had last seen Sam Newton at his fraternity in Colorado Springs. What was that—two—three years ago? Newton, from Sioux City, Iowa, had not been a close friend at the Springs, but they had been fraternity brothers. Sam had dated Rosemary and Kay and knew most of Bert's friends.

In the middle of the second beer, Sam voiced an idea. "Bert, if we're both going to be in bombers, why don't we get ourselves on the same crew?"

"Do they do things like that in the military?"

"Damned if I know. But we can sure find out."

They walked a few blocks past low-slung barracks, dodging second lieutenants at every step. Several enlisted men came by, popping smart salutes at the new officers.

"I feel like Lord of the Manor," Bert said.

"You're pretty casual on that return salute, Lieutenant."

"I could so easily be an EM, myself. Don't you get the feeling, Sam, that most people who pop you a big one are really laughing at you? What'd we do to deserve this tribute?"

"Hey, listen, buster, you earned it. Flying school is not that easy."

"I still don't care that much about being an officer. But if anyone tried to take these wings away, I'd yell and scream."

They turned in at a busy headquarters building. A long table stood in the corner of the room. A small dark-haired girl in a smart tan uniform looked up as they approached.

"Hello, again, Lieutenant," she said to Sam with a slight smile. "Can I help you?"

"Sure can, miss. My friend and I here are old friends from college. We work well together. Have you got the pull, young lady, to get us on the same bomber crew?"

It was like Sam, Bert thought, to make it a challenge—that was how things like this got done. Even so, he was surprised when she didn't reject the idea forthwith.

"If you'll both write down your full names and serial numbers," she said, "I'll check your orders. Look after my desk for a moment, will you, Alice?"

When she returned a few minutes later, her smile was pronounced. "First hurdle cleared," she announced. "You're both assigned to B-17s and headed for Alexandria, Louisiana. Before we go any further, I'll have to refer this to Captain LaForge.

"Perhaps you shouldn't get your hopes up," she added. "But if the Captain is in a hurry, and if he sees no particular objection, it could work out for you. You two must be good friends."

Late that afternoon, after a visit to the PX, they revisited the WAAF and presented her with a nicely-wrapped necklace along with their thanks.

Sitting on his narrow bunk, Bert wrote to Kay Bisenius:

> We are supposed to be shipped out tomorrow or the next day or next month. There are about 3,000 pilots living here in the hall for showing off Utah's best pigs—about 500 of us here in this room—grimy—weary—sad apples.

> I ran into Sam Newton. We have it fixed up so I'll be his co-pilot—which would be the end of the world. Somebody has given the word to throw every heavy bomber into the air.

Once orders were cut, there was no more leave. The Air Corps wanted them in phase training as fast as possible: to pick up a crew, learn the ropes, get aloft in a B-17, and— as Bert put it—"get our butts overseas."

The Air Corps had been punishing France and Germany with daylight heavy bombing for well over a year. Intelligence reports had convinced General Eisenhower and his staff that carrying the war to Hitler was taking its toll. Munitions plants, railway yards, marshaling yards, factories, air fields—all had been subject to intensive bombing by the U.S. forces. It was beginning to pay off.

But losses had at times been alarming, particularly during 1942, when there had only been three bomber groups based in England. Now, with ten times that many groups, the odds of survival had improved somewhat. Fatalities were still high, however, and new heavy bomber air crews—on B-17s and B-24s—were vitally needed. So leave was scarce, phase training shortened, and planes and men rushed to bases in England.

Alexandria, Louisiana, in the south central area of the state, was on the Red River. Like much of Louisiana, the terrain had wetlands, groves of hardwood, and fields planted to cotton, soybeans, tobacco, and grain. Bert knew the state only from passing through on his way to visit grandparents in Mississippi.

Sam Newton was worried. Soon he would meet the remainder of his crew—two other officers and six enlisted men. He had no choice in the assignment process. What if his men were not sufficiently trained? What if they didn't respect him as pilot in command? The ten of them would be going to combat together, into dangerous situations, yet he was entirely at the mercy of the Air Corps—or of pure chance—in whom he would be flying with and depending upon for the next several months.

The wait wasn't long. On Monday morning, their squadron adjutant handed Lt. Newton a list of names:

2nd Lt. Samuel Newton, Pilot, Sioux City, Iowa
2nd Lt. Bert Stiles, Co-pilot, Denver, Colorado
2nd Lt. Donald M. Bird, Bombardier, Oswego, New York
2nd Lt. Grant H. Benson, Navigator, Stambaugh, Michigan
Sgt. William F. Lewis, Engineer, Grand Island, Nebraska
Sgt. Edwin C. Ross, Radio Operator, Buffalo, New York
Sgt. Gilbert D. Spaugh, Waist-gunner, Winston Salem, North Carolina
Sgt. Basil J. Crone, Waist-gunner, Wichita, Kansas
Sgt. Gordon E. Beach, Ball-turret gunner, Denver, Colorado
Sgt. Edward L. Sharpe, Tail-gunner, Hot Springs, Arkansas

Pilot and co-pilot met their crew in one corner of the recreation room. Introductions went well. Yet it was a large situation for Sam Newton: he wanted to—he *had* to—get to know each man as well as possible in the next ten weeks. He was determined he would talk with each of them separately, get to know their personalities, backgrounds, likes and dislikes. And weaknesses.

In the first week they had their first flight in a B-17. With close to 100 hours in the aircraft, Sam felt he had been adequately trained. Bert Stiles had never even been in a B-17. The crew seemed to Newton to be fairly well trained. But he really didn't *know* that. It was his job to assess their training and their fitness for the job at hand. Quite a job for the twenty-three-year-old Sam Newton.

Bert wrote his parents on December 8:

> Our crew seems to be a good outfit. But this plane is really a monstrosity. It takes a horse of a man to bend one of these things into a turn, and there are 2,017,000 switches to learn and settings to know. Sam Newton, my pilot-roommate-boss, is going to have some sad days before I learn the score on this machine. The sport of flying is all over...we were supposed to fly yesterday, but our plane would not sit up and take notice...I kicked our instructor in the head jumping out of the escape hatch—which is a beautiful way to begin.

Despite his misgivings, Bert knew he was caught up in a great adventure. The B-17 Flying Fortress was not his first choice of warship to be taking into combat—more like his last. But he was assigned to it, and he would do his best to fly the airplane. But he would do his damnedest someday to transfer into fighters. There he'd find the exciting life he craved, far from sitting at the controls *(assisting* at the controls, really) of a flying boxcar with the maneuverability of a tackle on the New York Giants.

From an early age, Bert had enjoyed expressing some of his personal philosophies to his mother. He wrote to her in early December, just before her birthday:

> I guess birthdays don't mean much any more—it's just nice if somebody remembers you were born and is glad. I have an idea that of all the people you have run into in your life, most of them do remember and all of them are glad.
>
> *Especially me.*
>
> Here are the wings you wanted. They don't mean much to me right now because I can't fly the monster plane I'm assigned to. From here

to the end of the war I'll be doing something I hate. Because flying these big trucks isn't any fun, and the business we're in is pretty ugly.

I haven't found anyone I could talk to since I got in the army. And I'm getting out of the habit of doing any real thinking. Not much gets said that means very much—nobody knows what to say. It seems to me all my ideas and faiths grew up in those lost years from 1935 to 1941, and all my questing was done then. Whenever I get into an argument I find myself saying words I've said before when I had Powell and Krutzke and Sleepy to sharpen up with—and you and Dad. So I must be changing and maybe there'll be more changes.

I'm not getting anywhere in this letter, so be happy on your birthday— and I'm glad you were my mother and are my mother and will be my mother.

If there was a strain in flying a "monster," adjusting to Sam Newton's personality, and learning new skills every day, Bert had his special relief valve not available to other flyers at Alexandria. *Writing.* He still wrote short stories, some of which he never sent anywhere. And he watched the mails, hearing from Maxwell Aley once in a while, selling a story now and then. Aley forwarded $700 for a half-forgotten story he'd written a year earlier. He was delighted, not only for this reminder that he hadn't lost his touch, but for the money. Seven hundred dollars was several times his monthly pay as an Army pilot.

At night, on his bunk, Bert studied the flight manual of the Fortress. It was required reading, of course, but aside from that, he wanted to know as much about the airplane as he could. The more he read, the more appalled he became. It was too big, too unwieldy, too slow. It *was* a monster.

Oh, it had power, all right. Four Wright Cyclone radial engines (1200 horsepower each) drove the great hulk of metal and rivets through the air at 210 miles per hour, straight and level flight. The supposed maximum speed was 305 miles per hour, but Bert doubted it ever attained that speed except when it had lost its tail and was headed into the ground. Wing span was 104 feet, length 74 feet, and ceiling 36,600 feet. Not bad credentials—for a bomber. A powerful wing supported the engines, bulky and solid.

The young co-pilot decided he liked the appearance of the B-17 well enough: formidable, hulking, well-armed, a fullback of an airplane. It looked and felt solid and it was known for its remarkable return ability. He supposed Boeing up in Seattle had done as well as they could. But who could be happy sitting in a truck of an airplane flying straight ahead with limited maneuverability in attitude, course, or power settings?

And of course loops, rolls, or anything approaching acrobatics was impossible. The only time he felt any kind of thrill was during takeoff, when all four throttles were pushed forward to the hilt and the big plane slowly gathered takeoff speed. With vibrating floorboards and shaking engine mounts, Bert knew a form of excitement, but it sure wasn't like riding on the back of a soaring eagle. More like being tied to the rump of a rhinoceros in a jog trot.

There had been no expectation of a leave over Christmas; they were too close to overseas assignment. He couldn't even swing an overnight pass to visit his grandmother in Jackson, Mississippi. He wrote to her instead. He also wrote home a few days before Christmas:

> It is Christmas which is certainly the best time of year to give anything away. So I give this to you because I want you to use it. I don't know whether the house on South York is all paid for, but I would like to pay for some of it. I do not know whether the travel fund is built up to trip proportions yet, but I would like to help build it. And please telegraph Elizabeth and May this day that they each have twenty-five bucks more to play with....Serenade

He missed Colorado and the Rockies. He remarked to Sam that he was ready to go AWOL to be in the Springs or Boulder or Estes Park in the clean, crisp, snowy Colorado winter.

Midway through the ten week course, he finally began to feel relatively confident about his duties on the B-17, duties such as starting engines, reading off checklists, watching RPMs and manifold pressures on takeoff, and opening cowl flaps. Big, big stuff for a second lieutenant, he thought. On landing, he called off airspeed, handled the tailwheel, opened cowl flaps, monitored propeller pitch. Whatever the pilot, in his wisdom, needed from his right-seat helper.

And, of course, fly. Depending upon the personality of the pilot, most co-pilots expected to fly up to half the time. While he didn't shirk flying, he didn't look forward to it, either. He found it difficult work: monotonous, boring, and very tiring. The total opposite of a fighter plane, he thought, where he would be master of his own destiny.

In a P-51 Mustang he might find his Blue Lady often; in a Fort, the Lady would probably be too bored to bother.

He wrote his folks that they needn't worry about the ability of his pilot Sam Newton. He wrote: "The one who should be worried is Mrs. Newton, because when I take over there is really no telling what may happen."

The Silver Moon was a bar and dance hall on the edge of Alexandria where some of the crew personnel repaired for drinks, laughs, and relaxation. Sam and Bert usually went there on Friday and Saturday nights.

On a chillingly cold Friday night in late January Bert and Sam spent the early hours of the evening at the bar; there were a few others they knew present. The jukebox rumbled in the background. "I'll Get By" was the favorite ballad of the evening, "Mairze Doats" the most popular novelty tune. Then Sam told Bert he was leaving.

"Leave? Now? C'mon, Sam, the evenin's young."

But Sam left, hitching a ride with a couple of officers from another crew.

Bert looked at the bartender. "Joe, will you drink with me since my friend's left?"

"'Course, Lieutenant."

"Hey, the Lieutenant's name is Bert. Come on, now, let's hoist them. Anyone else want to join us?" he added, glancing around the room and earning some friendly glances but no takers. "Then it's you and me, Joe. What'll you have?"

Joe was a light-colored mulatto, with an open, friendly face and a direct way of looking at things. He was about twenty-five or twenty-six. Bert liked him a lot.

"No more beer," Joe said, with finality. "That stuff fills your gut—you spend half your time going to the can."

"What, then, buddy?"

"Want to go for something different? Listen, the boss is out of town and I've got all sorts of liquor there. Want to experiment?"

Bert gave him a bright smile. "A guy after my own heart. Sure. Let's figure it out as we go." Nimbly, he vaulted over the bar and began to take stock of the back bar inventory.

"Pick out some stuff, Loo-ten—Bert," Joe said. "Go ahead. I've got to wait on those new guys just came in."

Bert, who was not drunk but certainly not sober, either, began to gather bottles with the most exotic labels. By the time Joe had returned, he had lined up creme de menthe, creme de cocoa, gin, absinthe, sweet vermouth, and rye whisky. Then, with a flourish, he grabbed a fat bottle from the back of the bar—Southern Comfort.

Joe grabbed the largest martini mixer he had. He looked quizzically at the array of liquor. "All of it?"

"All of it, indeed."

They both poured liquor, helter-skelter, into the mixer. In went three jiggers of gin, a large shot of creme de cocoa, several jiggers of Southern Comfort, and liberal pinches of vermouth and absinthe. Joe added crushed ice and they took turns shaking it lustily. The result was a frothing, brownish, unappealing liquid. They surveyed it critically.

"It's not quite right," Bert said. "Something's missing."

Joe cocked his head. "Did we put any creme de menthe in?"

Bert considered. "Don't think we did." He grabbed the bottle and poured in a generous amount. "Hey, this is better—gives it a more pleasing appearance. Who knows— it might even improve the taste."

They took turns shaking it, then solemnly Joe poured the brown-green concoction into two beer glasses.

"Let's drink together," Joe said, raising his glass high. "That way we can die together."

They drank. Neither said anything for a moment. Then Bert spoke. "God, it's sweet. Too damn sweet. It needs some lemon or something. But—there's something about it: it seems to have a strange power over me. I need some more."

Joe, staring at him with wide open eyes, drank with him.

There was silence between them as they both considered the situation. Then Bert spoke again, abruptly. "We've got to come up with a *name* for it."

Joe smiled. "Better we flush it down the toilet."

"No, no, buddy. It's good stuff and we have to give it a proper name. Let's see—what does it remind you of? Dark castles on the moors? The wicked witch in *Snow White?* Or the Witch's Brew? Something like that. Got any ideas?"

"You name it, I'll just drink it."

Bert sipped again, thought a moment, then looked up, his face bright with triumph. "How's this? *Witches' Madness.* I think we have it, Joe."

They continued to sip slowly, careful not to inhale too much at one time. Neither suggested they quit. Bert thought it wasn't a bad drink for one they'd just invented.

It was eleven o'clock and they had finished their third *Witches' Madness* when Bert became aware of someone standing behind him. He turned. Standing there, staring at him with the loveliest green eyes he'd ever seen, was a tall young lady.

"Hello," Bert said.

"Hello."

"Where'd you pop in from?"

"Cape Cod."

"You mean Cape Cod, as in Massachusetts? You just came in from there?"

"I was there last summer. I was just thinking about it. I'd sure like to go back. Will you take me back?"

"First thing tomorrow," he said, then looked hard at her. Here was a bright wraith, appearing like magic out of the cold Louisiana night. And did she ever talk crazy. This was no ordinary doll.

"You've got green eyes," he said. "Prettiest green eyes in this town."

"Yours are brown. Sort of a golden brown. There's a sort of strange light in them now."

He gave her a bright smile. "Might be 'cause of this special brew. Want some?"

"Why not?"

"We call it *Witches' Madness.*" He poured some in a glass, handed it to her. Joe had gone to wait on a customer.

"Say, green eyes," he said. "Are you alone?"

She took a moment to grimace after tasting the drink. "What did you do, make this drink up yourself? Well, I'm not exactly alone. See that big captain coming out of the Men's Room? He's my date—tonight."

He spoke quickly, excitedly. "Go out with me tomorrow night?"

She looked directly into his eyes; she was just his height.

"Sure."

"Right here—eight o'clock."

"Okay, brown eyes."

"Say, what's your name?"

"Just call me June."

The next day, a Saturday, Bert borrowed an old bicycle and rode out into the Louisiana countryside. He needed to think about his new girl. Well, not his girl *yet.* What did she have? Aside from long, auburn hair, skin as clear as a mountain stream, and those so green eyes—well, what else was there? He didn't try to intellectualize his attraction to her; he only knew he *had* to see her that night.

He was at the Silver Moon before eight o'clock. The place was crowded but there was no sign of her. He had a beer; by unspoken consent he and Joe avoided *Witches' Madness.* After the second beer, it was 8:30. He had a third and it was past nine o'clock. He realized she had stood him up.

Of course, Bert reasoned, as he walked two miles back to base after midnight, this doesn't lessen my desire to see her again. In fact, it probably increases it. Maybe she planned it this way. I could call her—but, God, I don't even know her last name. It would be a week before he could attempt to see her at the Silver Moon. He prayed she would be there.

They flew Fortresses on simulated combat missions to various cities but never landed. They overflew Jackson, New Orleans, and Gulfport, honing their flying abilities, testing navigation skills, practicing gunnery. Crew photographs were taken; he sent one home to his folks. He wrote that they were "the cream of the nation and the pride of the fatherland."

On the second Friday night he caught up with June at the Silver Moon. The evening was everything Bert had hoped for.

Sam and Bert were friends on the ground, but it was often a bit strained in the air. Lt. Newton was in charge, and he had his way of doing things. When his co-pilot tried to put his own character into the flying hopper, Sam would frown, tell him how he wanted the particular task at hand done, and then watch Bert closely. The latter sometimes felt constricted, like a teenager too carefully watched by a demanding father.

If Sam Newton sometimes approached a martinet in the air, he was a different person when earthbound. He was a close friend and they did things together: movies, dating, beers at the O-Club. But Bert needed to escape from the crew at times—by writing, walks in the countryside, dates with June—and by finding an off-crew friend.

He found the right person in Alfred McCardle, a pilot on another crew in the squadron. "Mac" was from Pittsburg, and had been in the Phi Gam house there. Bert was delighted his new friend was a fraternity brother. Tall, good looking, sandy haired, intelligent, quick with the repartee, Mac was just the friend Bert was looking for. They tested each other with their pet theories on national politics, philosophy, war, history, prognostications for the future of the human race. Mac was an intellectual equal not so caught up in flying and his crew that he couldn't talk on many subjects—and argue, joke, compare, insult, commiserate. In short, a friend.

Training was winding down. There had been so much down time (mechanical troubles and weather) that they were already overdue to move out. Bert had ambivalent feelings about leaving Alexandria: he wanted to get on with the war, but he was having a great time with June. Her unconventional actions and thoughts kept him mesmerized. He thought she was a bit wonderful; wacky, of course, but quite a doll, withal. She stood him up again, then once again, never offering much of an excuse, never really apologizing. She was June and if Bert liked her, well, fine, they'd get along. If he couldn't put up with that kind of treatment, well, that was fine, too. She thought Bert was a dashing flyer with a romantic streak a yard wide, but he wasn't the only man around. She wasn't going to change for him.

Leaving Alexandria wouldn't separate him from his friend Mac. He and his crew would be in the same shipment, headed for the same destination—wherever that was. Bert was delighted they would go overseas together. They would stay best friends, he figured, perhaps stay together after the war, too—roam the world together.

On February 16 a new B-17G was assigned to them. He wrote to his parents that it was a "beautiful silver airplane, with staggered waist guns, an electronic supercharger, a sweet dream of a plane."

While sweating out inevitable delays, he wrote on March 1:

> Everyone is going mad...in a big gay way, and nobody knows where and why and how soon. The luck has held out for so long—it started when I drew you two for parents; and only two other people in the world have been that lucky since...so the world is round and for a while I'll be quite a way around the curve. And maybe I'll wander quite a way before I get back....
>
> So this is the way it is for me now—for your son, born in 1920, who will be coming home some day, I think and hope and wait for...and so say hello to the high mountains...and I'll come back sometime and we'll go fishing....

8

A SAD AND TWISTED WORLD

"I grew up to be in love with the
world...deep and bad and mixed up
and wonderful...."

Maybe the Americans and the Russians and the English and all the others
who had learned to fight together could crawl out of their Yaks and
Liberators and Lancasters and General Shermans and LSTs and jeeps.
Maybe they could sit down and smoke a cigarette or a pipe of peace.
Maybe they could get drunk first, and make love for a while, and throw
darts, and get good and hung-over. Maybe the peace-makers could sit
quietly in comfortable chairs on the moon, some place where they could
see all the world, and maybe help a little to tie it together....

The inevitable train ride landed them in Grand Island, Nebraska—their
final stateside stop. Midway along the boring, bumpy ride he wondered
why they couldn't fly. They were pilots, weren't they?

Grand Island was just another base. Bert didn't like the city as well as
Alexandria, which wasn't saying much. But they were treated royally—
fine food, few formations, lots of time off. Fattening them up for the
slaughter, he thought.

There would be no more leaves. After waiting out a two-hour line, he
telephoned his parents and asked for a few things from his room: some
books, long underwear, and his typewriter. He wasn't going to Europe
without his Corona.

Sam, Mac, another pilot and Bert went to town nearly every night at Grand Island. They had acquired a taste for sparkling burgundy. They would go to a bar, buy a beer occasionally, but basically drink from their own bottle. They were sitting at the edge of the dance floor on their second night in Grand Island when something made Bert look up—and there she was. Somehow, June had found him.

She stopped at their table. "Hello," she said.

"How did you get here?" Bert asked. He rose quickly and began to edge her away from the table.

"I came to see you."

"I can't believe that, June. You didn't seem to mind much when I left. How did you *get* here so fast, anyway? And how did you know where we were *going?*"

She smiled. "I really did come to see you."

"Sure. Have another big one."

"Okay, don't believe me."

"I won't." And he didn't, really, but there was doubt.

They danced and they drank and Bert tried to steer her away from another pilot who thought he had latched onto her.

He saw her when he could. She was swell, he thought, but how the hell can I ever come to terms with her personality? She was from the other side of the mountain. But he raved to Sam about her long hair, those green eyes, the warmth of her, that luscious body. Could I ever trust her, he wondered? He knew she had been married before, but knew no details. Her habit was just to smile when she didn't want to answer. Which was often.

Their silver new B-17 Fortress arrived and the entire crew inspected it carefully and critically. In spite of his open distaste for bombers, Bert was enthralled. He might not like the flight characteristics of the Fort but, Oh Babe, what a lovely, expensive toy this was to take into battle! They had been told they would fly it to Europe. They heard they were headed for the Eighth Army Air Force, headquartered in England, and commanded by General Jimmy Doolittle.

The day before their scheduled departure, Bert felt a need—a driving need—to write one final letter home:

> Maybe the luckiest thing of all about you two was that I grew up
> without anything phony pounded into my blood about Negroes or Jews

or Chinamen. Maybe I could have figured it out for myself; I don't know.

You are the kind of people I would fight for even if you didn't belong to me. You have been good for the world and for me. I'm glad we knew each other. Which is a bad way to say it, but there isn't any good way. No one has ever found a way to tell a mother and father how it feels to be their son and to be glad about it. Somehow our family worked. So my life hasn't been much like yours, I guess. But most of me is you, projected into the strange shifting intersecting planes of all the worlds a person lives in. Some of the things you are I hope I am—and some of the things you are I will never be....

So the way the luck built up, I grew up to be in love with the world...deep and bad and mixed up and wonderful...because I loved it when I was a little kid. So I think I have said enough for one afternoon. Anyway, goodbye, write to me, and some night when the sky is clear and full of stars I'll come back to York Street and knock on the door, and I'll be pretty glad to get there. Serenade...

But their departure was delayed by weather. There was time for one last party—with both Sam's family and crew involved. Sam's brother, Jim, from Sioux City, had not been able to get down to Grand Island earlier. But when Sam called him and told him of the delay, Jim and his family jumped right into their car.

Jim Newton brought with him his wife Mary Helen and her parents Walter and Dorothy Johnson. The Iowans also brought with them a suitcase full of whiskey—as if the flyers needed any more booze. The four visitors were staying in a small hotel near the center of Grand Rapids, but it turned out to be too small for anything resembling a first-class reunion.

"Sam," Mr. Johnson said, "We can do better than this. How could we possibly get your crew in here? I'm going to try to get in the Yancey—let me have your place by the phone, Bert."

"They sure didn't have anything when I called there yesterday," Sam said. "Booked solid with visiting families."

"Don't forget I'm in the hotel business," Mr. Johnson said.

Ten minutes later they were on their way to the Hotel Yancey, retaining their smaller room for sleeping purposes. The Yancey was Grand Island's finest—ornate, roomy, comfortable.

While the others settled in, Bert and Sam borrowed Mr. Johnson's car and drove to the base to pick up their crew members—those they could find.

By eight o'clock that night twelve or thirteen people were crowded into the hotel coffee shop for dinner; then they adjourned to their suite. The four civilians toasted Sam's crew several times. Stories were told, some even true. The non-coms, slightly nervous at first in this group of officers and their families, soon relaxed. The evening lasted until well after midnight.

There was another "reunion" involving the same group. Sam's crew was scheduled for a gunnery training flight the next day. Sam had an idea. It involved a little risk—but what the hell.

At exactly noon, their gleaming B-17 pulled a first-class "buzz job" over the highest point in Grand Rapids—the sunroof of an insurance building. Sam banked the huge four-engine craft over the building while Bert and several crew members waved and cheered. Below, they could easily see four figures waving amongst a crowd of bewildered spectators. Perhaps amazingly, they weren't disciplined for the stunt.

There was one more event in store before departure; this one also featured Sam Newton. At the Yancey Hotel in late afternoon, back from their training flight, Sam and Jim were shopping for cigarettes and stopped briefly to go to the men's room in the basement of the lobby. Jim Newton asked his brother about the Black Widow, the Air Corps' new night fighter. Sam told him some of the facts he had heard, adding that he thought it would be a potent weapon.

As they were leaving, an Air Corps Captain, non-rated, approached Sam.

"Lieutenant," he said. "I want to talk with you a moment." He looked meaningfully at Jim Newton, who stepped outside.

"Lieutenant, I just heard you tell that civilian classified information about one of our warplanes."

Sam blushed deeply. "That was my brother, Captain."

"I don't care if he was your grand-niece, Lieutenant," the officer answered crisply. "You know, there are spies around—they're not just in trashy war novels. You were saying some pretty damaging things."

Sam Newton could hardly believe his ears. "Sir, I read all that stuff in flying magazines. I'm a bomber pilot; I don't really know anything about Black Widows—except what I read."

But the Captain, who Sam decided must be in Intelligence, wouldn't let him go without getting his name and outfit.

"What was that all about?" Jim Newton asked, when Sam had emerged into the lobby.

"You don't want to know," Sam said, "And, besides, that bastard is still watching us."

Bert Stiles was directly involved in the aftermath.

Each day all officers were required to assemble for roll call. The following day some sixty or seventy officers were milling around in the base gymnasium awaiting the day's roll call. Abruptly, someone called "Attention!"

The group came to attention and all noise ceased.

Bert was standing in the crowd of fellow flying officers, but Sam wasn't present. He had wanted to see his brother one more time before Jim's family returned to Sioux City. Sam had asked his co-pilot to answer "Here" for him—to cover for him. This was a fairly common practice although it could be overused.

The Captain who had entered was a stranger to Bert. The officer stood on a low platform and announced, "Respond with 'Here' when I read your name."

The Captain began calling names in alphabetical order. After a few minutes, he reached the Ns.

"Newton," the Captain called.

"Here, sir," Bert responded.

There was a pause. The Captain looked around. "Where are you, Newton?" he asked.

Nervously, Bert raised a hand and stepped lightly apart so he could be seen.

The Captain took a long look at Lieutenant Stiles and said, "You know, there's only one officer I know in this group and it's Lieutenant Newton, and YOU'RE SURE NOT HIM."

Sam Newton had to appear in the Captain's office the following morning. There were no excuses. Surprisingly, the Captain did not recommend punishment.

So Lt. Newton had a shaky final week in the States—with a buzz job in a B-17, loose talk in a restroom, and being AWOL for roll call. By contrast, Lt. Stiles was an angel.

Their new B-17 flew off into the blue on March 20. Grant Benson, their navigator, would soon find out if he had mastered navigational training.

There were stops in Labrador and Iceland with layovers the order of the day. The weather was ominous.

There was time for writing, and letters poured forth from Bert's smuggled Corona. Most letters were serious in tone; he wanted to honestly record his activities and thoughts as they happened so that he would have fresh material for writing short stories, the great American novel, or whatever. He asked his mother to save all of his letters, which she would have done in any event.

In Iceland, where they were holed up for two nights, he wrote that the air was full of the North and the mountains, cold and sweet. He recalled other cold places he had visited: Sun Valley, Aspen, Berthoud. But it wasn't the same. This was not carefree, this was sad. He wrote home:

> It seems so senseless to be going off to war when we could be skiing. It's a sad, twisted world right now. The planes were taking off here today, a cool deadly, lovely sight. And then the snow got gooey and I fell in the creek…and I wished that Eddie Jo or Jack or Violette were around. And I can't go home tonight, Mom, all tired, and know you would warm up some soup for me.…

They landed at Presward Airport in Scotland during the afternoon of March 26, 1944.

During the spring of 1944, most airfields were crowded into a fairly small area of southeast England. In fact, there were 130 military airfields, including forty-two Eighth Air Force bomber bases and fourteen fighter groups. American fighters at these fields were usually P-51s and P-47s. Five bases were permanent RAF facilities built before the war.

The RAF bases were rumored to be classy, superior to the mass-constructed U.S. facilities. Housing was more comfortable, heating better, and recreational opportunities more varied. The English bases were known as the "Country Clubs of the Eighth." Sam and Bert, believing the rumors had a strong basis of truth, decided to buck for a converted RAF base. They even picked out the base they wanted: Bassingbourn, home of the 91st Bomb Group. Scuttlebutt had it that the 91st was the dream assignment: close to London, comfortable living, good combat record.

The train was right out of Conan Doyle or Agatha Christie, Bert thought. Quaint, creaky, romantic, but capable of a journeyman efficiency. Gazing dreamily out of the coach window, he watched the countryside become a patchwork of green squares, aimless lanes and hedgerows, hamlets with thatched roofs, and an occasional donkey pulling a cart. Again he thought of the many English novels, stories, and poetry he had enjoyed over his lifetime. He had a sudden feeling of "coming home." He wanted to get to know this country, then he wanted to *write* about it.

His eyes filled as each vista of lush landscape floated by. Strange how any land could be so many shades of green, he thought, with the lazy netting of crooked lanes wandering everywhere and nowhere. His eyes satiated with the landscape, he said the word "war" two or three times—and it just didn't make any sense. It was so peacefully lovely out there in the fields. Yet the people who lived here had fought since the beginning of time, since before the Romans. And they were still fighting.

Surprisingly, their choice of base had come true: the 91st Heavy Bombardment Group (B-17) in Bassingbourn. The former RAF base was about forty miles northeast of London, near the village of Royston, in Cambridgeshire. He wrote home that evening:

> Funny place, this place, and nothing like I thought it would be. But it's good to be here, and it'll be better when we get into this thing—and it will be soon. The whole idea is to be deep inside what is going on, and we're still on the edge. Maybe in a little while I'll know more about the war, what a war is, and how it gets that way. Anyway, I feel a little closer to the center and that's the only place to be, right in the center. So serenade...

A two-story house which looked something like a small college dormitory was the co-pilots' house, the home of the two pilots on the Newton crew. Bert took pride in that the house seemed to be named for him: "There's *some* advantage in being a co-pilot," he told Sam. After settling in, and with his roommate Newton out negotiating the purchase of a bicycle, Bert took stock of his room.

He looked for a moment at the jigsaw puzzle picture on his desk, a picture of a dame with a lovely chest under a sheet of plexiglass. "In case we run out of words while writing a letter," he told Sam. Nearby were a lamp, a radio, and a bucket used as a waste basket—also a saucepan for cooking eggs on the electric heater, which was shorted out most of the time. There was a fireplace with nothing to burn in it and two ugly blackout boards that stopped all the light from going out and all the air from coming in.

Above Stiles' bed by the window there were pictures of Margaret Sullivan with bangs, Jane Russell with legs, and one of a little dream girl named Doris Merrick. Close by was a photo of Ingrid Bergman with her hair grown out from playing Maria in *For Whom the Bell Tolls.* Then came Ella Raines, and in the corner a startling photo of Maureen O'Hara, deep red hair piled high.

Scattered around the girls were pictures of P-51 Mustangs. Every time he passed, Bert paused for a closer look at the crisp, sleek lines of the fighter plane. He blew them a kiss.

He took off his sweater, threw it on the bed, and groped in his foot locker. There was a book by Freud there and an atlas. Lying about was a book of poems by Rilke, a book on yoga, another on algebra, and a song book with words to a lot of songs no one ever heard of. A blue baseball cap from the Brooklyn Dodgers lay on the floor near some used gum wrappers.

Bert decided it was a room he'd like to live in again after the war. He smiled to himself as he envisioned carefree wandering around the country to see what England was like without the threat of war.

They had been informed that the commanding officer wanted every combat crew to fly two or three practice missions before taking the air over Germany. On their third day at Bassingbourn they flew a borrowed Fortress, seemingly all over England, and practiced assembling into formation, flying tight formation, gunnery, and navigation. It was a three-and-a-half hour flight and Sam and Bert were exhausted.

"Hope it doesn't take more than three-and-a-half hours to go to Berlin and back," Bert said, "or I won't last the course."

"More like double that," Sam said, dejectedly. "But, listen, buddy, your formation work was pretty lousy today. I can't fly this big crate all alone. You've got to work on that."

"Give me a break, Sam," Bert said. "Today was my first formation. I can do better; stay with me."

Later, they walked to the mess hall together. Just like cadet days, Bert thought, standing in line, serving themselves from steaming pots of mutton, boiled potatoes, and strange-looking vegetables. They were joined by Alfred McCardle, Mac to everyone, whom Bert had first met in Alexandria. Mac was a first pilot on another crew but spent more time with Stiles than he did with his own co-pilot. He had a room on the second floor of the co-pilot's house.

Halfway through their meal, Billy Behrend, who roomed across the hall from Sam and Bert, joined them. Dark-haired and with a few freckles strewn haphazardly across his nose and face, he was another co-pilot. His easy manner and perpetual grin usually led to instant friendships. Before they finished their dinner, the four flyers had hatched a plan for the night.

Billy Behrend, who could talk anyone into anything, obtained a jeep from some dubious source and the four of them took off on a narrow lane through the wooded area that they knew would lead to a paved road to Royston.

The dance was at the Royston Town Hall, a tall, stately building in the center of the small village. Arriving just as the dance began to get into full swing, they stood for a moment in a tight group. Then Bert spoke up. "The only thing to do is separate," he said, decisively. "Divide and conquer. Let's see who can come up with the best-looking English wench."

So saying, he launched himself at a tall, slim girl named Eleanor. She was about his height—possibly a bit taller—but she had such lovely green eyes and long dark hair that he didn't let this bother him. She was nineteen years old and lived with her parents in nearby Duxford.

The flyer and the young girl danced cheek to cheek; he was soon carefree and relaxed, the war temporarily forgotten. A little later they walked through darkened streets, huddled in their coats in the cold spring evening, hand in hand. Bert learned about her life in England, her brother who was in the army in Africa, her Navy boyfriend whom she was about to break off with ("Well, that's *good*," Bert said.) and her job in a Cambridge factory making ball bearings.

Bert told her a bit about his life of college, roaming, writing, and now flying.

At a corner pub, they could hear loud male singing. Bert, who had always been attracted by singing and music, steered his girl inside. He checked his right hand pocket: three half crowns, four sixpence, three pennies. Enough.

The pub, thick with smoke, was composed mostly of men of late middle age. Beers were being hoisted, dart boards were in avid use, and the song "Bless 'Em All" was just finishing. Bert, who loved the song, wished they would sing another chorus.

Instead, they began another number: "Underneath the Lamppost, By the Barracks Gate."

Eleanor was amazed to see that Bert's eyes were wet.

"I didn't know you cared about us that much," she said.

Bert took his time answering. "I care about you very much," he said. "All of you. England. Your parents. Your air raid wardens." He glanced around. "Your 'Lily Marlene' singers." He smiled. "Even your dart throwers.

"Eleanor—you people are just *great.* You've shown such incredible courage—you can't believe how much Americans, most Americans, admire the stand you've taken. Care about you? You're damned right I care. I love you—love you all." And he leaned across the small table to kiss her on the cheek.

The four flyers met at the front door of the Town Hall at midnight. There were handshakes with new friends, a final kiss or two with lasses they met, a last wistful look at the civilian life they had enjoyed so briefly.

Bert and Eleanor clung to each other for a long moment. He figured he would see her again—he knew where to find her.

Their approach to the base was the opposite of the exit route. Again, they proceeded without lights. There was no problem. Bert couldn't decide whether the MPs occasionally turned their backs on such goings-on, or whether the four of them were really *that* clever. Hell, if you could drive a B-17 for nine hours you should be able to navigate a jeep undetected for a few miles.

They entered the co-pilots house in perfect blackness. Sam tumbled into bed immediately and to sleep. Bert sat on his bed in darkness, looking out his window at the dark sky. A pale quarter moon glimmered above the airfield.

He walked softly out of the room, to the front door. He could see no lights anywhere. Sitting on the front step, he hugged himself to keep warm and thought of the night. What a glorious time night was: black, forbidding, magical, mysterious. It was a time to be out in the world, to sample its wares, savor its mystical aromas, flirt with the unknown.

This was a special moment: about to start combat, out with three swell guys, met a neat girl, the day off tomorrow, and this incredible night before him. He would write letters tomorrow, to Kay, Rosemary, Sleepy, his parents. As he sat there, shivering a bit but perfectly content, he mentally composed a letter to Kay:

> In England they have a merry way of spreading everything all over the
> map. This place is camouflaged between cows and towns and roads

and duck ponds and getting lost is a thing done with the greatest of ease.

This land of England is very much worth the living in. And I can see why they fight for it so valiantly. This "somewhere in England" is really nice. And this address—91st Bomb Group, APO 557—ought to last for a long while. It is supposed to be the break of breaks to go to the 91st.

It is one of the oldest groups and lives at an old RAF field and maybe we'll be living at a castle and digging up treasure on our days off and running around the greensward with much gaiety. And you should see this castle I live in. It is better than the Fiji house at the Springs.

9

SEEING GERMANY FOR THE FIRST TIME

> "The entire crew huddled back
> by the huge up-swept tail. He
> thought it was a little like the
> locker room at South High before
> a ball game...."

When the lights were out I lay there for a while, not ready to go to sleep. I wasn't scared. Not yet. I was just wondering a little—what the hell was I doing here? I'd been building up to this night for a long time. I used to dream about it at school, sitting there drinking cokes with Kay, reading the airplane magazines. I used to think about it all the time in the cadets. And now we were really here, ready to go to war. We were going out to kill the Germans.

He awoke with heart hammering, knowing the potential for death in the skies that day was real. And if I die, he thought, if Bert Stiles disintegrates, how stupid, how irrelevant, my life would have been.

The light was as bright as daylight as Lt. Porado tried to shake wakefulness into Sam Newton.

"Come on, Lieutenant," Porado said, "Breakfast at 2:30, briefing at 3:30." Newton still hadn't moved. Porado headed for the door. "I got a long list of wake-ups," he told Stiles. "Make sure he gets up, will you, Lieutenant?"

The co-pilot, his chest tight with undefined emotions, shook Newton's bed violently. The pilot turned over onto his back, opened his eyes, and fixed them on Stiles' grinning face. "My God," he said.

Food was plentiful: powdered eggs, bacon, pancakes, and hard dry toast. Bert said, "Can you believe what we are about to do, Sam? Going on a trip, a long trip, to help some other guys beat up on a town, or an oil plant, or a steel mill. Doesn't this seem like a pretty futile way to live?"

Sam Newton, his mouth full of pancakes, merely grunted.

The briefing was in a group of connected Nissen huts near the head-quarters building. There was a scramble for the aisle seats near the front. Chairs for about 250 crewmen faced a low platform. Sam and Bert glanced about looking for familiar faces. Some members of Sam's crew saw them and edged over. The room filled quickly.

Lt. Col. Sheeler, the Group Operations Officer, stood on the platform facing them, waiting patiently for the combat crews to settle down.

Bert thought the group, himself included, looked like a raunchy bunch. Most of the officers wore leather jackets and crushed officer's caps; a few had on leather flying helmets with the earflaps turned up. The enlisted men wore fatigue clothes and caps or black woolen skull-caps. Within a few minutes, a blue haze of cigarette smoke cast a gray pall in the large room.

Just as the noise began to abate, the colonel spoke. "Good morning, gentlemen."

There was instant silence. "In a moment we'll talk about the target for today and the formation you'll fly to get there. Then we'll be looking at the flak situation and the weather en route.

"Before we start on that," the colonel continued, "let me welcome the crews who are going on their first combat mission today." His leathery face broke into a half smile.

Bert looked sideways at Sam, a crooked grin on his face. Sam didn't acknowledge the look. Grant Benson and Don Bird shifted nervously in their seats.

"You new crews," he went on, "look to your flight and squadron leaders closely. Remember, they have the experience, you don't. Fly tight formation—I can't emphasize that enough. Just do as you've been drilled to do for months now. Follow your checklists, from pilot to tailgunner. We don't need any accidents or screw-ups before we even reach enemy terri-tory. Now, any questions before we get to the target for the day?"

He nodded to Major Thompson.

With a flourish, the major whisked the white cloth from the map to reveal a large-scale depiction of central Europe. "Take a close look," he said, using a wooden pointer to draw a circle around an area in the south central portion of the map. "This is Eschwege—your target!" He went on to describe it as an assembly base for fighter planes, a shipping point for German aircraft clearing to more forward bases. He held high a large aerial photograph of the fighter station.

The Assistant Operations Office came on and unveiled another map, this one showing known or suspected positions of German flak along the route to the target. "For you crews on your first mission, we're *not* routing you through flak positions." Bert brightened visibly. "But," he added, "know that the Krauts move their gun positions around regularly." Bert let his grin relax.

Each of the forty-eight B-17s flying that day was assigned a specific position in the 91st Bomb Group's formation plan. Four squadrons of twelve planes each. Three planes to a flight, four flights to a squadron. All very simple and straightforward, Bert thought. Bert looked for their plane number on the mass of data and noted they were flying right wing off the lead ship of the high squadron. He copied the information, as Sam had asked him to do.

The weather officer, a slim captain, used still another map to illustrate location of clouds, and spoke of visibility en route and temperatures at various altitudes. They would bomb at 25,000 feet; the day promised good combat weather.

The Operations Officer came on again at the end of the briefing. "Time hack," he said, and every crewman in the room prepared for the ritual. "Coming up on 3:58," he said, as if he were about to start a race at a grade school track meet. "10 -9 -8 -7 -6 -5 -4 -3 -2 -1 -Hack!"

The clicks were audible throughout the room.

"Good luck, gentlemen," the colonel said a few minutes later. "Give 'em hell today."

Bert Stiles followed the other co-pilots into an adjacent hut to pick up escape kits and food rations. Later, he dressed in a crowded equipment hut. Since he hadn't put on long johns—he hated them—he donned an electric flying suit, followed by coveralls and a leather jacket. The potentially life-saving Mae West jacket went on last.

By the time he had finished dressing, he was sweating.

When all the clothes he could find were on, he looked for something to do. God, he thought, I have to get off my feet, the truck won't be here for a while. His waist-gunner, Basil Crone, compactly built and dark-haired, came up similarly dressed. Without a word, they lay down on the concrete tarmac, their heads on their parachutes, and looked at the stars.

It was Tuesday, April 19, 1944. Bert Stiles was twenty-three years old. The Denver native had been in the Army Air Force for fifteen months, all of it spent in training—training for this first mission. Is this what it's all about, he wondered? So I can lie out here with brother Crone on a cold April morning waiting to go flying off into the sky to go bomb some poor souls? Hands clasped behind his head, staring at the blue-black sky, his thoughts swept upward:

> Oh, Blue Lady in the sky, how is it up there in the twinkling darkness? Hey, Lady Luck! Will you ride with me this morning in my giant B-One Seven boxcar? As long as you come along with me, Lady, I'll be all right. We're going to some place called Eschwege, O Blue Lady. We're going to bomb hell out of some fighter planes—and probably some women and children, too.

By the time the crew was jammed into the back of a G.I. truck, Bert had put his good luck symbol on hold and soon became caught up in an adventure he'd preened for since 1940. He felt exactly as he had when the starting basketball lineup was announced, when he tipped his skis over the edge of the downhill run, or when he threw a baited line into a cold Colorado stream.

The ten crewmen were squashed by parachutes, escape kits, flak vests, and their own bulky flying clothes. Everyone was talking in rapid tones, laughing nervously, shivering with anticipation.

The truck pulled to a stop beside a huge dark shape. Bert examined their B-17 closely. It was a borrowed one; their crew didn't yet rate one of their own. The Keystone Mama, a pretty good name, he concluded, whatever the hell it means.

The co-pilot had decided the Flying Fortress was a romantic looking plane, for a bomber, that is. Beautiful on the ground, sure. Sturdy and powerful, too, as you flew formation hour after hour, but, oh God, what a monstrosity to fly. I'll help Sam fly this thing; that's why I'm here. But it's Sam's plane, Sam's crew, Sam's responsibility. Thank God.

Bert busied himself with the co-pilot's duties: issuing emergency rations, checking oxygen outlets, directing the loading of equipment. He didn't have that much to do, and he eyed Sam Newton as the pilot talked to Roy Frantz, the crew chief. God, what a confident son-of-a-bitch Sam Newton is, he thought. While he was glad he *was* confident (God, how would it be to have a pessimist as a pilot?) it didn't make him feel any better about his own part on the crew. Co-pilot…helps the pilot…understudies the pilot…there if needed…maybe, just maybe, could bring the plane home if anything happened to the pilot.

He stood alone for a moment, looking across the field in the pale morning half-light, noting the dark shapes that were dozens of B-17 Flying Forts. They all looked alike, and yet each had its own character. A plane had a name, but did it have a soul? He decided to ask himself that after this first mission.

He swung himself into the plane's neck through the forward hatch. He turned left toward the nose and the pilot's compartment. He wanted to get his flak suit out of the way but it kept snagging on things.

"Damn it," Bert said to Lewis. "There ought to be more room in these damn things." Sgt. Bill Lewis, engineer-gunner, was installing two 50-caliber machine guns in his upper turret.

"Take it easy, sir," Lewis responded.

Bert could see Bird and Benson in the nose; they seemed completely tangled up with their guns, flak suits, and oxygen masks. What a way to fight a war, Bert thought.

They had time on their hands. "Start Engines" had been set for 0600; it was 0450 now. Sgt. Spaugh poked his head into the pilot's compartment and Bert said, "Come on, Gil, let's go back and look at the bombs."

They edged their way through the tiny radio room to the bomb bay. The armorers had already loaded the bombs—ten 500-pound high explosives—and Bert sat on his haunches and patted one a couple of times. It felt cold and dead; he thought they were ugly and terrifying. Ten bombs—big and blunt-nosed—that would go hurtling down onto the German countryside in about four hours. God! What kind of game had he gotten into?

When all the guns were installed, the entire crew huddled back by the huge up-swept tail.

Waist gunner Basil Crone said, "I hope the bastards come in on my side."

But Ed Sharpe, the twenty-one-year-old tail gunner, disagreed. "Not me. I hope they all stay in the sack."

Bert looked reflectively at the diminutive Gordon Beach, their ball-turret gunner. Beach was silent: he was a pretty quiet guy. He was thirty-four years old—elderly for air combat—but Bert already felt close to him.

Stiles had been on many teams—football, baseball, tennis, basketball, skiing—and, just lately, had begun to feel about this crew the way he had felt about his sports teammates. He had known them for nearly six months now, and he liked them. Most times, he felt he liked the enlisted men better than the officers. Sam Newton was a queer exception. He liked the pilot, and admired him, too—for his piloting abilities. He still couldn't believe they'd been able to team up together on the same crew. Since college, their paths hadn't crossed much until this crew assignment.

He's the first pilot, all right, Bert thought. So be it. I never did imply to anyone I could fly these monstrous bombers.

Yes, if he *had* to fly bombers, co-pilot was all right. But, oh God, Oh, Blue Lady, what would it be like to go to war in a P-51 fighter?

Now he stood at Sam's side as the pilot said a few obligatory words to his crew.

"Start engines at six," Sam said. "It's 5:15 now—we'll climb aboard in a minute." The group around him was silent; Bert felt unfamiliar vibrations all around him. "Okay," Sam said finally, "this is our first one. We might as well make it a good one. Let's go give 'em hell."

By 5:30, Bert had set himself up in the right-hand seat. Everything was plugged in; again he had time on his hands.

He stared out the small right window. He could see bombers in their hardstands, seemingly in every direction. About fifty planes in all, counting standbys. Ten men in each—500 men waiting in silence and darkness for the time to start engines.

A brilliant red flare arched over the center of the field. Dozens of pilots nodded to their co-pilots and engineers.

Sam Newton gave Bert a tight smile. "This is it, buddy," he said. Newton glanced behind him to Bill Lewis, who was standing between the pilot's and co-pilot's seats, watching everything closely. Stiles unlocked the primer and set it to Number One. The pilot hit the starter button for the same engine; the inertia starter in the wing set up a shrill whine. Within a moment, a small amount of raw fuel charged into the engine.

The first pilot kept his hand on the starter button. After a few moments the engine coughed several times, belched blue smoke and settled into an uneven throbbing.

Bert, fascinated, kept one eye on the Number One engine instruments, the other on the scene out his right window. God, he thought, forty-eight engines turning over, nearly in unison. Across the field, in each hardstand, propellers coughed, twitched, sometimes sputtered, then caught and held steady. Soon there would be 192 engines—less an inevitable few that failed to catch—creating minor hurricanes.

His spine tingled. This was the adventure he'd been seeking all his life. He had written about high adventure, dreamed about it, romanticized it. Now here it was! The vibrating power from the four engines surged upward from the floorboards, flowing through Bert's body to his mind, a mighty stimulus to his always vivid imagination.

As Keystone Mama rolled tentatively out of the hardstand, brakes squeaking, Sam lifted a gloved hand in a salute to Roy the crew chief; he received a formal salute in return.

The imagery of the gesture brought a fleeting analogy to Bert's mind: Roy the father entrusting his favorite daughter to a rowdy crew setting forth on a long arduous date.

Sam taxied the heavily-loaded bomber from the hardstand to the taxiway and followed a line of similarly-laden airplanes, wing and tail lights blinking.

As co-pilot, Bert had never received detailed instruction in the B-17; he had gone straight from advanced flying school in Texas to Salt Lake City, where he had joined Sam on the crew. He'd flown the bomber often enough in Alexandria, Louisiana, but this was not instruction, it was simply learning to be Sam Newton's co-pilot. Far from the same thing. His formation time at the stateside staging base had been practically non-existent.

He knew the loaded B-17 carried more than ten tons of bombs and gasoline. This included 2,780 gallons of gas when full. Total plane weight topped thirty-five tons. He and Sam had checked the runway length at their Bassingbourn base; it was barely 6,000 feet. With a full load, that runway length was the minimum required to lift the B-17 from the ground—so the textbook said.

They had been briefed, over and over, that the takeoff in a heavily-laden bomber was not a routine maneuver. The loaded bomber was about as frisky as a dozing rhino.

Even taxiing at five to ten miles per hour was an adventure to Bert. With brakes wailing above the engine roar, he watched, fascinated, as Sam's hands caressed Numbers One and Four throttles in smooth turns, then gunned the tail wheel around a turn just ahead of the heavy bulk of the fuselage. It was like driving four trucks simultaneously, each loaded to the hilt, while avoiding collisions with similar trucks.

A dirty gray vista had replaced the night blackness as they approached takeoff position. Forts were stacked head-to-tail in front and behind.

As soon as the Fort ahead of them began its takeoff roll, Sam lined up Keystone Mama, leaning on the footbrakes while slowly moving all four throttles forward into the full power position. The plane strained and vibrated and the engine roar was deafening. Bert sat mesmerized by the thrill of the moment, by the sheer power waiting to be unleashed, and, for just a moment, he felt a sense of glory in the deadly pursuit of war.

When Sam lifted both feet from the brakes Bert waited for the monster to jump forward like a bird released from a cage. He knew better, but he could hope. The Fort, shackles free, rolled forward slowly, with agonizing deliberateness. We can use every inch of that 6,000 feet today, he thought.

The Flying Fort built up speed at a frighteningly slow pace. Bert watched the instruments and called off airspeed while Sam, eyes riveted to the runway, began the pull-off at 120 miles per hour, with about one-third of the runway remaining. At a thumbs-up signal from Sam, Bert flipped a toggle switch to bring up the wheels.

Keystone Mama climbed straight ahead, slowly gaining altitude. The co-pilot's job on the climb was both inside and outside the plane. He watched engine temperatures and pressures for unusual readings, and kept his eyes wide open for planes on collision courses. Presently, he edged the cowl flaps closed to maintain recommended cylinder-head temperatures.

Outside Bert's small window, he watched in wonder as they drifted upward through a pale overcast. God—what made this big hunk of metal actually fly? Wisps of clouds flickered past like wind-blown, gray-white tatters.

The co-pilot watched Sam's large, leather-enclosed hand ease back on all four throttles to reduce manifold pressures slightly; later the pilot also cut back on RPMs to maintain a steady 500-feet-per-minute climb.

The interphone crackled. "Navigator to pilot," Grant Benson's voice sounded crisp and businesslike.

Newton nodded to Stiles, who pressed the mike button on the steering yoke. "This is the co-pilot," he said. "Go ahead, Grant."

"Fly 155 degrees for four minutes thirty seconds—now," Benson said. "Assembly point coming up very soon. I'll monitor VHF for instructions from Group."

Stiles said, "Roger, Navigator," and glanced at Newton to make certain the pilot had received the message.

Although both pilots were watching closely for other planes, the sky was suddenly full of Forts, seeming to come from all directions, at varying altitudes. One Fort, gleaming sliver in the sunlight, appeared to be at exactly their altitude, on a collision course.

"My God, look at that fool!" Sam yelled, and banked sharply to the right.

"The sky is full of maniacs," Bert yelled back over the engine roar. Sam gave him a tight-lipped smile.

Without warning, Keystone Mama, caught in a slipstream, bounced violently and slipped off to the left. Newton steadied it, bringing it back to straight and level. Prop wash from other bombers was a constant probability.

Their assembly orders were to gain altitude with a constant course for thirty minutes and level off at 13,000 feet. Then, they would fly a reciprocal course for another thirty minutes to reach the southwest corner of Bassingbourn airport at approximately the same time as other squadron planes. After forming on the leader, they would seek the Group Lead B-17 which, at least theoretically, was in the immediate vicinity.

Many things could go wrong with this plan, and frequently did. At the end of thirty minutes, Sam told his co-pilot to make a 180-degree turn to the right, watching out for other aircraft. As soon as Bert was well into the banked turn, they were quite suddenly in the midst of a parade of bombers. Planes were above, below, on all sides.

What a stupid way to die, Bert thought wildly—colliding with friends over the green pastures of England. Assembling a group of airplanes is a madman's business.

Newton grabbed the yoke, yelling, "What the hell is going on?" Bert let go of the wheel as if it were a red-hot ember while Sam Newton brought Keystone Mama back to straight and level. Abruptly, there were no planes in sight. Sam looked sideways at his co-pilot, then said, "All right, she's yours again. Complete the turn to a heading of 260." Bert thought he detected a hint of apology in Sam's demeanor.

Co-pilots in every plane in the squadron were looking for a green flare, and suddenly there it was, in the distance at about 11 o'clock high. Bert punched Newton's arm and the pilot gave him a triumphant grin.

They formed at 17,000 feet, flying off the wing of the high leader. By this time, Bert's face was soupy with sweat, his oxygen mask was binding, and he found he could hardly move his shoulders in his electric suit. His head ached miserably. How can I handle eight more hours of this crap? he thought.

For the next half hour they flew tightly off the wing of their element leader while other bombers joined up. Their Group leader made a gentle turn to allow stragglers to catch up.

Despite his intuitive distrust of bomber flying, specifically the B-17, Bert gloried in the parade of aircraft. Silver ships sparkling in the sunshine, he thought, and laughed aloud at the unwitting alliteration. We must be strung out for miles, he figured. One thousand or more boys aloft at one time in just this one section of sky. How many were married? How many were fathers? What states were they from? How many from Colorado?

His dreaming ceased abruptly as Sam touched his gloved hand and motioned for him to take the controls. Bert flew formation carefully, gingerly. He had a real problem with holding the big plane in tight, and he had told Sam this often. Sam had been generally sympathetic, but he had made a key point: "Hey, buster, I can't fly it alone. You've *got* to do your part in formation—that's what most of the flying is in combat. Come on, let's go over it again. Small moves on the controls, instant reactions. *That's all there is to it, buddy.*"

That's all, is it, buddy? Just like that? That's about as tough a job as there is in flying. Tougher than flying a beam right down the middle; tougher, yes, than flying a link trainer. With absolute concentration he was able to hold the Fort within the wingspan of his lead plane. God, we're in close. Is this really necessary? One or two itsy-bitsy miscalculations and we're all dead. Bert used the heel of his left hand to make minute changes on throttle settings. But his right hand gripped the yoke in a furious grip. ("Relax over there," Sam had told him more than once.)

As long as he concentrated fiercely, he seemed to be all right. But after five minutes of riveting attention, he felt rivers of sweat pour down his chest. His right arm was stiff, his attention span began to waver.

They were over the Channel now and a light cloud cover had formed. Through the filmy substance, Bert could see the mighty group of Fortresses, each marking the sky with silver tracks. What a pretty sight, he thought, and what an impressive display of leashed power. He decided he wanted to remember this moment—and write about it, perhaps even tonight.

Again he felt Sam's heavy hand on his, and, with alarm, watched as the pilot moved all four throttles forward in a minute but distinct movement. With a start, he realized he had allowed Keystone Mama to fall back, well out of formation.

"Get on the ball!" Sam yelled. "You gotta stay in there. Jesus, Bert, stay alert."

Bert watched his pilot fly for a minute, and, despite his own sense of dejection, marveled at the way Sam flew. He could move throttles a quarter of an inch once in a while and keep the plane in tight formation. God—do you learn this or are you born with it? When you take a quick look at a formation, it always looks good. Static death, standing still in the air. Even the ships out of position look right. Then, if you watch for a minute, you'll see the constant swing and play. Hundreds of pilots are easing up on their throttles and easing back—or inching forward.

Their flight path took them across the Dutch coast, still in tight formation. The lead navigator must have been on the ball; they wove around flak positions and didn't encounter any of the deadly steel until they had crossed the Zuider Zee. But another wing off to their right wasn't so lucky—or skilled. Bert saw his first flak from a distance. Although he knew better, he wrote about it later as "pretty black puffs in a blue sky, harmless looking stuff."

They reached 20,000 feet, still climbing slowly. A flight of P-47 Thunderbolts flew over at three o'clock high, then disappeared into the sun. For a minute, the interphone chatter was incessant. The sight of friendly fighters was uplifting indeed.

They were two hours out from Bassingbourn. They had seen no enemy fighters and only a little flak off in the distance.

So far, so easy, Bert thought.

Sam was flying when Benson said, in majestic tones, "For those of you who have never been to Germany before, have a look. We're over the Third Reich."

Bert leaned as far forward as he could, and stared out his side window. The land was all chopped up into little fields and tiny towns. The fields looked just as green as those in England, the towns just as cute. Germany was the enemy, he thought, but they used the same sun down there; the sky was just as blue. But for some reason known best to God, they had to be killed. They were Germans, the hated Nazis.

How sad, Bert thought, how unbearably, unbelievably sad. He was seeing Germany for the first time and he was *bombing* the country.

Bert Stiles amused himself by sorting out his feelings on a scale of ten: perhaps two parts confusion, another two parts terror, one part each for cold and exhaustion, and the balance—four parts—for boredom. What had happened to glory and pride?

A flight of P-51 Mustangs flew past. Bert stiffened in his seat, eyes glued to the streaking planes. For a moment, just for a moment, he could see himself in that single-seat fighter, riding with the sun, cruising through the sky in carefree style. Could he ever swing a transfer to those devils?

Sam waggled his wings at the American fighters while Bert sat there with mouth open, eyes wide. He thought they looked like angels, shining angels. Then they were gone, headed back to England. A note of realism crept into his thoughts as he realized they had gone as far East as their gasoline allowed.

When Bert took over the controls, he at first held formation as tightly as Sam had. Then, unaccountably, the Group on their left began a slow right turn in front of them. Their Group had no recourse but to chop throttles. Bert, who had been making small adjustments successfully, suddenly found all of his minute adjustments meaningless—and dangerous. He overran the lead and had to bank to the left—his blind side—in order to avoid a possible collision.

He glanced at Sam. The pilot looked tense, he thought, but didn't take the controls back. Bert pulled all four throttles back for a moment or two, but he held it too long. Keystone Mama faded well out of formation. With Sam watching closely, Bert put power back in slowly, held it, them moved them forward again. The Fort slowly gained on the leaders and Sam relaxed a bit.

He chanced a quick look around. There were Forts everywhere—the United States Eighth Army Air Force in action, Jimmy Doolittle's pride. What were there—maybe 500 planes in the air now? Close to 5,000 men? He shook his head violently. No time for thoughts like these now, *he* had the controls.

The interphone squawked; it was tail-gunner Sharpe again. "Flak at seven o'clock," his voice came booming through. "Look at the stuff. It's all over hell."

"Take it easy on interphone," Sam yelled at him.

They were deep into Germany now and enemy anti-aircraft shells began to pop regularly in black and white puffs above them, below, alongside.

Fear suddenly clutched at Bert's stomach. He felt like a duck in a shooting gallery.

Colonel Putnam led the forty-seven trailing Fortresses in a series of slender turns to confuse the flak throwers. They were at 25,000 feet. Intellectually, Bert knew flak was deadly, but he couldn't come to terms with the extent of the danger. So far they were just a bunch of puffs in the sky. So far. He was reminded of his grandfather Wilbur's pipe on a winter's day in Denver.

Flak—with the sole objective of knocking down aircraft—could come from guns anywhere from 40 mm to 88 mm. The ground installations included guns of several sizes, but it was logical, Bert thought, that the heavy guns would be concentrated around likely targets.

He ran over in his mind the definition of the two types of flak: predetermined or "aimed" flak, aimed at a group of airplanes. Scoring hits from this practice was chancy considering shells had to climb 25,000 feet and hit a plane traveling at perhaps 240 miles per hour ground speed. But it happened all the time.

The other flak type was "barrage." The enemy simply aimed at a spot in the sky and filled that spot with its killing steel—until an airplane passed through it.

"Anyone see any fighters?" someone asked on interphone.

"Naw," came an answer, "the German fighter boys heard that Lieutenant Newton was flying today so they stayed home."

Bert glanced swiftly at Newton and saw him purse his lips and wondered if he was going to do any chewing. Then he remembered with a start that as co-pilot he was supposed to be interphone monitor. "Co-pilot to all crew," he said, crisply. "Let's have iron interphone discipline." God, he thought, that doesn't sound like me. Then he added, more naturally, "Don't goof around on interphone."

He released his finger from the mike and could tell, without turning his head, that Newton was looking at him.

Maybe I made a few points with old Sam, Bert thought, and then again maybe I didn't.

He was still thinking this over when he noticed with amazement that the bomb bay doors of the lead ship were open.

Benson broke the interphone silence to say, laconically, "We're at the I.P." The Initial Point was the base from which the bomb run would be run.

There was something terrifyingly inexorable, Bert thought, about a sky full of bombers bearing down on a target, bomb bay doors open to the wind. There was no compromise possible. This was their answer to the Nazis: destruction and death from above.

But there was always a price, he thought. Here we are, compelled to fly a straight-in course, constant speed, no maneuvering. And there below are a hundred or more guns trying to knock us out of the sky.

Bird was watching the lead ship intently. When the bombs finally fell, topsy-turvy, the bombardier immediately toggled their bombs out.

With the bombs away, there was a moment of respite. The formation loosened and everyone on Keystone Mama was ogling the ground to look for smoke, fire or other evidence of devastation.

Bert was mesmerized by the scene spread out in front of their plane. Forts all over the sky spilling their guts out on the unseen enemy below. Here they were, ten reasonably decent young men from good homes and not-so-good ones, up here at 30,000 feet raining hundreds of tons of high explosives on those below. Certainly, some of the people on the ground— perhaps most of them—were soldiers expecting to be in the line of fire, but how many civilians, how many *children,* were receiving the same dose of death? How many cute, blonde youngsters would scream and shriek and cry for their mothers as the hell rained on them from above?

Bert gulped and shuddered and suddenly wished he were high on the slopes of Pikes Peak, skis carving a trail through soft snows, nothing more on his mind than how to drag a B minus out of Biology.

Bombs were still falling from neighboring B-17s. Bert watched in fascination as thousands of oblong shapes dropped like leaden weights from yawning bomb bays.

"Radioman, see if all our bombs are away," Sam said.

"Wahooooo," someone from the tail or waist said, "look at all that smoke!"

Then everyone was talking at once, interphone discipline forgotten. Sam pulled Keystone Mama into a looping swing to the left, well away from their former heading. There had been no flak, which was amazing.

Bert glanced at Sam. The pilot's face was a study in relief and determination. Understood, Bert thought. Relief in getting off this damn bomb run, determination to get home in one piece.

"We missed it all to hell," Bird said from the nose. "I couldn't even see the target."

Sam's face tightened but he said nothing.

The squadron began a gentle descent to about 22,000 feet in order to throw off the flak throwers. With Sam at the controls in a turning letdown, Bert was free to look for bomb damage. Below, a town was smoking like hell; it looked wiped out. Was *that* their target? Perhaps they would never know, and that was probably for the best.

The B-17s, which had scattered somewhat after the bombs had fallen, now reassembled at the rally point. They would also fly home in formation.

Their target, Eschwege, was not deep into Germany; within a few minutes, Grant Benson, the twenty-two-year-old navigator from Michigan, announced, "We're in France now. We're out of their goddamn country."

Again, Bert could not tell the difference. The fields, rivers, hills—they looked just like Germany *and* England! Are all those guys down there suddenly good guys? He spotted what might be a barn. I'll remember that, he thought. A place to hide if we have to bail out. Maybe there was a hayloft where some dark-eyed French girl was waiting with a couple of jugs of wine. But then maybe there would be a storm trooper with big boots and a bayonet to comb through the hay. His imagination, always in high gear, had created a scene straight out of a Hollywood B movie.

Past feelings of locker-room camaraderie flitted across his consciousness. This was a fine group of men, he decided. They had accomplished something together. Mainly, he thought grimly, not getting ourselves splashed all over the sky.

And their B-17 Flying Fort still lumbered along with impunity after half the marksmen in Germany had taken pot shots at it. His chest tightened. And yet, and yet, he thought, how can we speak affectionately of our airplane? What is it but an assortment of nuts, bolts, wires, gauges, needles, motors, gas tanks? It doesn't have a heart; it simply gets you home if you treat it right—and are lucky. But if your Blue Lady is looking the other way, you are dust in the sky, never to be seen again. He shrugged—God, he had to stop analyzing everything.

As Keystone Mama approached the coast of England, he recognized the White Cliffs of Dover, although he had never seen them before. He was reminded of numberless books, movies, and plays he had experienced about the country they were approaching. It was wonderful to be in the sky, one of many warplanes, streaking for the England of history.

A lifelong reader as well as an admitted romantic, Bert felt a special place in his heart for the island empire. How could you top, in all literature, the character of Falstaff? Or Robin Hood, King Arthur, Richard the Lion-Hearted, Tom Jones, or Sherlock Holmes? For a moment, he felt an exquisite longing for the reading adventures of his childhood days in his basement room on South York Street.

The general order had gone out that morning: look sharp as you overfly the green fields of England, for Generals Doolittle and Spaatz were visiting Eighth Air Force bases. And so was the old man himself, Winston Churchill.

Bert Stiles didn't worry about looking sharp. At that moment, as tired as he'd ever been in his life, he didn't much care.

Still in their letdown, at about 3,000 feet, Bert could easily see cyclists on narrow roads framed by hedgerows, pigeons flying, flocks of sheep in large meadows, and green fields everywhere. The sky had a silken texture, pale and dim. Yellow afternoon sunlight lit the hedges and fields. It was a beautiful afternoon, as remote from war as was Colorado Springs.

They had broken formation by the time Benson brought them home to Bassingbourn. As Sam banked onto the final approach, Bert suddenly had a joyful feeling. He had survived the first mission. But there was a jolt of guilt there, too. He knew other bomber jockeys were dead, wounded, or taken prisoner. Again his chest tightened.

Keystone Mama set down in a perfect full-stall landing. Sam taxied the huge airplane back to the hardstand. There, Roy, their crew chief, waited, the end of a long vigil.

"We been to the war," Sharpe said from the tail.

"But we're back now," Bird said with finality.

"Wonder if we killed anybody?" Lewis asked at Bert's elbow.

"I'd be satisfied if I knew we'd hit the fighter park," Sam Newton said. "Well, we'll find out in de-briefing."

They had been in the air for seven hours and thirteen minutes and over enemy territory for more than four hours. It was almost two o'clock—, twelve hours since wake-up call in the predawn. Did we do much to shorten the war, Bert asked himself? Did we win? Did we lose?

When the final switch had been cut, Bert sat still in his seat, so tired he could hardly move. His hair was spongy with sweat and his eyes felt like they had been sanded down and wrapped in a dry sack.

He looked up to watch a B-17 taxi by. It had half its tail blown off. *God, that could have happened to them.* What kind of magic allowed a plane so badly damaged to return?

Bert dropped his flak suit, two layers of jackets he had removed at lower altitudes, and his Mae West and oxygen mask—all the encumbrances of combat flight—out of the forward hatch, then dropped through himself. He stared at the bomb bays—as empty now as his stomach felt. Think on this, Stiles: eight hours ago we loaded 10,000 pounds of high explosives on board. Then we ferried it nearly a thousand miles across three or four countries. Next we hit a button and—presto—they all fell out—on places we had generally aimed at but had no assurance we'd hit. Or on people we *hadn't* aimed at but could have hit. This is war, Stiles.

The gunners were offloading their guns; Bert helped Lewis carry his over to the truck. Most of the crew were there but they were generally silent. No one had decided whether to be happy or sad, fulfilled or dejected.

Then Sharpe said, "Well, we're not virgins any more."

On the truck, Stiles lay back in a pile of flak suits and closed his eyes. Well, we've been to war and now we're home, he thought. As simple as that. One down and twenty-four to go. There weren't any holes in us or the plane—a pretty good feeling. He decided right then that he didn't want to be anywhere else in the world but here, with these guys—these guys on his crew.

Bert wouldn't have been true to himself if he hadn't written home the night of his first mission:

We're part of the wrecking crew now. We've started down the road to destruction. From where I sit in the airplane it is impossible to tell just what is going on. I can't say where or what we did or how well we did it. But you can read the papers.

It is a very beautiful world and when you climb out of that big airplane after driving around where you're not wanted all day, it is quite a place to be in, and it is nice to be standing on grass, looking at trees....

There isn't much else to tell. We are full of colds and sore throats and I am having birth pains with a wisdom tooth. I bit myself at chow the other day and I am still wounded. And I tried to climb on a horse who lives next door and he ran out from under me.

No mission tomorrow—so I'll sleep well tonight. Serenade...

10

WHILE THE LITTLE KIDS WAVED

"Then it'll be time for you to
wander down on the river and put
in a good word for me to the Blue
Lady."

*And when you get there, after coming from England across the channel
with a load of bombs, with the Alps on one side, and the green sunny
world of Alsace and Lorraine all shot to hell by a war on the other,
then you know that it all belongs together, the whole world. It's so big
you have to work fast to think of it all on the same projection. For the
first time in my life I saw the world as really round, one big world. I
knew if we had enough gas we could fly over all the people and wave
at them, or smash all their little roped-off worlds into blood and
jagged pieces....*

During the next eight days Sam Newton's crew flew five more missions.
The second one had been a "milk run" (no flak, no fighter opposition,
shorter than normal) to Calais in France. The next day was the opposite: a
maximum effort for both men and machines—to Munich. It was a nine-
hour effort.

Flying across the green fields of France, through the clean sky, Bert
marveled at the Alps, white and jagged, poking up here and there. The
armada of Fortresses turned East to parallel the mountains, and penetrated
deep into the Reichland.

Bert knew his duties: check the RPMs periodically, keep an eye on the manifold pressure, give the cylinder head temperature gauges a quick occasional glance. But this was part-time duty; he had time to look out the small co-pilot's window at the craggy, majestic slopes of Switzerland.

The Alps reminded him of home. The rainbows would be hitting in the little feeder creeks high in the Rockies and the ice melting fast in the high lakes. The cutthroats would be red and fat and beautiful, ready for the catching.

Over the tops of the Alps, he knew, were the dusty roads to Rome, and South from there were the steamy jungles of Africa. Bert could feel everything he'd learned about geography coming into focus. Mentally, he tore the world map off the schoolroom wall and pasted it on the Fort's grimy window.

He looked up ahead, toward Munich. Somewhere up there in a high valley was the doomed castle of Berchtesgaden. And well past there was the land of Comrade Stalin. He felt at one with destiny, with history, with supreme adventure.

He glanced at Sam to see if he might need relief, then checked the engine instruments again, his eyes sweeping the ten-to-two o'clock circuit for fighters. He decided he would get the help of eight or nine others.

"Co-pilot to all crew," he said, pressing the mike button on the wheel with his right hand and holding his throat mike tight with his left. "We're well into enemy territory. Keep your eyes open for fighters."

He could hardly believe he'd said those words.

With nothing left to do, Bert stared out his side window. Out there was Japan, and atolls and archipelagos and moon maidens. Somewhere lost in all that ocean was Australia, Easter Island, Tahiti, New Zealand—he would see them all someday. And out in another somewhere were the yellow beaches of California and the hot and heavy power songs of Detroit and Pittsburgh.

His thoughts turned to personal memories:

> I've hitchhiked across it, and flown over most of it, and skied down parts of it, and been pulled over some of it in a little red wagon. It was a large world that should be one great world. But it'll never be worth a goddamn as a world until it is tied together and knitted together so it functions as one world.
>
> Some people have been dreaming of one big world for a long time and doing their best to make it come true. Willkie went all the way around

the world in a Liberator and wrote a book about it. And Marco Polo wandered all the way to China and came back to tell about it. And the hooded Jesuits sailed out across all the oceans to spread the word of a man who believed in all people.

Snap out of the daydreaming, he thought. Get your mind back on flying and this damn mission. His return to reality was just in time to respond to Sam's request for 2300 RPM as they weaved around some flak.

After dropping bombs through a haze over Munich, they quickly turned off the target and headed for England. As they made the turn westward, Bert noted the sky was stained with smoke, the targets ablaze and cooking. He had time to think:

> Maybe boundary lines have their uses and all the other barriers built up by men on the ground, but the air flows pretty smoothly over all boundaries and from 20,000 feet it is pretty hard to see any good reason for them.

> We could fly our B-17 over all the little roped-off states and wave at the people and buzz in low and make the roofs flap in the prop wash, or go up high again and line up the cross hairs on the local steel mill or the opera house and watch the bombs drop.

> And while the little kids waved at us their houses would topple and the lights would go out, and the bomb dust would strangle the living air.

Fighter aircraft came streaking by. Were they ME109s or P-51s? They looked a lot alike. It seemed to Bert they were just playing around until one broke into a dive that ended when it hit the ground in a cascade of smoke.

"Jesus, did you see that?" Sharpe said. "Somebody just crashed down there."

"It looked like a P-51," Crone said.

"It was an ME 109," Spaugh said, positively. "There goes another one," he added, wonder in his voice.

Several enemy planes were getting through the tight bomber cover. Bert and Sam watched helplessly as three bombers peeled off, some trailing smoke, most probably headed for Switzerland and internment.

A Fortress blew up nearly in their faces. Bert watched in horror as pieces of aircraft came fluttering past his window. Suddenly, he was overwhelmed by a wave of deep pity for the human race and its barbarous habits of war. He felt he was already on familiar terms with death. He knew it could happen to him— abruptly, mercilessly, needlessly. The very thought of being on *any* terms with death forced the wind from his chest.

In the next three days, they flew eight-to-nine-hour missions to Metz, Brunswich and Avord. They carried 10,000 pounds of high explosives to Brunswick, flying on the left wing of E-Easy, and Bert, who could see better from his right seat, did most of the flying. He was looking into the sun most of the way.

Bert could feel Sam's tenseness. When Bert allowed the plane to fall behind by a plane's length, Sam knocked his co-pilot's hand from the throttles.

"I'll fly the sonovabitch," he said. "You sit there."

Bert sat there and swore at him. But later, when he had the controls back, he worked hard to keep it in close, jockeying the throttles until he thought his left arm would fall off.

The flak batteries from Brunswick threw up a hail of steel.

"Keerist," Bird said, softly, "Jesus Keerist!"

"How we gonna get through that crap?" Crone said.

They flew right through the middle. The only satisfaction they got was kicking their bombs out when the lead ship did. The entire formation immediately wheeled off South into the clear blue sky, away from the deadly mass.

As they overflew the Zuider Zee near the coast, the lower clouds were breaking up and they could see chunks of Holland.

"Lieutenant Newton," Sharpe called from the tail, "Don't slow down any. The flak is tracking us back there. No more than maybe fifty feet behind us. Keep moving."

Bert figured the Kraut gunners had the altitude and the direction but their airspeed was just a little off.

"Okay now," Sharpe said a minute later. "I thought they had us ticketed." His voice had returned to a deep bass.

The P-38s wheeled over their formation on the way home, easy and sweet, driving out to the left for a look around, swinging back, then whipping off below somewhere.

"Thanks, little friends," Bert said aloud. The wailing, banshee sound of the Lightnings thrilled him to the core. If he couldn't fly a Mustang, he thought, he would settle for a P-38.

When their plane had been bedded down in the hardstand, Bert had ambivalent feelings of elation (God, I've finished five missions—one fifth through) and depression (How many kids have I killed *today?*) I'm in this goddamn air circus and I can't get out. What's the matter with this world, anyway?

He couldn't figure her out—did she really care for him? In Alexandria, she had treated him royally or poorly, depending upon her capriciousness or perhaps by the position of the moon in the galaxy. But then to follow him to Grand Island—what kind of girl *was* she, anyway? As with many of his stateside girl friends, Bert thought of June occasionally—wistful thoughts laced with romance, tinged with regret.

She had written to him—three times now—her letters expressing what might pass for love. Her kind. He re-read her latest and tried to figure it out:

> Just thinking of you tonight, so thought I would drop you a line. Thought you might be a little lonesome. Lord, never thought I'd miss anyone like I miss you. When you left, G.I., it seemed as though all the fun in life had also left...it was so darned lonesome. I would certainly appreciate you if your were around now. Is it too late? Hope not...

Bert felt sort of sad about her. He doubted he loved her but he'd sure as hell had a good time with her. Was that love? She had been a gay little girl in the States. Now all the boys were gone to war and she was building B-29s in Kansas and going straight home nights. Or so she said.

He felt so drawn to her that he had to sit right down and write a long letter to this perplexing half-love.

They watched with horror as a heavy bomber group just above and ahead flew directly into a nest of steel. A Fortress took a devastating hit: flames splashed and licked toward the trailing edge of the wing. The pilot skidded the plane off to the left trying to extinguish the flames, but he must have known it was hopeless because he ordered his crew to bail out.

They all watched men fall out of the airplane. "That's six," Lewis said quietly, after a moment.

The stricken Fort swung around in a flaming 180-degree turn and blew up about 300 feet below them.

As Sam flew, Bert sat transfixed. Whose crew was it? Did he know those men falling out of an airplane at 30,000 feet? Did one of his drinking buddies go down with the plane?

"Fighters at two o'clock," Lewis said quietly.

"Fifty-ones," somebody else said.

"Hope so," said someone who sounded like Sharpe.

The fighters swung past the nose and both Newton and Stiles felt they were acting queerly for escort pilots. Then they were swinging again, this time toward them. One gray and silver plane rolled over on his back, crosses up, with all guns firing.

"Hey!" Bert yelled, but his microphone button was stuck.

It was all over fast. The only shots taken were by Sharpe from the tail. The MEs were maneuvering for another pass when a flight of P-51s chased them out of their air space. Cheering, hysterical and undisciplined, jammed their interphone.

They had encountered flak and fighters within a five-minute span but nothing else on the entire trip. Sometimes it happened like that.

Bert wrote to Rosemary that night:

> We've crossed the channel into the heartland six times now. The raids go by so fast they're all mixed in my mind. We've got an airplane of our own now. Cool Papa. She's named for Sam—they used to call him that in school because he was such a major operator. We're getting the name painted on her and a picture of a dame with no clothes on. There's a sergeant here specializes in bosoms. He must have lovely dreams.

> I'm so tired of sitting in the co-pilot's seat, I think I'm getting cancer of the buttocks. The cheek bone on the left side throbs at high altitude and at times it rings like a gong. Every trip seems to have a call for a three o'clock briefing. Two in the morning is a good hour to come home but a very wretched hour to crawl out of the sack.

"Mac" McCardle, the Pittsburgh kid, lived on the second floor of the co-pilot's house. Since they had become friends in Alexandria, Louisiana, Bert had realized he was his best friend. Mac was a first pilot on another crew, but was closer to Bert than to officers on his own crew. They had spent quality time together in the States in a sort of debating society: politics, war, girls, future of the world, whatever. When Bert wasn't chasing June, he wrestled Mac for the attentions of a little doll named Lois. Lois seemed to prefer Mac, and that was all right, Bert decided. Excitement traveled with Mac. Any place he was could never be dull. And he was easy as hell to talk to.

"Mac, do you know what the best day of my life was?" Bert asked as they sipped beer at the club. The weather had closed in and a standdown had been posted for the morning.

"I could guess, buddy—but I don't want to embarrass you."

Bert ignored the remark. "It was the day I got out of high school. I was so damned anxious to get out into the world, travel, start learning something other than out of books."

"So how you doing so far?"

"About a B minus. I've seen the West Coast—Los Angeles, San Diego, San Francisco—and spent a lot of time in the Northeast, particularly Connecticut. And of course lots of states in between. Minnesota, Illinois, Wisconsin…"

Mac sipped his beer and studied his companion. "And now you and I are seeing Europe courtesy of the Army."

"Can't count Europe—seeing Germany from a B-17 is out of bounds. I *do* count England. I'm glad I'm here rather than in Italy or the Pacific.

"Don't misunderstand me, Mac. I'm not anti-books. Far from it. But travel should be a part of book-studying, given about equal time." He leaned back, clasping his hands behind his back. "I've neglected the studying part—I don't feel too good about my formal education so far."

"Going to continue it?"

"I want to—yes. Not at Colorado College. I've finished with that stage of my life. I've thought of Chicago, Harvard, maybe Stanford. But I doubt my grades are up to it."

"There's a big choice out there of what to take, Bert," Mac said. "Any ideas?"

Bert laughed. "So many it makes my head swim. "Math, philosophy, psychology, literature, creative writing. And economics, Mac. You know, economics is just a hell of a fancy name for simply the way people live together."

"Interesting thought—the kind that should be spread around colleges and offices."

Bert sipped his beer, eying his friend. The club was beginning to fill up. Cigarettes were filling the air with thick smoke, and the haunting strains of a new war song floated across the room from a juke box. *"Long ago and far away…"*

"Just look at the education we've gotten here so far," Bert went on. "Locating a German factory by navigation, pressing a toggle switch at just the right time to kill the people who can't get out of the way, finding the lead ship in a sky full of maniacs..."

"Not a whole hell of a lot of use after the war," Mac said.

"Education has got to be number one priority after the war," Bert said. "Schools should be the cleanest and best-built and most carefully planned buildings in the country. And there shouldn't be that much difference between Yale and Ohio State and a school like Slate Creek School, up near where I live. Schools should be better kept up than banks—because there is greater wealth stored in them."

"And of course the buildings themselves don't do the job," Mac said, warming to Bert's topic. "It's the teachers, the books, the classes that count."

"Right. An education should teach a man how to think, and teach a little humility along the way, too. It should get a man to open his mind, to realize he is a part of mankind, that there are people essentially like him all over the world."

"Amen."

"And this same education, Mac, should teach how a society functions. That's where economics comes in. People have to work to survive and the study of what they work at and how they go about it—hell, *that's* economics. And it includes just about everything done by and to mankind."

"The teacher makes the class," Mac said. "I don't care how potentially boring a subject can be—with an outstanding teacher it becomes an outstanding class."

"Right again, buddy. A good teacher is priceless. They can sometimes even awaken intellectual curiosity in a dullard. What occurs to me, Mac, is that this war is taking people out of schools before their time. They're still going on back home, I suppose, but with far fewer students. And in occupied Europe, they're mostly just closed down, I suppose. What a pity."

"One more beer, Bert? Remember—no flying tomorrow."

"You bet one more."

When Mac returned from the bar with two bottles of Stout, he said, "Drink this slowly, Bert. This stuff is *potent.*"

"One more thought, Mac—it's sure not original, but I think it's important as hell."

"Fire away."

157

"There's got to be truth. And justice. All of education has got to stress those two—or we're all lost in a maze, and we'll never be able to claw our way out."

"Truth and justice, yes. And something else. Love and laughter. Without them it would be a dull world indeed."

"Hey, that's *my* line, buddy. I believe that as much as anything we've said tonight. You know what my creed is? 'Take it easy.' Have a good time, relax, take it *easy.*"

Mac smiled. "I know that's your creed, Bert. You've told me six times in eight months now."

Later, alone in his room, Bert felt the need to express himself in a different way. By letter, of course. To Rosemary Harley—dear Rosemary. He ended it this way:

> After you have become a Red Cross lady, have them send you to take care of the 91st—and me. You've got to come over. I don't know whether a girl like you would like England as much as some of the wandering males, but for me this is a damn good island and I think I know why these lads fought for it back in 1940.
>
> We've been having a high old time, but it should start roughening up any time now...and then it will be time for you to wander down on the river and put in a good word for me to the Blue Lady....

The day began with little things going wrong. They had stayed in the sack and missed breakfast. Sam forgot his name tags, Bert his G.I. shoes. They had to wait for the truck to their plane. And Cool Papa was out for repairs; they were to fly Shoo Shoo Baby, a plane they had heard ugly rumors about.

It was May 25. It would be their eighth mission.

Sam found oil dripping from Number One engine. He looked up to see his crew chief, Roy, standing beside him.

"I checked that leak earlier, Lieutenant Newton. I been watching it. It's a little thing. I think it'll be all right."

"How many other little things are there, Chief? Better tell me all you know about this crate."

His crew chief gave him a rundown. Shoo Shoo Baby had twenty-four missions without an engine change, the windows weren't bullet-proof, and there had been some complaints about the power.

"We were up half the night testing it, Lieutenant. Ran fine on runup. I couldn't recommend scratching it."

Newton frowned, looking at the dirty windows, the peeling paint, the tired look. A B-17 may be a beautiful thing in the air, he thought. But on the ground it's just a huge, ungainly hunk of metal. And this one is a goddamn crate.

Bert wrenched his shoulder trying to prime the engines.

At the green flare, Sam pushed throttles full forward and Shoo Shoo Baby intensified its vibrations, shivered, and stammered—but barely moved forward down the runway.

"What the hell's wrong with this SOB?" Sam roared.

With agonizing deliberation, Shoo Shoo Baby picked up speed and lumbered into the gray mist.

When Benson called Bert to give him the heading, his voice came through shadowy and fuzzy. Even the interphone was faulty.

They climbed through heavy haze toward their position in the high squadron. During the climb Bert noticed the cylinder head temperature on Number One engine topping 200 degrees—too high. He opened cowl flaps and noticed that the propeller was throwing a wash of oil back on the cowling.

Crone's voice came through static on interphone. "Number One is smoking a little," he said. "We ain't on fire, are we?"

"We might be soon," Bert said. "Keep an eye on it."

They were flying in haze, practically on instruments. There was no horizon, no sky, no England, just a soft gray mist. The formation was lost all over England, wandering around in haze.

The interphone crackled. "My goddamned heated suit is shorted out," Sharpe said from the tail.

"My oxygen indicator doesn't indicate," Beach said from the ball turret.

The fuel pressure rose slowly; the oil temperature on Number One was on the climb. The tension in the ship was rapidly growing into a threat.

"This is a goddamn crate," Sam said to Bert. "Why did we have to draw this sonovabitch?"

They were headed to Leipzig, a target they had heard too much about. A place that drew German fighters like a honey pot. It was also ringed with anti-aircraft emplacements.

Neither pilot mentioned aborting the mission. It wasn't that it was cowardly—often it made good sense. But after the early call, the preparation, the waiting, to go back without credit for a mission? And deny Hitler their ten thousand pounds of high explosives?

Number One nacelle was covered with oil now, and oil pressure had dropped five pounds while fuel pressure was slowly rising.

Then, with an abruptness that startled both pilots, they stalled out—the airspeed indicator was defective, too. For a moment they hung in the blue mist, then Sam punched the nose down and brought the Fortress back under control 500 feet below their formation.

Sam looked at Bert, raising an eyebrow. "What the hell is going on? That was *close*."

"Think someone is trying to tell us something?" Bert yelled.

Then Crone was back on interphone. "I think I got an oxygen leak," he said, his voice not entirely under control. "The gauge is falling off."

Bert, flying now, was having serious trouble catching up with their formation. The throttles weren't sliding well. Sam took over and had the same difficulty.

Later, they pulled up below the lead flight, but this was their only reference. The horizon still hadn't appeared.

"You tired old bastard," Bert said to himself. His quick imagination created a scenario with Number One giving up after they crossed the Zuider Zee, and Numbers Two and Three throwing in the towel on the bomb run, directly over the famous Leipzig killer flak.

At 15,000 feet the formation began a slow climb. Bert jacked up the RPM to 2300 and turned the superchargers full on.

At his side, Sam checked the power instruments, noting the widening distance between Shoo Shoo Baby and the formation. They were a mile behind and losing altitude, too.

Sam made a decision. Shoving the nose down, he jerked off his oxygen mask, and swore all the way around a 180-degree turn.

"Pilot to crew," he roared. "We're going home. We're not taking this goddamn crate anywhere."

Relief washed through the ship like a cool wave.

Our first abort, Bert thought, as Sam let down slowly. Maybe we could have made it—maybe the wagon would have held together. Maybe Doolittle would be sore. Maybe Spaatz would give us ten extra missions.

Over the green fields of England, Sam yelled in Bert's ear: "We could feather Number One—it would look better."

Bert gave him a tight grin and shrugged slightly.

"Guess not," Sam said, and completed the letdown.

Their ground crew were out at the hardstand as they taxied in. The Chief seemed to be looking at something on the ground. As Sam swung Shoo Shoo Baby around, the squadron jeep roared up. Bert figured the Major would be wearing his C.O. look, ready to start chewing.

The crew was silent as they unloaded personal gear. No one looked at anyone else. The sun shone wanly through a ubiquitous mist.

The crew chief and one of his men were up on top of the nacelle of Number One engine almost before the propeller stopped turning. After a few minutes, Roy climbed down and came over to where Sam and Bert were chatting with the squadron commander.

"She wouldn't have took you there," the chief said. "Number One is all through."

It was amazing how the Chief's words brightened them all.

"It ain't natural," Crone said, "us being here this time of day."

As he hunched back on the truck, his head on his parachute Bert felt as beat up as if they *had* gone all the way.

Bert remembered earlier times with Rosemary in a letter to her that night:

> So everything is new and everything is very old and the past has faded into a dream that never happened. The end of each mission when we are letting down over the Channel is sort of like the end of Hell Week in that first year of school...and we wonder...where will we go tomorrow?

Aside from Mac and Sam and his crew members, Bert's best friends were Billy Behrend and Fletch. Fletch was James Fletcher, a pilot from across the hall. There was something about Fletch that was easy to take. He was open-minded, outgoing, unwilling to be serious very often. Bert was in his room a lot, for in that room was the best collection of pinup girls in the entire Eighth. There wasn't a brassiere in sight.

There was a little girl in the upper left corner of Fletch's room whom Bert said good night to every night. Her name was Doris Merrick and she was the pinup girl in *Yank Magazine*. She was small and blonde and had a funny sort of what-the-hell look on her face. After the war, he thought, he'd go to Hollywood and take her to a drugstore for an ice cream soda. They'd go down to Balboa and lie on the beach and get brown and knocked out from too much sun. At night they would go to the *Rendezvous* and dance to Bob Crosby and drink sparkling burgundy.

So he said, "Good night, my sweet," to Doris while Fletch blew kisses to a redhead in the corner and Billy made eyes at a gal in a black bathing suit. But, gosh, Bert thought, Fletch and Billy are both married—they can't put their hearts into it like I can. Bert closed the door on Fletch and Doris and sat in front of his typewriter to compose his Friday letter to his folks:

> We're due for a couple of days in London. Sam is pretty shot tonight and has been rough to get along with. My formation flying probably drives him nuts. I thought once that maybe under fire an aircrew would turn into the biggest thing in a lifetime, a bunch of guys all for one and hello comrade. But this crew just hasn't worked out that way—they're just a bunch of really good guys.

> Dad—soon you will be having a birthday. If my luck stays, when I come back we'll lock up the house for a couple of weeks and head for Wyoming or down near Creede, or maybe Montana...and we'll see if we've lost the touch. So wander up to the high country and say hello for me...happy birthday.

11

WHAT CAN YOU TELL A GUY'S MOTHER?

"I never before knew how much I
wanted to live in the world, just to
live, just to *live*...."

*I'm up here at 27,000 feet and unless one of your flak artists gets lucky,
I'll be home in England in a couple of hours, and I won't know who I
helped to kill, or whose legs were blown off, or whose houses were
smashed in. I'm up here where it's clean and blue, where I'll never
have to smell the dead ones, or help clear out their half-rotted bodies.
I won't know and I won't care, because I'll be so tired and all I'll care
about is hitting that sack....*

The two-day pass began in a daze. Bert Stiles was so shot with fatigue
that he didn't even look out the dusty train window until they were
halfway to London. When he did, he found the same casually neat green
England he had come to love: the hedgerows, gray smoke curling from
chimneys, old men in long coats puffing their pipes sitting in the sun at
tiny way-stations. It was a coldish day and there didn't appear to be a
war anywhere around.

Bert loved trains, symbol of travel, of freedom, of romance. He thought
of the towns he'd gone into on trains: Denver, Chicago, Philly, New York,
Los Angeles.

Sam and Bert came into King's Cross Station, picked up a cab and headed for Piccadilly.

"No Red Cross clubs for me," Sam said, as he tried, without success, to relax in a fast-moving cab. "I'm sick of the Army."

It flashed across Bert's mind that they were also sick of pilots and airplanes—and each other.

The driver found them a hotel lost in a court off St. James Street. They lay on green silk bedspreads on the twin beds and drank three double scotches while they considered the immediate future.

Later, uplifted by the alcohol, they were ready to wander. But their moods and temperaments were too dissimilar for them to stay together long. They lost each other in a corner pub and Bert wandered off looking for new friends. He found one in an RAF bomb-aimer at the Ritz Hotel and they were joined by a Free Frenchman at the Savoy. They drank Scotch until it was gone—then found some Pimms Special.

Later, alone again, Bert tacked up a lonesome street in bright moonlight. Cool night, steady night, he thought, with no flak and no 109s in the clouds.

The girl came out of the shadows, carrying a fur. Her voice was soft. "A bit of love, Yank?"

He felt she looked good with the moon in her hair but he wasn't in the mood for a bit of love. He wanted all the love or none at all.

Bert awoke first back at the St. James and stood over Sam, looking down on the sleeping face. Sam was quite a sight, sleeping away, dreaming his wild dreams.

When he finally stirred, Bert asked, "Hey, you still sleepy?"

"No, I'm Sam," the pilot said.

He'd said it a thousand times before, but Bert always laughed.

They attended church at Westminster Abbey. Most of the time they just looked up at the great stained windows of that timeless, candle-lit sanctuary, an island of peace in the heart of a city at war.

Sam went off to meet a new friend and Bert wandered again. He watched the barges and the riverboats on the Thames River, listened to Big Ben, and waited for Churchill to show up at Number 10 Downing Street. He queued for a bus ride without knowing the destination. Everywhere he looked there was London and more London. There were too many uniforms, he thought, too many Americans, too many dirty-faced little kids.

Some stores and houses were smashed, some were still startlingly intact, and he thought it was somehow strangely wonderful.

He saw a girl on the edge of a crowd and he laughed when she laughed. They ate in a little Russian place on Oxford Street and drank nut-brown ale until closing time in a pub called the New Moon Arms. They threw darts with some Royal Engineers and lost three times in a row.

Her hair hung dark and loose and her eyes were clear and deep. She was Russian and Czech with perhaps a little Polish and French thrown in. Her name should have been something long and full of vowel sounds, but she only said, "Call me Mary."

Mary had to go to work at midnight, so he said goodbye in the shadows with the moonlight full and sweet in the streets.

After midnight in a darkened London—where was he? Somehow he found his way back to the lost hotel. Sam wasn't there, so he walked back outside and stood listening to the city, dark London under the moon. He marveled again how intensely he loved the night.

It came to him with swift clarity that England was home, more home now than the Springs or Denver. Standing there in the dark doorway, shivering slightly, he thought of the names of England, names that were romantic and mystical and as ancient as the world. Land's End and Cornwall and Devon. Charing Cross and Coventry and Canterbury. And some pretty oddball ones: Nutt's Corner and Leighton Buzzard and Southend on Sea.

England! Ever England! He knew the green and storied island was not a paradise—there was cruelty and crime and cussedness the same as in America or Ceylon or on the island of Manicura. But the mixture of literary and historical mythology seemed to seep from the dark earth, or rode the gray mist from the skies, or kindled a reflection in a little girl's eye— thoughts that made him want to shout or swear or stamp his feet in undefined desire.

The food and the goodwill and the drink and the taste of romance concocted a heady potion. It was at that moment that an unspoken desire to remain in England after the war became a *decision* to do so. God, please let me live out this war—and let it end, let it end *soon*.

Late Sunday evening Bert and Sam returned to Bassingbourn from their short leave. As brief as it had been, Bert felt refreshed and alive once more—things were in perspective.

"Think we'll get Cool Papa for the next one, Sam?" he asked as the train neared Royston.

"Brother, I sure put a pitch in for it. Clean and neat and *new,* that's for me. No more of this tired metal."

"Is it out of the shop yet?"

"Should be. It was probably ready today."

"Then maybe someone else flew it today. Think so?"

"Nah," Sam said, "It was *promised* for us. Besides, I don't think there was a mission today. Still bad weather. Hope there's more weather tomorrow. I could use a little sack time to rest up from London."

They signed in at the squadron orderly room. The duty sergeant walked over to talk with them. "Oh, Lieutenant Newton," he said. "You know that ship you been waiting for?"

"Yeah." Sam tensed; he was ready to battle for it.

"It went down today."

"What?"

"On the Munich mission. And there was a real snafu, I heard, in assembling. There were—"

"You sure it was Cool Papa? Who was flying it?" Sam had turned white.

"Some guy named Mac something."

Bert stood there stunned, head reeling. He finally found his voice. "Are you sure? Was it Lieutenant McCardle?"

The Sergeant sensed something. "Yes, sir," he said. "First Lieutenant Alfred McCardle. He was pilot of Cool Papa today. Went down over the coast."

"Any chutes seen? Any reports in? What does Intelligence say?" Bert pressed his hands hard, face down on the counter, as if trying to dig a hole in the plaster board with his fingers.

"Sir, you'll have to talk to Captain Martin on that."

Bert stumbled out of the orderly room, face hot, eyes watering. God! Not Mac. God—you didn't let Mac get it today? *Why,* God? Mac was, Jesus Christ, the best guy...God, God...

Clambering aboard his bike, he rode furiously out into the country, heedless of the blackout, thinking of his friend. Mac had plenty to go back to—a scholarship to Harvard Law School, a girl who loved him, a passion to help change the world.

Later, Bert found some of the flyers who had been on the mission. It had been flak, right at the coast. He was the only one who went down that day. One out of hundreds.

He checked the bulletin board. His own crew—Newton's crew—wasn't flying tomorrow. That was good, that was bad, it just didn't matter a damn.

He stood alone in darkness, staring at the sky, thinking his thoughts. He forced himself to think about Mac *now*, before he slept on it, while he was still in the day that Mac died.

A guy goes down but, strangely, everything else goes on. You keep waiting for him to come back, as if he's been on leave. But, in a quiet moment, he just checks out. It doesn't mean anything at first. You just say, Mac's gone, Mac went down, Mac's had it, and you don't really believe it yet.

And then you wake up some night, after you've been arguing with him in a dream. And you walk into the mess hall, and save a seat for him before you remember. It hits you slow, like a cancer. It builds up inside you into something pretty grim and ugly. Why did it have to be him? Why did it have to be at all?

The next day he started a letter to Mac's mother. But what can you tell a guy's mother? She was there first. She knows what was inside him. Most people don't change so much after they leave home. What's there is there, and it comes from her and his father, and his brothers and sisters, and his teachers, and the kids on the block.

I could have told her Mac was the one guy I could talk to and get something back every time. I could have told her Mac was my best friend, that I liked him tremendously. But I wasn't anyone to her. I'd only be a name.

Bert remembered Mac's bitching. He hadn't thought much of the condition of the world. Stupid people drove him nuts. He wanted to *do* something—get working on changes needed in the world. He was the kind of guy the world could use after the war. He had a mind and he wanted to use it—and maybe he would have been a pretty big guy in the world before he stopped.

Bert remembered a talk he had with Mac a few nights before. They had been sitting on Mac's littered bed, dance music from the Armed Forces network in the background.

"We can't hear the kids crying," Mac had said.

"What did you say? You'd better explain *that* one."

"Sure, Bert. We see the smoke, the smoke from a destructed target. Pillars of smoke hiding—what? Death, horror, mayhem, lost babies, mothers in anguish. Jesus, what are two good people like us doing here? Why should I be here, precisely *I?* I'm Alfred F. McCardle of Washington, Pennsylvania, and there's only one of me. This man-form you see in front of you is the only existence I have—will ever have. My life is of enormous value to me. So, why am I sitting in a tin bomber miles high in the sky, letting—actually encouraging—perfect strangers to shoot my ass off?"

"We're all condemned to die, Mac. It's just a matter of when."

Mac looked hard at him. "Well, I've decided not to die, not just yet."

"You'll outlive us all, buddy," Bert said. "You've got too many things going for you. Including Lady Luck."

But in the end, Bert thought as he stood looking at the darkening sky, all Mac had lacked was a bit of luck from his own Blue Lady.

Newton's crew didn't fly for a few days. Bert had plenty of time to think—and to write. On May 5 he began a bittersweet letter to his parents:

> One of my buddies took our plane over to France and got it shot in half and himself with it. A lot of our comrades are gone; the one who went down was the best of all. I've thought a lot about this world—sometimes, after we've come home from a long haul, I ask myself whether I ever knew before how much I wanted to live in this world, just to live, just to *live.*

> It seems to me that if enough people in the world were really in love with it...then it might work out. Could National Socialism grow up inside people who laughed at the sun, and made love in the moonlight, and wondered about the wind? The words come slowly now because I am sad and tired. The way we fly is a way of living I hate beyond any words. But there's only one way to end it, I guess, and that is to win it.

But B. W. and Elizabeth Stiles' son was apparently not so tired that night as he had expressed to his parents, for it was late that evening that he began writing what was to become both a labor of love and a source of anguish for him: an autobiographical novel which he named *Serenade to the Big Bird.*

He had flown nine missions, he had lost a close friend. He was enduring a troubled relationship with Sam Newton. He was having a love affair with

England. And he was ready, he had decided, to put it all into writing. Book-length writing.

Actually, he had already written portions: stories he had sent to Maxwell Aley in New York and to two London editors. His short pieces had appeared in *Yank* newspaper and others were placed by Aley in the U.S. He intended to use most of this material in *Serenade,* perhaps slightly rewritten. Stories entitled "A Co-pilot's Education," "Portrait of the World from 20,000" and "This is Where I Live" would appear as chapters in the proposed book.

A few of his stories were autobiographical, but most used other names for himself as if a co-pilot with a different name was Sam Newton's right-seat helper.

He figured his sketches would double as chapters in his book. He had great fun writing it. As always, he loved to express himself, to create, to seek emotion and meaning on the written page. He would return from a mission exhausted, disenchanted, even morbid. But with a shot or two of whiskey at de-briefing and sometimes a few more at the Officer's Club, and a meal and a shower, he would sit on his bunk and create—or rather re-create—actions, thoughts, and deeply philosophical feelings about going to war in a bomber.

Often it was hard going. He put *himself* into his book, and spared neither his feelings nor his reputation. He admitted to his readers that he was probably a failure as a co-pilot.

More important, he tried to expunge some of his guilt feelings about being part of the killing. Yet they were far from erased. Writing about the bombing, the horror, the probable murder of mothers and their kids, he relived his experiences, enduring them by day, writing about them at night. It was a difficult time for the young warrior-philosopher, and he inevitably became emotionally charged by it.

Thoughts tumbled out of his head and onto the typed page, sometimes disorganized, often bitter, at times lyrical. There was a longing implicit in his words—longing for a better world, for Bert Stiles to be a better person, for the mountains of Colorado, for the politicians to settle the war in some way other than by killing. And he wrote about a dog:

> Some mornings there is a black dog with white feet out by the trucks. I like to lie beside him and scratch his stomach and rub his ears and wish he'd be my special buddy. I call him Blackdog. He used to go on

milkruns to France but he got flakhappy and tried to jump out of a waist window. So now he's on ground duty and comes to see us off in the morning. Someday I'm going to have an English setter, a white one. Maybe he'll love me more than anybody...

To Bert, Sam Newton was an enigma. He had known him for over five years—through fraternity, B-17 training, now combat. Bert felt he should know him well—and yet he didn't. Sam was big and gruff and funny. *Humorous* funny. He said some things that made Bert break out in laughter. He had a curious sort of mind; sometimes it was like a knife. Nothing much got by him; nobody Bert knew was faster or keener on the comeback.

Pilot and co-pilot never talked about the war. But they did talk—about going home and places they'd go and the girls they'd run after. Bert never tired of listening to his friend tell about his big times. Some nights they would lie there in their beds and talk for hours, about nights in Omaha and L.A. and Denver and the guys and girls they used to know.

In the air it was different. The chemistry disappeared. Bert figured Sam had to have a fellow pilot he could trust completely. He never got to the point of knowing what Sam wanted before he asked for it. And if he did something before Sam called for it, it was usually wrong. They wore each other out in the air.

Neither of them worked on it enough to smooth it out. When they got back on the ground they were so glad to be back that they didn't want to think about airplanes. Bert read a book or beat on his typewriter; Sam slept or wrote to his girl Barbara or went somewhere.

Bert was not a loner but he was perfectly happy being alone. He would be deliriously happy being with someone he particularly liked. In the old days it would be Rosemary or Kay or Sleepy. Now it would be Billy or Fletch or Sam. He would be stimulated beyond all measure by a good conversation or rapid repartee or a bang-up argument. If drink were available, that would add something. If not, so be it.

One of his special alone times was during the hour between "Stations" and "Start Engines." With everything in readiness for winding up the engines, other crew members would talk quietly, kid a bit, sit alone, even play cards. Bert would often find a place in the nose or outside on the grass if it wasn't too cold. The night before he would have written the words on a slip of paper of a favorite song he wanted to memorize.

"My heart tells me this is just a fling," he would sing, knowing the words by heart to "My Heart Tells Me." The lyrics to "Summertime" and "No Love No Nothing" would follow. Usually, he sang to himself. He figured the psychiatrists would ground him if they heard about it. But he wouldn't trade those alone times for anything.

Like all military bases everywhere, Bassingbourn was alive with rumors; they flowed out of offices, living huts, the flight line, the latrines. The leading grapevine topic was the coming invasion. Through May and early June, every time Lieutenant Porado woke them up someone would say, "It's D-Day." But it never seemed to be.

Then on the sixth of June it was.

It was only twenty-nine minutes into that day that the imperturbable Porado woke them. "Breakfast at one, briefing at two," he said.

"What the hell is this?" Sam said. They had been in bed only an hour or two.

Shuffling to breakfast, the only light was a faint glow from the moon, curtained off by a low overcast. Warplanes droned overhead; Bert figured they were RAF planes returning from Germany. From the flight line came the roar of Wright Cyclone engines being run up by the line crews.

There was an inordinate number of rank at chow—whole tables full of captains and majors and light colonels.

"Maybe this *is* D-Day," someone said.

Nobody laughed—it wasn't worth a laugh any more.

Doc Daugherty was there. "I'm going on this one," he said. What was going on? The Doc usually didn't fly with them.

At the flight line, the Public Relations Officer—Major Maclemore— was there, shining in white scarf and pressed flying clothes.

"You must think this is D-Day," Bert said to him.

The P.R. man nodded and winked suddenly.

Weariness evaporated. Bert and Sam quickly tuned in on the tension in the room. They were in on the big show. Finally.

The Base C.O. addressed a hushed group of combat flyers. "This is it today," he said. "This is invasion. You will be flying in support of ground troops."

The excitement was a tangible thing.

"Tanks on the beach at 0725," one of the briefing officers said a moment later. "Troops to hit the beach at 0730."

"There'll be 11,000 aircraft in the skies," another added.

"You *must* stay on briefed courses," a third stated. "No abortions—you can't go down—you can't turn left or right."

The 91st was bombing by six-plane squadrons. Newton's crew was to hit a wireless-telephone station five minutes before ground troops hit the beach.

A big yellow moon came through just before takeoff time.

Forts were circling everywhere as they formed at 17,000 feet in the murky dawn. Planes were stacked every 200 feet in elevation. Later, Bert wrote in *Serenade:* "The sun was a deep bloody orange in the East, and the fading yellow moon lay in a violet sky. The tattered overcast pulled itself together South of London, and became a steady blanket, puffed up here and there in soft cumulus."

They hit propeller wash once, so violently the pilots nearly went out the top. All the ammunition in the turrets jerked out of their boxes. Crone called, "Hey, someone get me down off the roof."

Well below, P-51s and P-38s were coming in low, strafing the shore installations. The medium bombers—B-25s and B-26s—were just above them, and somewhere offshore the foot soldiers were waiting to wade in.

Just before they crossed the coast, the undercast thinned and Bert could see a curve of landing boats, perhaps fifteen of them. Their guns flashed intermittently, brightly, against the dark sea. A minute later they dropped their bombs; there was no flak, just Forts, endless streams of them. Their formation turned West, then Northeast back to England. From the placid skies above, it was impossible for Bert to imagine the blood and death and hell below.

"The poor bastards," someone said on interphone.

Their planes had supported ground troops, Bert knew, but they were now on their way back to their obligatory shot of whiskey and their baseball games and their warm huts. The ships had supported them, as well, but now the sailors were below decks in relative comfort. Only the foot soldiers stayed on, never out of gunshot range, seldom out of danger.

The Air Corps would still truck the bombs over, perhaps for a long while yet, but it was no longer their private flying show. The boys who fought their battles the slow hard way had the bright lights of history on them now.

Bert wrote: "Blood is the same whether it spills on aluminum or the mud of Normandy. It takes guts whether you fly a million dollar airplane or wade in slow with a fifty-dollar rifle."

After landing and unloading, Bert lay down in the grass behind the tailwheel. Later, still alone, he walked to the co-pilots' house and joined a group of flying personnel who were waiting around the radio in Fletch's room. General Eisenhower's speech stirred them mightily and they learned the invasion had been a smash success.

He went to bed June 6 still thinking of Eisenhower's invaders. He thought of the grimy guys in the grass, moving down the roads, crawling through the brush, and he hoped they made it okay.

He turned on the lights—Sam was still out talking somewhere—and began a letter to his parents. He needed to at least start writing *something* this historic day; he would finish it tomorrow.

> By the time you receive this, you will know much more than I do about the invasion. But we were there, we were there in our serene sky, cut off from the whole affair by a layer of stratocumulus. I saw a few landing barges shooting like mad at something, and the mist closed in again…the future is a great glow tonight…and maybe I can help a little to tie it together…I hope so…Serenade.

The next day, a standdown, Bert lay around all morning, thinking of Tuesday, June 6. Toward noon, several new crews came in, looking virginal. They chatted with them, gave them the low-down, exaggerated some things, down-played others.

He headed for the mess hall at noon but the new crews had taken over the place. Giving it up, he returned to his room and took to his typewriter to add to his *Serenade* journal, still not through thinking or writing about D-Day:

> A Fort lives in the sky, from three to six miles up, and the only real things are the throttles and the feathering buttons, the engine gauges and the rudder pedals, an oxygen mask full of drool, and a relief can half full of relief.

> The flak is real when it clanks on the wings, and knocks out your number one oil-cooler. The rest of the time it is only a nightmare of soft black puffs and yellow flashes outside the window.

> I've seen what a knee looked like with the kneecap clipped away, and a waist-gunner with his brains all over and his legs shot off just below his flak suit. That guy was just as dead as any of those in the surf today. A dead one lies just as still in the sky as in a mudhole.

But most of the time you don't live with death in a Fort the way they do in a ditch. The smells don't get to you and every night as long as your luck holds out, your sack is ready and waiting, soft and dry.

Bert had fallen asleep over his journal when Lieutenant Porada came around in mid-afternoon to announce: "All crews down to Operations."

Bert jumped up. "Porada," he said, "It's *daylight*. What are you doing here? Don't you live in the dark?"

They took off in mid-afternoon and flew West, then South. The target was an airfield, a place called Kelvin-Bastard, not far from Lorient. Bert was flying when Europe loomed ahead through the softening sky like a huge stepping stone on a garden of dark water. The sun was sliding down through the soft blue toward the sea.

The flak started just after bombs away. The first puffs were just outside the co-pilot's window. Bert could easily see the dull flashes as the shells burst. There was an ugly clank somewhere and he knew they were hit. Quickly, he scanned the instruments: engines okay, instruments reading true, propellers still attached to the engines. His stomach tightened suddenly. He knew helpless fear from those soft black puffs. Nothing to do but sit there and pray the luck holds.

Oh, Blue Lady, are you still out there? Haven't heard much from you lately. Are you still on my side? Are you the same Lady who let Mac crash? Will you turn on me, too?

Then they were out of it, turning home. The wide, choppy channel loomed ahead. Once you were out of it, he thought, flak never seems quite real until the next time.

His tiredness started at the knees and ran on up to the eyes, but he felt good, glad to be in a descending airplane, glad to have his friends around him, glad that the day was nearly over. It was dark then and the stars were coming through over England.

They picked up their new B-17 two days later. Named Times a-Wastin' by their crew chief, Roy, none of them could figure what it meant. But Sam and Bert decided the ground crew deserved the honor; they put the big bomber to bed every night and fixed her up when she got scratched.

The Group artist had painted a picture on the airplane's nose of Snuffy Smith breaking out through a newspaper with a machine gun. But it was not the picture Bert had asked for. He had written to his sister Beth, who was studying at the School of Music in Rochester, New York.

> Hello, little sister...we are getting a new airplane and we need a design for the side. I figure you have the talent to draw us one. Here is my idea: a very fat man...without clothes...sitting on a block of ice...looking at a dame without clothes...who is flying in with propellers on both nacelles.... Thanks, pal. And just think...your work may soon be flying over the finest museums in Europe.

Beth Stiles easily found time to render a drawing for her flyer-brother. She sent it posthaste and eventually received a note from him:

> Thank you, komrad, for the job very skillfully and beautifully done...take care of thyself at school and when you get to New York next call up Mrs. Aley, for she is a tres fine gal...and how about writing a letter to this far land? And Serenade...

Late that afternoon a group of enlisted men from two crews—Newtons' and Langfords'—played a classic game of baseball. With still an hour before chow, and bored of writing in his room, Bert strode over to watch.

"Hey, Lieutenant Stiles," Sharpe said, "we can sure use you. We're behind nine to four, or something like that. Pull rank and come on in."

"Nah, Ed, I can't do that," Bert said. But Bill Lewis, who was playing second base, called time and walked over to him.

"Take my place, Lieutenant," he said. "I've already made four errors and I got to write a letter anyhow."

So Stiles, who had played second base for the freshman team at Colorado College, filled in for his Engineer-gunner. As he trotted onto the field past Sgt. Sharpe, he said, "Hey, Ed, can't you cut back on that 'Lieutenant' stuff. I'm Bert."

It was already the sixth inning of the seven inning game and Bert got to bat only once, slashing a single to right. He also made two throws to first for outs but fumbled a grounder. Just like high school, just like college, he thought. Fielding, .667.

Late that night, after hearing there'd be no mission on the morrow, he thought of God in the abysmal sky above, and mentally composed a letter he would write to Sleepy the next morning:

> I wonder what other people's Gods are like. Mine is very real and close. I guess I was brought up in a Sunday-school way—but I don't

go by it. I am a Christian in the sense that I think Christ must have been wonderful. So many church-goers are so fervent and have no person-alities worth mentioning—that I don't go anymore.

There was a new moon last night, a slim, silver curve low in the sky and the P-51s were up there playing around in the moonlight. You can wish on new moons, you know, and last night I wished: *please let me fly one of those little jobs…please give me a P-51….*

12

EVEN GOD MUST BE
A LITTLE BIT AFRAID

"Everything becomes simple. The
only thing that matters is to keep on
living, to be happy...."

*Maybe someday people will just be able to live. Maybe someday most
of the people in the world will be able to take it kind of easy and choose
their own way into the clear.... I'll throw away my pinks and the battle
jacket I bought for five pounds and if I never climb into another B-17
except to show my kids the instrument panel, I'd be crazy happy...but
the war has to end first and it's our turn now to fight....*

He found her just before chow one night after he had returned from a mission
to Berlin. She was a nurse, just a little girl with her nose turned up. She had
green eyes and a soft tan and she was lovely. She stood at the bar with two
other girls, unaware she had stopped all normal activity in the room.

They sat at the same table, across from one another. Their smiles came
at the same time. He said, "What are you?"

"Air Evac," she said. "C-47s."

"You evacuating us?"

She smiled again. "No, just looking."

Her brown nurse's slacks seemed made for her. Bert closed his eyes
and transported her into a white formal coming down the steps into the Cafe

Rouge at the Pennsylvania Hotel. Glenn Miller stopped the band to look at her. Bert bowed formally and steered her into a chair. After champagne, they danced. It was a lovely picture.

"Look," he said now, "how would you like to wander tonight?"

"All right..." She was laughing, but she was doubtful, too.

"Where are we going?"

"We can throw darts, or wade in some ditch, or look at the moon, or just drink."

They took a cab into Royston and found the Kings Arms. She was from Philadelphia. They talked about a girl he knew in Philly and some vague relative of hers in Denver. Noticing a large diamond on her finger, he asked what it meant.

"I'm engaged," she said, smiling again.

"You're—*engaged?*" he said, mocking surprise and masking disappointment.

"To a Spitfire pilot."

When they didn't talk it was best. It was almost like back at Colorado College, at Rusty's, drinking. She was out of the past, a dream of other days, when there was woo in the moonlight and laughter all around. He closed his eyes again and she was a girl named Eleanor he had taken to the Senior Prom at South High School.

She didn't talk much. She wasn't having a big time in England but she was getting by. Her life now was mostly plasma and bedpans. She held together the badly wounded until they could be flown out to the operating tables somewhere.

Sitting there, looking at her, the English ale changed to a Zombie and the smoky room became the Rainbow Room, and there was Goodman music from somewhere.

Walking home in the quiet countryside, the world sank low. She was pretty, she was built, and she was American. He could visualize her in sweater, skirt, and saddle shoes; he could see her sucking on a coke straw. And his imagination conjured up a vision: she and he, all ruffled up, riding home in a rumble seat.

She was a symbol of something that was always there in a corner of his mind. A girl with brown shoulders, in a pink formal with a white carnation in her hair, dancing through the night. A symbol of everything he'd left behind.

It was habit now. Tenth mission—Calais. Don't think about it—just go. But did any day start right that began at 0200? The powdered eggs were tasteless. The real eggs had grown old and died.

In the truck, it was so dark Bert couldn't even see the faces of his crew.

Chief Roy was leaning on Number One propeller when they arrived.

"Everything okay?" Bert asked.

"Everything's okay. We put some relief tubes in the cockpit and the nose."

"Good deal. You're a saint, Chief."

Climbing up through the forward hatch, the co-pilot dropped his oxygen mask on the concrete.

"I'll be a sad sonovabitch," he said.

"Naughty, naughty," Lewis chided. "Wash your mouth out."

Stiles heaved his parachute into the right seat, noted the oxygen supply, and checked that all fuel shut-off switches were off. Then he crawled out and went back to the tail to hand out escape kits. Sharpe was sitting in his narrow seat, sweating and cussing his guns.

"We get any candy, Lieutenant?" he asked.

"Maybe."

"I won't go unless we do."

The plane looked okay—two wings, one tail, four engines, all present and accounted for. Bert gave each tire a kick and called it a check. When Roy said a plane was ready, it was ready.

Everything done, no duties left, still forty-five minutes to "Start Engines." He kidded with Sharpe for another few minutes, noted the hard laughter (too casual, too strained?) of the other crewmen, then retired to his favorite place—behind the tail in the soft grass, head pillowed by his flak suit. Eyes wide open, he stared at the dawning sky, his thoughts tumbling out.

The sky is a mighty mysterious place. A big canvas drawn over our pitiful lives, ubiquitous, changing, mysterious. God, I love the sky. I've read stories about it, dreamed about it, let my imagination go wild about it. Are you up there on this wild blue morning, O Blue Lady?

I feel a strong pressure in my chest, a kind of ecstasy, forceful but not definable, an unknown. I have the sudden thought that I am in charge of my life, after all. I will fly these bastard B-One-Sevens, then breeze aloft in P-Five-Ones until the war ends in a blaze of victory.

I'm 23 years old and still a blind, naive kid, I guess. I'm here to do a job and I'll do it right now, by God, and I'll come out of this, I know I will. I'll be *positive* about *everything*—and I'll help Sam fly this airplane and then go whirling away to fighters, and then...and then....

He looked at the bombs on his way through the catwalk above the bomb bays. Big, ugly, dead things, coming alive only long enough to kill everybody around. We climb up about five miles, he thought, and kick them out—and haven't the faintest idea what happens when they connect. Does the earth break in half? Does the sun shatter in the sky? Do the leaves wither? What a hell of a life a bomb leads.

They took off into the soft cream of morning and headed for Calais. It was an easy flight in the red-gold of the early sun, but it was cold—the cockpit heater went out.

Since the invasion, tension had lessened. Even the formation was loose when the togglers flipped the bombs out. There was a mangy fur of flak off at two o'clock low. They let down after bombs away, into a hazy level of contrails from the planes ahead. Looking back as they banked, they could see a dream world of white plumes and following trails.

Sharpe sighted 109s at three o'clock low, then Crone saw some P-51s going after them. Mustangs came moaning in from all directions. The tail gunner gave them a blow-by-blow account of a dog fight at four o'clock low. Times a-Wastin' let down in formation through a widening hole. Sam eased out a little and dived down through a bulging cloud, and he laughed like a circus clown.

Soon the patterned loveliness of England showed through the cloud holes and they went on home.

After early chow, Bert went out alone on his bike, past a bronze barn and down through some yellow fields. A swallow came up on the deck and channeled up over some high weeds. Some day, he thought, I'll have to get a swallow to check me out. Compared to a swallow, a B-17 just doesn't have it.

At the end of the road he left his bike and climbed a fence. In the middle of the grass he lay flat on his back and gazed at the sky. Well, he thought, second time today I've stretched out on the ground. The air was fresh and windy-clean and the blue of the sky faded deep into forever. He thought:

Every time I come out here I get a feeling of intense awareness of being alive. Everything becomes simple. The only thing that matters is to keep on living, to be happy. I don't want anything, I don't miss anything, and yet...and yet...I miss everything, I want everything....

He rolled over and lay with his face in the grass. When he sat up two horses were standing close by, looking at him. They were big and red and fat. He still had part of the mission candy bar in his pocket; he held out some chocolate. The first horse sniffed at it. The second, the one with the white foot, took it all. He patted the horses for a while, until they got bored and went back to a corner of the field.

There was an alert on for the following morning. He knew, because he had checked. He wished he hadn't.

He rode slowly and sadly back while it was still light enough to see his way. Time to write maybe one letter, or a few pages of *Serenade to the Big Bird*. No more than that. Two o'clock briefing came early.

"There's going to be some changes on the crew," Sam Newton said casually. They had finished breakfast and were in their room, trying to decide what to do with the rest of the day. The mission had been scrubbed, but there was a rumor there might be an afternoon flight. Another rumor, *rumored* to be a live one, was that real brass would be around, Generals Doolittle and Spaatz and even higher rank, the boss of the Air Corps, General Arnold, and the Army Chief of Staff, General Marshall.

"Changes, what changes?"

"Well, for one thing, Bird's probably gone for good. They like him at Group. 'Course Beach is at the Flak House for a few more days. And then Jack Oates needs checking out."

"Oates is getting his own crew?"

"Yeah."

"You going to check him out?"

"Yeah."

"So—then—what happens to me?"

"You get to hog the sack for a while. Lucky dog."

Bert got up from his bed, walked around the room, suddenly restless. "When does this start?"

Sam shrugged. "Well, buddy, if there's a mission this afternoon, Oates will be on it as co-pilot."

Bert suddenly felt tired. "So you asked for Oates?"

"I didn't ask for Oates. He was *assigned* to me to check out as first pilot."

"But you didn't fight it. C'mon, Sam, we're old friends, we've been through a lot together. You can level with me. Am I all washed up?"

Sam's voice steeled. "Damn it, Bert, you have twelve missions. You're halfway through. You'll finish your tour almost as soon as I do."

Bert plowed right on. "I guess you're saying I'm not coming back to your crew?"

Sam held a long shrug. "Your guess. Maybe not. If not, Bert, it's been great having you—"

"Oh, c'mon, Sam, knock it off," Bert said, angrily. With a long look at his pilot, he strode rapidly from the room.

In mid-afternoon, all scheduled air crews were called to the flight line. The parade of Generals was there to watch takeoffs. Bert slept through it all; he didn't awaken until 1930, after it was too late for evening chow. Walking to the Red Cross hut, he drank tea and ate waffles for an hour and talked to the resident nurse, Greata. She was from Bryn Mawr. About 2130 he walked to the flight line to look for returning planes. It was all quiet.

Standing there, eyes skyward, he thought about his crew. How was old Sharpe doing? Perhaps a 109 was sitting on top of a cumulonimbus waiting for him. And Oates? He would do fine. He decided Sam would keep Oates and request they chloroform Stiles. Everybody stood around. Nobody said much; you could feel the tension like a tangible thing.

At 2200 hours Stiles figured his old crew had been lost for good. Without him, their luck had turned sour. At 2205 he had laughed himself out of that notion and decided that without him their chances were about 50 percent better.

"God, why don't they come back?" some G.I. said.

And then came a faint hum of engines from the East, soon a steady roar. The first group came over the field and the low squadron peeled off. They were flying a beautiful tight formation.

The Red Cross girl had been counting. "They all made it," she said. "Every one."

Bert didn't wait. They were home. He wasn't on the crew any more. They didn't need him.

June was still writing, but less often now. The letters were flattening out; no more poetry.

If only I could fly across the miles of blue water and could hold you and soothe you, believe me that's all I'd ever ask of life. If only I had things to do over—I would have realized a few things that never entered my head. Maybe, when this war is over, I'll have a chance to prove to you I've changed.

Reading her words, Bert was deeply touched. He thought, however, that it was time to stand back and look hard at this affair. Was there anything left? He felt she might turn out to be a really good gal for some guy, or she might wind up being a sad sack all the way. He had a clear picture of her now, but it wasn't in technicolor. He tried, but couldn't bring back the way he had felt when she walked across a room. If it had mattered, it might have been sad.

He slept in most days now—he was unneeded, an extra co-pilot, a black dog wandering around the squadron. The brass announced mission requirements had been increased to thirty. Bert's depression was complete. Now he had eighteen to go.

On June 21, with Bert still involuntarily grounded, Sam took his crew on a particularly tough one. Ed Sharpe told Bert about it that night. Bert reflected that Sharpe the tail gunner and Stiles the ex co-pilot had gotten on the verge of a close friendship. Sharpe threw a lot of big words at Stiles and Bert threw others right back at him. Both of them became experts at thrust and riposte.

"It was to the Big B—Berlin," Sharpe told Bert. They were sitting on Sharpe's bed, facing each other. Sam was at the Officer's Club. "We were in the low squadron, tucked in tight. Got hemmed in—so Lieutenant Newton just got the hell out and into an open slot in the high squadron.

"Then somebody called in that a formation of Mosquitoes was headed our way—we couldn't figure that out. About that time Crone woke up: 'Them are ME 410s,' he said.

"They came in on a tail-pass and I remember saying, 'Here they come' in a weak voice. The first one was shooting right up my tail-pipe and I shot right back. Then—damn if the ME didn't sag off and begin to fall apart. And the pilot bailed."

"So you *got* one?" Bert yelled.

"Yeah, yeah. Confirmed."

"Hey, great, Sharpie."

The tail gunner grinned widely and shrugged happily. "Anyway, then the 20 millimeters began busting all around us and up ahead the Forts began to get it. A '17 fell out of formation and began to smoke. We counted nine chutes from that one. Then a couple more Forts went down. It was something else again.

"Not that I was watching falling bombers. 'Cause the 410s came again and *all* of our gunners were shooting away like mad. God, what a sight! Ross shot one down, too. The simple Kraut was flying formation with us and Ross shot his head off.

"And Lewis shot one high off the tail, shooting straight back."

"God, you guys were *great,*" Bert said, in awe.

"And then it was Crone's turn."

"What, old Crone got one, too?"

"Yeah, he hit a 190 comin' in about nine o'clock. He sent it into a spin, flaming, and it just went on into the ground."

"Oh God—I wish I'd been there. Listen, Ed. Do you know how Sam and Oates did?"

"Well, they about went nuts. Lieutenant Newton pleaded with someone to tell him what was goin' on."

Bert reflected on how it must have been: all fourteen 50-calibers shooting and Forts and fighters throwing up all over the sky.

Sharpe chuckled. "Listen to this, Lieutenant. Sam Newton was screaming on interphone, asking were we hit, who was doing the shooting, what the hell was goin' on. And so I said to him, 'Sir, will you please shut up?' And he did.

"Anyway, the 38s and 51s took us home and we had an easy ride back. And—listen. At the interrogation we all got jagged on scotch. And we was all talking with both hands and drinking coffee and dunking doughnuts and trying for more scotch. And Lieutenant Newton was walking around wearing his two .45s, and one of the other pilots said, 'Some outfit you got, Sambo.' And the lieutenant said, 'I *told* you I've got the best crew.'"

Bert smiled at Ed Sharpe, reflecting his happiness over the success of his old crew. "God," he said, his voice husky, "You shot down—what—five, six? You *have* got the best crew."

"*We* have the best crew," Ed Sharpe amended. "It's *your* crew, too—Bert."

Bert Stiles flew six missions during the next three weeks, all as a fill-in co-pilot. There were no problems with pilot or crew, but he never felt at home. He was the outsider, the sixth man again. Targets were all over the map: an airfield in Toulouse, a power plant in St. Pol, a munitions factory in Hanover.

Sam Newton was still his roommate and they still talked about the old days—but seldom about flying.

The day Sam flew his last mission—his thirtieth—Bert, who had not been scheduled, rode his bicycle out to the flight line about two o'clock. Leaning against his bike, he watched as the Forts came home, one by one. And then there it was, safely on the ground, the plane carrying his old crew. Besides Sam, Benson, Crone, Sharpe, and Lewis had finished up together.

Bert met them at the runway turnoff and ran alongside, waving, as they taxied in. As Roy and his crew chocked the plane in and Sam cut engines, Bert stood looking up at the pilot's compartment. Sam had a huge grin on his face.

Everyone was in a quiet daze.

Bert walked up to his former navigator. "Lieutenant Benson, I presume."

"Old bertstiles," Benson said.

"You're all through!"

"We're all through." But they wouldn't really believe it.

Don Bird, who had finished his missions the previous day, joined them and he and Bert found some water in the equipment hut. They filled up half a dozen flak helmets.

"I christen thee a sharp son of a bitch," Bert said to Sharpe as he dumped a helmet full of water over his head. A moment later, Bill Lewis, sipping coffee, got the same treatment from Bird. Basil Crone, who had been hiding somewhere, came out and was met with a deluge from both Bert and Bird.

Later, alone, it hit Bert Stiles—hard. His old crew was through, they were going home, and he still had seven missions to fly. They were the crew he had come with—but now they were leaving him behind.

The Squadron Operations Officer, Captain Martin, told Bert he might as well take advantage of being on the unassigned roles and take a couple of days off—go to London. Bert couldn't find anyone to go with him;

everyone was flying. But he didn't look too long; it might be a good time to be alone.

A couple of hours after leaving Victoria Station, he decided London was the loneliest city in the world, with the loneliness hanging over it like a curse.

He ate dinner at the Savoy and drank a whole bottle of red wine. On top of the scotch he'd had earlier, the liquor deepened his lost feeling.

The buzz bombs were still coming. They'd started just after D-Day, hour after hour, night after night. No let up, no end in sight. The pressure on the people must be hell, he thought.

Piccadilly Square was depressing. Uniforms everywhere— English, Australians, Poles, Swiss, Americans. And old people, women of all ages, and so many little dirty-faced children.

He knew how to get around now. From Leicester Square to Piccadilly, and from Piccadilly to the Strand or Trafalgar or King's Cross or Charing Cross. He went to a matinee and saw *There Shall be No Night.* An older English couple in the next seat gave him some of their candy.

In the late afternoon he took the underground tube to King's Cross, then to Waterloo, then back to Leicester Square. There were people there, anyway.

He spoke to several. There was a Canadian between trains, a South African Red Cross girl on her way to Cambridge for a date, and a dubious blonde who thought he was trying to pick her up. Well, perhaps he was.

He had nowhere to go—and it would be the same anywhere. At Bond Street Terminal he stood in the dusty station looking around. People were bedding down for the night, a row of bunks were filled, and most floor space was covered with papers and blankets and coats. Cave dwellers, he thought, his chest constricting, getting their caves ready for the next raid.

A little girl nearly at his feet was waking up. She didn't seem to have anyone caring for her. She had white-gold hair in sleepy disarray. Her face was streaked with dirt and tears. A weary-faced woman looked at him without interest. He tried to smile but it didn't come off very well. She didn't smile back; perhaps she was out of smiles. He looked from the woman to the child and lifted his eyebrows.

The little girl didn't seem to be scared. He thought he had never seen eyes so blue before, not an ordinary blue but warmer and softer.

"Hello," he said, "I thought I stepped on you."

She fixed her blue eyes on him, but said nothing. Bert thought she looked about three years old.

"How old are you, honey?"

"Five." Her voice was soft and shrill.

She sure didn't look five, he thought. "Want some gum?" It was the only thing he had to offer.

She shook her head.

"I do." It was a boy in short pants with the dirtiest knees in London.

Bert gave him the whole package. Beechnut.

"Thanks, Yank," he said in a high, shrill voice. Then he simply vanished.

The little girl kept looking at him. Then—did he imagine it?—her eyes softened.

"Want to go for a ride?" he asked her.

She didn't know what he meant.

"On my shoulders," he said. He turned the palm of both hands down and patted his shoulders.

Her mother smiled faintly and he lifted the girl high for a look at her world. She didn't weigh much. Then he put her on his shoulders and whirled her around in a couple of circles. She gave a delighted little gasp, then began laughing, very softly.

Trains roared by every few minutes. Two women, sitting with backs against the wall, smiled at him. A one-legged man with thick glasses looked long at him.

Later, he put the little girl down and she looked up at him, eyes wide. She laughed again and her cheeks glowed.

"Prettiest eyes in London town," he told her.

"Thank you very much," the little girl said. She lay down on the cement and covered herself with a coat. Her eyes showed that entrancing blue for a moment and then she was asleep.

Standing over her for a moment, watching her fall asleep, his mind moved back a couple of years:

> Somewhere back there, somewhere, a long time ago, there were beds and sheets and blankets, and moonlight and a fresh wind coming through the window into my room. And somewhere over there, across an ocean, a thousand years ago, there had been laughter and peace and love.

Peace is just a word here, just a wish to the new moon, just a prayer to
every dawn. But for a little while there had been laughter from a little
girl while the trains screamed through the tunnels deep below the war
outside. And there is love—all around—and suddenly it presses in
stronger than fear or tiredness.

By the time he had returned to the Red Cross, looking for his bed, the
loneliness had gone.

In the morning, shaved and spruced up, he stopped in to see Major
Arthur Gordon, a peacetime editor of *Good Housekeeping.* The major had
heard about Bert through Maxwell Aley and had invited him to drop by his
office near Grosvenor Square.

The editor placed a file of Bert's writings on his desk in front of his
visitor. "I've been hearing about you from Maxwell," he said. "And now
I've been reading some of your things. Good stuff, Lieutenant, I hope you'll
keep it up."

"I intend to, sir," Bert said. "There are so many stories to tell." He
hesitated. "I've been working on a longer piece, too. A sort of anthology.
Weaving all my short works into book length. Trying to tie it all together."
Bert went on to tell him about how he worked nearly every night. And how
he felt readers would want to know how one pilot felt about flying the "big
bird" and dropping bombs for a living.

Major Gordon seemed interested and asked a few questions. Bert
couldn't decide whether he was just being polite or was really interested.
Later, Gordon took Bert to lunch.

His spirits were still high when the train pulled out that afternoon. So
he wasn't on a crew, so he still had five or six missions to go? So what? He
was still a writer.

It was an incongruous situation, one which honored combat aircrews,
but one which they had been *ordered* to attend. But why *wouldn't* they want
to receive air medals from the brass?

They showed up in Class A uniform at 1600 hours one Sunday. Fifty
or so from Bert's squadron were there, looking slightly sheepish, fidgeting with unfamiliar ties, most wanting to be elsewhere. But their
country wanted to recognize their daily forays under fire, so they'd go
along.

"Medals?" Bert asked Sam. "Are we heroes or something?"

Captain Martin read off the names alphabetically. Bert couldn't remember any other occasion in England when they'd had to stand at attention. When the Captain had finished, the base Public Relations Officer took over. Major MacPartlin read off the citation, words that included "exceptional gallantry" and "cool courage."

The ceremony had been scheduled for the tarmac in front of the hangar, but rain forced them inside the hangar. In the near background, a B-17 engine was being tested. No one seemed to note or care that the Major's remarks were mostly lost in the engine roar.

When Stiles' name was called, he stepped forward, saluted smartly, and thought he heard MacPartlin say something like "Glad to have you with us." Back in line, Bert opened the box. He thought the medal was nicely done—pretty and lettered neatly. The citation which went with it was mimeographed.

"My name was typed in," Bert wrote later. "The mimeograph was about out of ink and the 'exceptional gallantry' part was pretty thin. I hoped they weren't trying to tell me something."

A long letter followed that Sunday night, one that epitomized how he felt about God—now. He decided he would re-read it when he returned home—to recapture his feelings when he was fighting a war.

> My God lives up in the sky. He is so wonderful, and beautiful, I can only sense Him. He is always there, whenever I want Him. I don't worry whether he is finite or infinite. I hold up my hands and He takes them. For an instant I'm not here, I'm out there, in the starry night, riding the wind, intensely, wonderfully happy. I know that while I live on this plane, I will never completely get up there...only for an instant at times, and sometimes I long intensely for death. For then I will go up there, up into the blue blue....

> In a way the war has intensified all these feelings; in a way the war has mitigated them. How can anything be halfway normal in a war? In a war, I think, even God must be a little bit afraid....

13

JOURNEY TO A WAR

"I felt the ground and I wanted to
take my shoes off. Every time I
breathed, I knew it...."

*Wash Park School started getting me ready for this, for B-17s in
England, and strawberries, and Munich through the overcast, and
Berlin with the 190s slowrolling through the formation, and Toulouse
famous for its accurate flak...it was that kind of school, remote from
a world where the storm troopers rode into Paris, detached from a
world where the English kids drank their tea and took the Spitfires up
for the late afternoon flight, oblivious to a world where the Poles were
starved and slaughtered....*

To the people back home, it wasn't often that any particular bomber base stood
out over any other in the E.T.O.—or in any theater of operations. But Bassingbourn, home of the 91st Group, had a claim to fame. It had been about a year
earlier, on May 17, 1943, that the Memphis Belle had flown its twenty-fifth
and final mission. That B-17, piloted by Captain Robert Morgan, was the first
American bomber to finish a tour of twenty-five missions.

Bert had arrived at Bassingbourn months after the Memphis Belle had
finished its missions, and he had not met any of their crew. Still, his
romantic nature thrilled to the knowledge of their accomplishment. He'd
heard that their crew had made a highly successful tour of the U.S.,
promoting the use of heavy bombers for daylight raids.

About the time Bert was putting the little girl on his shoulders in the bomb shelter, a man named Ted Malone visited Bassingbourn. Malone was an on-the-spot reporter and commentator for Westinghouse Electric. Billed as "Human interest reports of the men who are making history in the war effort," the reports were broadcast by shortwave every Monday, Wednesday, and Friday from London.

Malone was an experienced interviewer and reporter, and his reports were designed to capture the essence of the war in Europe. Some of them were quite effective, even memorable.

On July 24, 1944, Ted Malone broadcast from London, beginning his presentation this way:

> Hello there! This is Ted Malone overseas. I hope you will forgive me if I do something a little different tonight. I was up at an Eighth Air Force heavy bomber base the other day, the home of Memphis Belle, General Ike, and Yankee Doodle. A grand bunch of fellows, and I promised them I would say hello to you tonight.

Malone went on to pay tribute to several former 91st men, beginning with Captain Sid Hantman, then recuperating at Walter Reed Hospital in Washington D.C. He also mentioned Sgt. Henry Street of Dryfork, West Virginia, who volunteered for a second tour and had completed fifty-two missions, "just about a record," according to Malone.

The reporter described Capt. Charles Hudson of Bakersfield, California, who kept right on firing his machine guns despite a wrist broken by flak. "Did you know that Hudson always flies in his pajamas?" he asked. "He overslept on his first mission and shoved his clothes right on over his pajamas. It was a good mission, and he has worn them ever since for luck."

A little later in the half hour program, Malone described Bert's friend Lt. Arthur Maclemore of Washington, D.C. who had flown seventy-two missions to date, sixty-three with the RAF before joining the Army Air Corps. He had to be fished out of the North Sea twice.

Malone described a recent mission when Maclemore was acting as co-pilot and ran into a heap of trouble:

> Lieutenant Sam Newton of Sioux City, Iowa, was Lt. Maclemore's pilot on a run over Berlin. They lost ten ships all around them—to fighters and flak—and their ship Times a-Wastin' got its share, too. The oxygen and hydraulic systems were shot out, control cables partly shot away, and an engine shot up, so they just barely made it to the field....

When Bert heard about it, he was happy for Maclemore and Newton, but he couldn't help remember that it should have been Bert Stiles flying co-pilot that mission to Berlin. Or—he asked himself—would they have made it back at all if he were in the right-hand seat?

Lt. John W. Green was a newly-installed pilot in the 401st Squadron. A former co-pilot for Captain William Thissell, he had been moved to the left seat when the Captain had been promoted to lead pilot. The rest of Thissell's crew were delighted. They had been afraid they'd draw a new first pilot rather than the co-pilot they'd trained with.

Before the restructured crew could fly any missions, they of course needed a co-pilot. Jack Green asked for Bert Stiles.

Bert knew Green slightly. He had met him when Green had moved upstairs in the co-pilot's house to replace the former occupant, who had bailed out over Switzerland.

Stiles dropped in to see his new pilot in his room.

They talked for a few minutes, becoming acquainted, then Bert said, "And so I guess you're stuck with me."

"You mean you're stuck with *me*," Green said.

They grinned at each other like a couple of schoolboys. "I think you'll like the crew," the new first pilot added. "I'll tell you about them when we have a chance."

Bert liked the way he talked. Green had lived in the Philippines; his father had been commissioner of police there during MacArthur's days. Later, he had gone to an unusual sort of progressive school in the southern California desert called Deep Springs College, then switched to Stanford just before the war. He had been in Pre-Med.

Bert told him about his own abortive experiences with progressive education at South High School. They laughed together at their common educational adventures.

Green said he intended to return to Stanford. He was an open-faced fellow with a high forehead and a small mustache. After eating together, they talked into the night in Green's room.

As Bert said good night after midnight, Green put a hand on his shoulder. "I'm glad it was you I got," he said.

Bert stood there with his mouth open. He didn't trust himself to speak for a moment. He couldn't think of anyone recently who had said they were glad Bert Stiles was on their club.

Finally, Bert said, "I'm glad, too, Jack. And maybe we'll stay lucky." Solemnly, they shook hands on it.

The next day, a standdown, Bert rode his bicycle to the Public Relations Office and talked to the P.R. Officer. He asked for the files on Crew 2109.

Bert read the files for nearly an hour. Along with what Jack Green had told him, he formed a pretty good idea of the men he would be flying with:

Navigator—Martin L. Bulion from New York City. He was a Flight Officer who had been a student at NYU, a quiet fellow, fair, tallish, friendly.

Bombardier—Robert L. Simmers, from Detroit, married, short, portly, sandy-haired, outgoing.

Top-Turret Gunner—Gilbert Bradley, from Shamokin, Pennsylvania, former bottle inspector in the old Reading Brewery. He had brown hair and was tallish.

Radioman—Thomas McAvoy was from Lawrence, Massachusetts and was a former railway traffic man. He had brown hair and was of medium height.

Ball-Turret Gunner—Harlyn Bossert. According to Green, a quiet classic of a gunner. From Cassville, Wisconsin, he had worked in a factory. Dark-haired, very slender, handsome, a lady killer.

Waist Gunner—Roy Tolbert, who hailed from Greenwood, South Carolina, was the crew clown, an excitable type. He had been a clerk in a cotton mill and later a mechanic. Fairly well built with brown hair.

Tail Gunner—Erwin Mock, from Hobart, Oklahoma, was described by Green as best tail gunner around. He had worked at Douglas Aircraft and was of average height and had a round face given to a habitual grin.

During the rest of the day, after he had met his new crew, Bert put together names with faces. He liked what he saw.

Three days later they flew to Munich.

Their target was the JU-88 plant. It was July 16, 1944. It was the crew's twenty-first mission.

Bert didn't even get to bed the night before. He was brushing his teeth just after midnight when the call came.

It was ten-tenths overcast, which meant, Bert wrote later in his book, "We didn't see the wine country or the Rhine or snow on the Jungfrau, or anything at all of the world except the sky, and the sun on the cloud cover."

Two Forts blew up on the mission, but Bert knew none of the crewmen. Three B-24s from another Group had to sink down through the undercast and were reportedly shot down by Focke-Wulfs.

It was overcast and the only way they could tell it was Munich was by the heavy flak, some of the worst in Germany.

On the way home, Mock called from the tail. "You *think* we hit Munich, but you don't *know*."

Bert didn't smile. He was thinking of another tail gunner, ready to return to the States soon. Sharpe had said he would get out to Denver to see Bert's folks. Sometime. Bert hoped he would.

He missed his old crew, and yet...and yet...there was something about Green's crew, and especially Green himself, that gave him satisfaction. 'Satisfaction?' Hell, that was too tame a word. Trust, pride, camaraderie? No matter the precise word: it felt *right* for him just now.

He sat at his typewriter again that night:

> I wish you could meet Green...you should have seen him today...he was so wonderful...steady and easy...You ought to see this crew...it's sort of like walking out of the fog into the clear—to look for something so long, and then to find it.
>
> The Lady was there today, and she came in close and put her hands on mine and said, "Take it easy, Little Boy," and we walked through the valley.... That's a beautiful sentence, don't you think? Yea, though I walk through the valley of the shadow of death.... Serenade...

They flew three missions in the next four days, with about fifteen hours of sleep during that span. They headed well up into the Baltic to Peenemunde seeking out a robot plane research lab. Bombing was at 26,500 feet, the payload forty-two one-hundred-pound incendiary bombs made of rubber and gas. McAvoy and Tolbert had forty-two safety pins to pull. Clear weather and excellent results.

Flak was heavy and when they landed they found holes and jagged tears all over the horizontal surfaces.

They led the low group of the wing to Lechfeld the next day. Bert sang to himself all the way to altitude through gray and diseased clouds, but he knew he wasn't letting Green down. Not once had the pilot had to give him a direct order.

At 22,000 feet, just before 0600, Bert paused to marvel at yellow down on top of soft gray clouds. Then, before his eyes, the down changed slowly to gold and soft orange, with thin layers of pink above and one bright arrow of a cloud pointing at the sun.

Just before reaching the I.P., which would lock them into the bomb run, B-17s immediately behind them were hit by ME-109s. Excitedly, Mock reported in from the tail:

"The Forts are really getting it! I got in a few shots, but they're pretty far back there. My gosh—Jesus! There's two going down at once. One has its tail shore off, completely off. And there's a man falling free."

"Any chutes, Erv?" someone asked.

"No chutes. None."

This time they carried fragmentation bombs, thirty-eight one-hundred-pound clusters. Their aiming point was the airdrome barracks. From what they could see, the results were devastating.

There was a sky full of flak at two o'clock, white flak, heavy stuff. Bert wrote later in *Serenade:* "In the Wing ahead a Fort powdered. A chunk of it slipped down onto the wing of another. The Tokyo tanks blew. Half a Fort plunged down into the element below. They all went down in a sickening blown-up red mass of Forts and tears of flame."

Even with flak still exploding all around them, Bert could wait no longer. Motioning to Green, he unhooked seat belt, flak suit, oxygen mask, and headset, and climbed down from his perch. He had to take his gloves off to hold the relief tube in place and tried not to notice the cold. Is it worth it, he wondered, as relief flowed over him? Why not just cut out all water for two days before each mission?

As they let down over the English Channel, Bert carefully un-wrapped an oblong package. Within a moment he showed Green his prize: three tortilla-shaped pieces of powdered egg omelet—for the return journey.

"Want some?" he asked Green.

The pilot shook his head violently.

"Hey, Brad, you want some?" he asked the engineer.

The gunner made a gagging noise.

"You don't know what you're missing," Stiles said.

Green and Stiles grinned at each other as they hoisted after-mission scotches. Bert believed Green liked him okay, but he had to get something else out on the table.

"Jack, tell me something, will you?"

"Sure, Bert."

"How am I doing? I mean, how am I *really* doing? Am I doing my part? I mean, goddamn it, just kick me—anytime—if you find me goofing off. I want to be the best damn co-pilot in the Eighth."

Green's grin had not faded. "Don't worry about it, Bert. I don't know about you and Sam, that's your business. But you've been doing great—just great—with me. Believe that."

A little later, after checking the bulletin board, they learned they were scheduled again the next morning.

"After today, with flak *and* fighters, tomorrow's trip *can't* be any worse," Green said.

About 0400 the following morning, Green had some second thoughts. Mission Number Twenty-five would be to Leipzig. It was reputed to be the best fortified city in Germany.

At the equipment hut, drawing supplies, Bert saw Gordon Beach, his former ball-turret gunner. Beach was flying with Lt. Bob Langford's crew now. This would be his last mission.

"We're the last of Lieutenant Newton's gang," he told Bert.

"And I'll be the *very* last," Bert said.

With less than four hours sleep, the co-pilot was so tired he felt drunk. But as they assembled into formation and headed over the Channel, he didn't feel sleepy, just dazed, from his toenails to his scalp. He swallowed and tried to stay alert.

They were flying Little Patches, Ship Number 678, carrying ten 500-pound demolition bombs. They came in over Holland, crossed the Rhine River just inside Germany and flew South almost to Frankfurt. Their heading was 120 degrees, direct to Leipzig. They were at their bombing altitude, 26,000 feet.

Bob Langford, with Bert's friend Jim Fletcher as co-pilot and Beach as ball-turret gunner, was in the high lead and doing a good job of it. There were eight B-17s from their squadron among about thirty in the group. They were well back and below most of the Eighth Air Force that day.

The sky was a soft but steely blue. A soft fuzz lay over a thin undercast. The ground showed a pale green through the holes.

Bert thought: *We don't belong up here.* He could feel the quiet threat of death all over the sky. Somehow, he knew they would be hit hard this day. He thought:

The lady named Death is a whore.... Luck is a lady and so is Death...I don't know why. And there's no telling who she'll go for. Sometimes it's a quiet, gentle, intelligent guy. Lady Luck strings with him for a while, then hands him over to the lady named Death. Sometimes a guy comes along who can laugh in their faces. The hell with luck, he says, and the hell with death. And maybe they go for it...and maybe they don't.

The Lady of Luck has a lovely face you can never quite see, and her eyes are the night itself. Her hair is dark and lovely. And the lady named Death can also be lovely and sometimes she's a screaming horrible bitch...and sometimes she's a quiet one, with soft hands that rest gently on top of yours on the throttles....

The co-pilot was monitoring VHF and Green was on interphone. Abruptly, someone from Wing spoke up on VHF: "Tuck it in—bandits in the target area." Their target time was about a half hour away.

Then, with no warning, just before the I.P., a black Focke-Wulf slid under their wing and rolled over low. Every gun on Little Patches opened up. ME 109s and more FWs came from three directions at once, in four major waves, parallel but also stacked up. Each wave consisted of thirty-five to forty fighters, each painted a shiny black or green.

Sgt. Bossert tracked one FW from six o'clock to two o'clock with his fifty-caliber guns firing all the time. Then he watched with incredulity as the German pilot threw off his canopy and bailed out. The German wore a black flying suit; Bossert was tempted to keep right on firing as he floated past them.

The MEs came up to about 400 yards and lobbed twenty-millimeter shells at their droning Fort. One shell lodged in their Number Two main gasoline tank. Flame burst out, flared, then died down.

Bert flipped to interphone in time to hear Mock say from the tail: "Here they come again." His voice was cool and easy, like in church. Every gun on the plane was firing steadily. The air was nothing but black polka dots and firecrackers.

"Keep your eyes open. Keep 'em out there," someone said. It sounded like Bossert.

"Got one at seven o'clock," Mock said.

Bert saw two Forts blow up at four o'clock. Fear was hot in his throat and cold in his stomach.

A trio of gray 109s whipped past under their wing and rolled away in a dive. *Black crosses on gray wings,* he thought, *shooting fire and death.*

A fighter came directly at them at 10 o'clock. Bulion and Simmers powdered him, he rolled over and fell away, and there was smoke and fire everywhere.

Bert looked hard at Green. The pilot was hunched over, concentrating and intense. But somehow, Bert thought, he looked calm. Green caught his glance. "Better give me everything," he said and Bert jacked up the RPMs to the hilt.

Fighters were queuing up again to their rear, dozens of them. Getting set to come at them again, fifteen or twenty abreast.

The Fortress flying off their left wing had already fallen off, under heavy attack. Now Bert saw with horror that their other wingman, on the right side, *his* side, had somehow lost a stabilizer. He could see blue sky through it. But the rudder still worked, still flapped. Then, as he watched, the left wing flared up and he fell off to the right. God—that was Bob Hanna's crew. He watched them go down in a steep dive. Bert's mouth sagged open, his eyes bulging with shock.

Up ahead, low, was Bob Langford's crew, but then abruptly *he* was gone, sagging off at three o'clock. At his side, Green slid Little Patches under the lead squadron, taking Langford's place in formation. Langford was in a dive with four or five fighters after him, coming in, firing, swinging out, then coming in again. Twenty-millimeter fire was all over the sky.

Bert felt the weight of a dozen flak suits on his chest. Beach was in that ball...poor goddamn Beach. And Fletch, from the co-pilot's house, was probably already dead.

Later, Bert wrote:

> There didn't seem to be any hope at all...we were just waiting for it...just sitting there hunched up...jerking around to check the right side...jerking back to check the instruments...waiting for the big one. They came through six or seven times, queuing up, coming in, throwing those 20s in there...we were hit...again...again. The whole squadron was blown up, burned up, shot to hell...look at that Fort going down: only one got out...

"Here they come again," Bossert yelled on interphone.

"There—four o'clock level."

"Take that one at six o'clock."

All the guns were hammering again. The vibration was frightening.

Jack Green's B-17 was the only plane left in the high element, tucked in tightly under the lead, snuggled up almost under their tail guns. They could see shell cases dropping down and going through their cowling, smashing against plexiglass, chipping away at windshields.

"I see Mustangs back there," Mock said from the tail, his voice calm and matter-of-fact, but somehow vibrant, as well.

Bert thrilled to the knowledge. His voice trembling, he rasped into the interphone: "How many, Mock, how many?"

"Four, maybe five," he said.

"Uh, oh," someone said. They were hoping for many more.

Bert saw a burning Fort nose down towards them. He punched the wheel forward. Green gave him a tight smile and nodded.

During all of the attack they had been on the bomb run. Somehow, Bob Simmers concentrated through it all. They closed up still more and "salvoed" their bombs on their target.

Bert Stiles' mood was vicious: *I hope those bombs hit home,* he thought, *I hope to hell they did.*

Green turned away from the target and motioned to his co-pilot to take the controls while he looked for B-17s still in the air. After a moment, Green held up five fingers: only five planes in the squadron still aloft. God: seven out of twelve lost. Bert flipped back to VHF and immediately heard, "Is my wing on fire? Will you check to see if my wing is on fire?" He gave his call sign; it was their lead ship.

They were already underneath and Green pulled closer.

Bert could see better than Jack Green. "You're okay," Bert yelled. "You're okay...baby...your wing is okay. No smoke, no flames, stay in there, baby." It came out more as a prayer.

A moment later they heard, "I'm bailing out my crew." The lead plane banked off to the right and Bert began to see people come out. All my buddies, he thought.

Bert reached over and touched Green, drawing a long look. *What a guy,* Bert had time to think. Then he touched the control column. And what an airplane. Still flying...still living.

Everyone was talking on interphone and nobody knew what anyone else said. Then it came through to all of them; all those guys, those good guys, cooked and smashed down there somewhere, dead or chopped up or burned or headed for some Stalag.

The fighters never came back. The ride home was easy. The sky was a soft unbelievable blue and the thought of death and terror was incongruous as hell.

When they left the continent behind, they began to come apart. Green took off his mask. There didn't seem to be any words, but they tried to say them, say anything.

"Jesus, you're here," Bert said, finally, clamping his open left hand on his pilot's shoulder.

"I'm awfully proud of you—of them," Green said quietly.

Bradley came down out of the top turret. His face was nothing but teeth. Bert mussed up his hair and he beat on Bert.

The interphone was jammed.

"All I could do was pray," McAvoy said from the radio room.

"You can be the chaplain," Mock said, laughing a little.

"If they say go tomorrow, I'll hand in my wings," Tolbert said emphatically.

Bert could still feel the weight on his chest. Langford down...that meant Fletch and Johnny O'Leary...and Beach, his buddy from Denver. And all the others; he knew them all.

They saw a beach through a hole in the clouds—white sand and England. They had never seen anything so beautiful in their lives. They were home. They had been sent out to get knocked off and they had come home, anyway. Home...

Bert's chest still felt like he was wearing six flak suits as they taxied past a beat-up Fort just turning into a hardstand.

"Jesus, that's Langford," he said, pounding Green. Their tail was shot, one wing was ripped. It was one sorry Flying Fortress, but it had come home.

After Green cut engines, people crowded around. Everyone wanted to know where the other planes were. Jerry, a crew chief from the next hardstand, came up and asked about his plane. They had to tell him: blown up—shot down—straight-on-in-dive.

The twenty millimeter that hit their own wing blew away part of the top of Number Two gas tank and an inspection panel. Their gas tank hadn't blown only because it had been empty.

Bert wrote later about that homecoming:

> I stood by the tail and looked at the holes. I felt the ground and I wanted to take my shoes off. Every time I breathed, I knew it.

I could look out into the sky over the hangar and say thank you to the lady of the luck, the Blue Lady. She had been there all along.

But I was all ripped apart. Part of me was dead, and part of me was wild, ready to take off, and part of me was just shaky and twisted and useless.

Back in his room in the co-pilot's house, Bert and Jack Green sat across from Bob Langford and kept telling themselves it was him. Then Jim Fletcher came in. "Jesus," Bert said, and just looked at him. Fletch had a smile a mile wide.

Later, Bert went over to see Gordon Beach, just-retired ball-turret gunner. He had shot down three fighters, maybe four. He had used every shell he had aboard.

"I guess they can't kill us Denver guys," Beach said.

A little later, Green came around again, smiling. Bert wanted to touch him, to tell him he was glad he was on his crew, to say—to anyone—that it was the best goddamn crew there was. But he didn't say anything like that and neither did Green.

Bert started a letter to his parents, but didn't get far. Suddenly, he came apart and cried like a kid. He could watch himself and hear himself, but he couldn't do a thing about it. Later, he finished the letter:

The Lady is cool and quiet and infinitely lovely. I'll never need her as badly as I did today.... I am deeply aware of just being alive. Earlier, when I started this letter, the pieces of me just fell apart. bertstiles was nothing at all...just tears.

You ought to see this crew. It's sort of like walking out of a cloud into the clear. Every guy here has tied himself to every other guy...and we are closer than anything has ever been. It's okay now. But it will all come back, slow, and we'll start again.

17. Bert Stiles in early 1944—just after receiving his wings as an Army Air Corps pilot.

18. Sam Newton's crew—ready for combat—in early 1944 (l to r) front row: Sam Newton, Bert Stiles, Grant Benson, Don Bird. Back row: Bill Lewis, Gil Spaugh, Ed Ross, Gordon Beach, Basil Crone, Ed Sharpe.

19. Bert rides his beloved bicycle at Bassingbourn, spring 1944.

20. *Billy Behrend and Bert Stiles relaxing in front of the co-pilot's house.*

21. *Sam Newton's combat B-17, Times A-Wastin'.*

22. *A squadron of B-17 Flying Fortresses setting off on a bomb run over Germany.*

23. *Cockpit of a B-17. Pilot flies in the left hand seat.*

24. Lt. Jack Green, first pilot on Bert's second crew.

25. *Lt. Jack Green's crew in front of Mah Ideal after Bert Stiles joined them (l to r, front row): Bossert, Bradley, Tolbert; (back row) Mock, McAvoy, Stiles, Simmers, Green.*

26. *Kathleen (Kattie) Regan, shown here with her brother John, an Air Corps pilot.*

27. *Fighter pilot Stiles and Nancy, a friend from the American Red Cross, in front of a P-51.*

28. A B-17 in formation off the left wing. "C'mon baby," Bert would say, "pull it in a little closer."

29. Tar Heel, assigned to Bert Stiles when Capt. Jim Starnes departed on leave to the States.

30. First Lt. Bert Stiles in front of his P-51 in November 1944.

31. Graduation photograph of Lt. Bert Stiles in November 1943.

32. Co-pilot's house at Bassingbourn.

33. Harry "Swede" Soderberg, flight engineer, and Jim Fletcher, co-pilot, seem proud of the wing damage after returning from the mission to Leipzig, Germany.

34. A look from the co-pilot's window at No. 4 engine, feathered.

*35. A B-17 from another Group heads for the ground after being
shot down by fighters.*

14

THE KILLING WOULD GO ON

"There is luck and there is horror...and there is laughter and a
tearing kind of loneliness...."

*It is summer and there is war all over the world...it has spread from
Normandy to Brittany and the American columns are swinging in
towards Paris. There is still plenty of war in Russia. The same war is
still going on in the islands, and in the sky over Japan.... I can only
think of it in terms of moments and chunks and stretches of eternity
measured in minutes...so far I've lived through it. So far the lady of
luck has let me come through.*

"I'll meet you in Piccadilly at high noon," Bert said to Jack Green late that
night. Bert had asked to see his squadron C.O., Major Lord, in the morning.
He would miss the early train to London.

Crews who had been on the Leipzig raid had been issued passes—in
effect, they were kicked off the base for a mandatory rest. Sometimes the
brass weren't totally dumb, Bert thought.

At 0900, his uniform sharply creased and with his new silver bars
attached, Bert presented himself to the Squadron Operations office and
asked to see Major Lord.

"Well, Stiles," the major said, returning Bert's salute. "This can't be
about P-51s again. Your request has been denied."

"I know, sir. I wanted to get your best advice."

They talked about it. First Air Division had no openings, and they were receiving a steady supply of fighter pilots from training schools in the States.

"But I have *combat* experience," Bert said, "something those kids in the States don't have. That's worth *something*."

Lord liked Stiles and he decided he would buck it up again. If Stiles wanted to fly *that* badly...he told the young flyer he would keep his request alive.

"Oh, Stiles," he added, "we have an opening for R and R. Today. I'd like you to fill it."

Bert had nothing against a week of "rest and relaxation"—he had been looking forward to it—but he had wanted to visit London with Green and the others. Still, he wasn't about to upset any applecarts.

Thinking about it as he packed his B-4 bag, he decided this could be good timing. He would take *Serenade* with him and work on it, perhaps even finish it. And a week without planes and flak and death. He could read, sleep late, perhaps even fish. And the Red Cross girls who staffed rest homes were supposed to be something!

An RAF Lancaster, a four-engine veteran of earlier days of the war, picked them up in mid-afternoon. Combat veterans usually attended rest homes as full crews, but often enough attended individually. Sometimes, three or four each from a dozen Air Corps bases would make up the complement. Bert knew the others from Bassingbourn by sight only.

During the short flight South, Bert wandered up to the cockpit and chatted with the pilots. They were night combat veterans temporarily assigned for easy ferry duty. Bert found them not unlike his fellow Army Air Corps pilots.

The British bomber landed at RAF base and was met by three U.S. Army trucks, each driven by a G.I. Bert sat in the front seat along with a sad-faced navigator from Great Ashfield who, he found out later, had lost his entire crew while he was on sick leave. Already, Bert could feel his nerves unwinding, his muscles relaxing. His romantic nature pictured a huge English country house on a hill. And, suddenly, there it was.

The driver had pulled into a long lane, at the end of which was a large, sprawling Tudor style home sheltered by giant trees and surrounded by shrubs, green lawns, flower beds, and woods. An air of serenity prevailed. Even the badminton and volley ball nets didn't obtrude. Hidden from immediate view were the dog kennels, makeshift baseball diamond, and motor and bicycle pools.

Bert Stiles was enthralled. Later that week, he described it in a letter to his parents:

> Furze Down is something never equaled anywhere in my time, a big old English country house right out of a Victorian novel. And it is beautiful country. England is so beautiful it gets you after awhile...Connecticut was like that. This is a civilized sort of beauti-ful—hedges and little houses and thatched roofs and gardens.
>
> And this House—Furze Down, funny name—no kidding, you can see why the aristocrat is so entrenched. If I'd ever get into a house like this, I'd never leave until they knocked me out...big and easy, it is, and wonderful...

They were in time for late tea, served by Inch, the butler, in real tea cups, not the usual army mugs. Tea was served in a sunny garden room overlooking a flagstone terrace and a lawn beyond. Bert looked at his own long, straight, hard fingers grasping the fragile teacup. Are these the same fingers, is this the same hand, that gripped the co-pilot's wheel with such viciousness just two days ago over Leipzig? Amazing—the different faces—and fingers—of us young warriors.

After tea they were shown around the house: living room, formal dining room, breakfast room, drawing room, game rooms, closets filled with sports shorts, sweaters, tennis sneakers, and corduroy pants, theirs to use all week.

They met the Red Cross Director for Furze Down. She was an attractive lady perhaps three or four years older than Bert. She explained the "rules" of the house: civilian clothes all day, all the milk they could drink (real milk), but no alcohol to be brought into the house, though beer and drinks would be served on special occasions. And report in and out when you leave Furze Down. Sports were encouraged. There was pool, bicycling, lawn bowling, fishing, table tennis, volley ball, badminton, croquet. Visits to special places of interest (Winchester Cathedral, Lady Arundel's castle) would be scheduled. And there were books and records (Glenn Miller's "In the Mood)" and photo albums and high tea and conversations and tall tales in front of the fireplace.

So these were the "rules" of Furze Down? Well, he decided, he would just have to put up with them.

After the introductory session Bert walked up to talk with the Red Cross director and introduced himself.

"Glad to have you here, Bert," she said. Bert quickly noted her lovely complexion and how well she looked in her Red Cross uniform. She was slim and not very tall. Her name was Kathleen (Kattie) Regan. Bert immediately decided he liked older women.

"It almost seems I've met you before," he said.

Kattie smiled. *"That* line has been used before."

"I've got better lines than that in my hip pocket," he said. "I'm from Colorado Springs; where are you from, Kattie?"

"Boise, Idaho."

"Boise, hmmm. Only person I know there is Kay Bisenius. I used to go with her. Perhaps I still do, I'm not sure."

Kattie was looking at him in amazement. "Do *you* know Kay? Why—she—she used to go with my brother, John."

It was Bert's turn to be surprised. "Go with your brother? Let me think...I know she fell for some Boise fellow who went out to Santa Clara to college...she went out there, too, to be near him. She ended up at Cal Berkeley for a year or so."

Kattie was smiling broadly. "That's Kay Bisenius, all right."

"I heard she and your brother didn't click in the end," Bert mused. "Anyway, she left Cal and went to Colorado College. That's where I met her. What a screwy world, Kattie."

They talked for a half-hour, comparing notes, much to the chagrin of some of the other officers, who would have liked to know their hostess better. Before he left her, Bert, always a fast worker, prevailed upon Kattie to go on a picnic with him the next day.

They rode bicycles along a country lane among the green fields, waved gaily at grazing cows, dodged pot holes filled with muddy water. Abandoning their bikes, they propped against an oak tree, sipped tea from a canteen, and nibbled on sandwiches the Furze Down cook had prepared.

"Gosh, Kattie, this is what I've been waiting for all my life," he said.

"It is a bit of paradise in the middle of war," she said.

"I don't enjoy being a bomber pilot, Kattie," he said. "I don't like any part of this." He paused; he had suddenly become serious. "What I do enjoy, what I do want—is simply my own patch of earth—somewhere—with someone. And that someone is a big mystery to me. I don't know that there is any girl who can put up with me.

"You don't know the girls I've known—Rosemary, Nancy, Kay, June. It's a big question, bigger than I can handle. But I've got to let this war soak in first. I've got to come to terms with it—if I can. And then, after the war, I want to roam the world a bit before I rejoin it." He looked sheepishly at her. "Gosh, Kattie, I apologize. Here I am with a darn pretty girl in a lovely spot, and all I can do is talk about myself—and other girls."

Learning of Bert's passion for fishing, Kattie Regan arranged for him to fish at the nearby estate of a retired banker, Sir Charles MacGregor. Bert thought he looked a bit like C. Aubrey Smith—white hair, ruddy features, prominent nose. Bert wrote to his father about fishing:

> Sir Charles owns a chunk of the River Tess, maybe the most famous trout stream in England. He loaned me a fly rod and I netted a big old brown the first day. But fishing for English trout is a pretty fancy business. They take only dry flies that are laid six inches above their nose. The English way is to know every fish in the stream and then sit and watch for an hour or so and see what they are taking; then tie a special fly; and then put it in his mouth and catch him. Marvelous.

The young flyer, with his compatriots, slept late, read in bed, had late breakfasts, and didn't wear shoes all week—except at dinner. The butler named Inch was right out of the movies. He was built like a penguin—impeccable and unflappable. He adopted the American flyers. He told Bert one night in semi-confidence that serving them was his "war work."

So Bert could have spent a completely lazy week—table tennis, an old favorite of his; fishing, an all time favorite; bicycling, pool, checkers, chess, group singing, and some mild flirting along the way. But he saved time—he *had* to—for something else: writing.

His Corona typewriter had made the trip with him. So had a notebook with *Serenade* written across the top. He had all he needed.

Because there was so much going on during the day, he took to his typewriter at night, usually after ten o'clock. He would sit in an alcove off the library, banging away, oblivious to a late-night conversation, hand-holding, gin rummy, or a letter-writer in the corner. He needed no reference books, no thesaurus, not even a dictionary. He could tighten up his writing later. He had what he needed: his *memory,* that cavernous storehouse of experiences, colored with imagination, flavored with idealism, and fleshed out with strong verbs.

He wrote *Serenade to the Big Bird* as a first-hand account of his life as a B-17 co-pilot in the United States Army Eighth Air Force. He wrote with compassion, with insight, with excitement—and sometimes with tears in his eyes.

He wrote of his relations with Sam Newton, not sparing himself; maybe he *was* a lousy co-pilot. He wrote of his trips to London, of his love for everything English, of the excitement of being part of a crew, of his craving to be a P-51 pilot. And he wrote, most of the time with jarring detail, of some of his missions over Germany.

Re-reading several chapters in the corner of the library at Furze Down, he realized he had become a confirmed pacifist, that he truly hated war. War was a great adventure, no doubt, especially when you were twenty-three years old. He supposed it had come along at the right time for him; he had not been a success at college, his writing career was progressing all too slowly, and he still needed to indulge an inexorable drive to roam and feel and taste the world. The war experience was an imperative. It was forcing a tremendous new perspective upon him.

He wrote his narrative as he felt, with honesty and clarity and forceful-ness. Straight and true.

He wrote rapidly, using his little notebook to look up facts about missions: names, places, events. Not that there was that much detail in his book. It was short, succinct, almost terse. He loved writing it, and he finished it on his last night at Furze Down. It was midnight, but he was far from sleepy. He wandered around the quiet house, looking for Kattie. Surprisingly, he found her, fixing a cup of cocoa in the dimly lit kitchen.

He stopped in the doorway. "Kattie," he said, "I think I've finished it—finished my book."

"Bravo, Bert. That's good for a big hug."

His face was radiant. There were tears in his eyes—and in hers. After a moment, he said, "Kattie, you've helped me with this—you'll never know how much. Just by being here."

They sat at the kitchen table together, drinking cocoa and eating ginger cookies. She was silent; she suspected he needed the relief of talking.

"God, how I hate war," he said. "Writing *Serenade* was a great experi-ence, Kattie, but the subject matter—killing, maiming, blind hatred—I can do without forever. I've lost so many friends. God, that Mac! What a guy he was." He paused, looking at his lap. "Now—tomorrow—we go back to it."

"You only have a few more missions, don't you, Bert?"

"Eight or nine, Kattie. But if I could only get into fighters I would climb right out of that boxcar forever."

"Bert—I don't know you very well—and perhaps I don't have a right to ask this—"

He looked up at her. "Kattie, right now you have as much right as anyone in the world. Ask away."

"You hate killing. Yet you want to transfer to P-51s—" He was looking at her with the world's sadness in his eyes, "and—well, go right on killing there?"

"It sounds illogical. And feeble. But I want to fly a *real* plane, Kattie. I want to feel the wind blowing across my face—to climb, dive, soar, be free, to be on my own." He paused, rolled his eyes. "I know that doesn't answer your question."

Her voice reflected his sadness. "And—the killing would go on?"

He looked at her with infinite weariness, tears crowding his eyes. "Yes—Kattie—the killing would go on."

Bert walked across the down the next morning to say goodbye to Sir Charles and Lady MacGregor. He found the old gentleman at breakfast in the garden, overlooking the River Tess. Bert accepted a cup of coffee. "I've enjoyed meeting you so much, Bert," Sir Charles said. "Will you come back to see us?"

"I may have to go AWOL, Sir Charles," Bert said, "but you can count on me fishing with you one more time. At least."

"I asked you in here, Stiles, because there's a chance now. Perhaps a good one."

Two days later, Bert Stiles was in Major Lord's office. The Squadron Commander's words thrilled him.

"Things have changed—they always do. The 339th Fighter Group are shy a few pilots—and they might need you—say in two weeks time. They're in the Third Air Division—and they fly nothing but P-51s."

Bert glowed.

"But understand this, Lieutenant. You're still on flying status here as a co-pilot on Green's crew. He was asking about you while you were at the flak house. You'll be flying tomorrow morning. When the fighter transfer comes through—if it does—we'll yank you right off a B-17 and put you in a Mustang cockpit." He paused for a moment. "You know, Stiles, sometimes I envy the hell out of you. Flying a fighter." Another brief pause. "But other times, I think you're out of your mind."

During the next week, there was little time to think about fighters. Green's crew, with Stiles as co-pilot, flew four missions. The first target was a jet-propelled airdrome at Chartres, France. It was a milk-run. Still, a Fort was knocked down by flak in the element behind theirs. Two days later, it was another airdrome: Mulhouse, France.

A few days later Bert was in the station hospital. "I'm giving birth to a gourd on the left jaw," he wrote home. "I won't fly for a while due to the wisdom of teeth."

While in the hospital, he wrote to Rosemary:

> Bo, it's getting so big and mixed up that I don't know whether I'll ever be able to put myself together again...there is the past and you and the mountains and the way the hills get smoky blue up the side of Monument Creek, and my folks...and this typewriter...and there is the big bird...and there is Mac...and all the other guys who are shot to hell and burned up and smashed...and there is the Blue Lady, so blue and serene and out of reach...and there is luck and there is horror...and there is laughter and a tearing kind of loneliness...

> Maybe I can learn to make love better than anyone in the world...so I could tear the heart out of someone—just spin them away into a mad, red, beautiful heaven in the sky...but there is something steady that comes in warm and easy and says here you are...and here I am, and together we are something we will never know...and there is no way to tell how good it is...and if you should go away, then part of me would die.

By the time Bert was released from sick leave, Jack Green had finished his tour of duty, but was still on base. But Bert still had five missions to go, and went back to a "fill-in" basis as co-pilot—the old "black dog" concept. He still awaited fighter orders. Most other friends had left. He knew orders for his return to the States would be forthcoming soon. Slowly, he became resigned to going home. But—damn it—he wasn't ready to leave England.

And then it happened. One minute he was talking with two new arrivals, Lieutenants Good and Thomsen, telling them some truths about flying combat. The next he was in Lord's office. He had been taken off orders to go home; new orders would be cut assigning him to a fighter group.

He found John Green in the Club contemplating a dark beer.

"Jack, this is *it*. I'm off to fly the little birds."

Jack Green clasped the grinning Stiles by the shoulders. "Bert, that is *great*. Just shows if you want something hard enough and long enough, you'll get it."

Bert told him about the refresher course he would need to take at a training detachment in northern England. "Then I'll be assigned right next door," he said. "At Fowlmere."

They talked for awhile, sipping beer, in the Nissen hut which served as the Officer's Club. Before they separated, they made plans, definite plans, to meet on the beach at Santa Monica exactly one month after the war in Europe was won.

Before he left Bassingbourn, he wrote Rosemary again, letting her know of a long-time and strongly-felt philosophy:

Remember when we talked about doing something in the world, a kind of holy grail—which was also senselessly beautiful, romantically noble, and grimly magnificent? Well, Bo, some day I will be free—to make love to a woman—to catch a fish—to ride a wave—to have kids who are brown and smart and kind and in love—to be able to get close to a Chinese—have him understand me—and me him—and the same with an Englishman and a Mexican and a Sinkiangese and a Kashmirian...

So someday after the war is over, I'll come back to see you. Maybe it won't be long and maybe it will be a thousand years...I wish it was tonight. There is no more sense to this letter than throwing rocks at the moon. I can't tell you how good it would be to be alive in Colorado again...so, so long for awhile, Bo, just be someplace I am, when I am....

By the time Bert Stiles arrived at Fowlmere, home of the 339th Fighter Group, he had more than ten hours in the AT-6, his old Advanced Flying School plane. He felt confident he could make the switch from right-seat bomber flying to fighters, confidence which was raised a level when he met his old friend Billy Behrend at the fighter base. Billy, now a veteran P-51 pilot of six weeks or so, had one ME-109 to his credit.

"If I can do it, you sure can," Billy told him.

"Hey, I haven't even been in the cockpit of a Mustang yet."

"Don't be in a terrible hurry, Bert," his old friend said. "Get as much practice in the '51 as they'll allow you. Don't rush out to tackle those Krauts. They'll be around for a while."

"Tell me every damn thing you know about the Mustang."

"Hmmm. Might take five minutes then. Seriously, Bert, the best advice I can give you is to read the manual in both directions, twice. Then sit in the cockpit for an hour or two to fix the position of every control, every instrument. Be worth every minute, chum."

Bert fixed Billy with a steely eye. "Methinks everything you've just said is as straight and true as the P-51, itself."

He wrote to his parents a few days later:

> This outfit has knocked off about 50 planes in the last three days—and three guys I knew from cadet days have gone down. It is the same ugly war. Our flight leader is Captain Olander and he is wonderful. Lieutenant Hrico is a good guy, too.

> So far I've waxed everyone in the squadron in ping-pong. And I get my laundry done by a nice little old lady. So far everything is really going good. I have a pair of silk gloves and a pair of chamois and gauntlets, too. And I have a new chute and a clean flying suit and my name is on the board...and I really *belong* to this outfit.

On September 26, 1944, First Lieutenant Bert Stiles took off in a P-51 for the first time.

15

SOMETIMES THERE IS FOREVER

"So it is Thanksgiving, cool and
deep in the mud of England. It is
sort of queer and beautiful to be
alive."

*I was lucky enough to be born below the mountains in Colorado. But
some day I would like to say I live in the world. In the end it is only the
people who count, all the people in the whole world. Any land is
beautiful to someone. Any land is worth fighting for to someone. So it
isn't the land. It is the people. That is what the war is about, I think.
So if we can get through with this war, I'll get started....*

The North American P-51 Mustang was considered by most airmen to be
the finest all-around fighter in the war. With a Packard Merlin inline engine,
it developed 1,720 horsepower and a maximum speed of 437 miles per hour
at 25,000 feet. Its wingspan was thirty-seven feet and it had a length of just
over thirty-two feet.

The fighter weighed 7,125 pounds empty, but loaded with fuel and
armament topped 12,000 pounds. While it had a service ceiling of 41,900
feet, it seemed to be most effective between 25,000 and 30,000 feet. With
its maneuverability and speed, its best use developed as a high-altitude
bomber escort. It had a range of 2,300 miles.

Sitting at the end of the runway, ready to go, Bert Stiles felt a thrill
beyond any anticipation. When the tower flashed the green light, he raised

his right thumb skyward and shouted "Tally-ho," holding the last syllable for several seconds. Then he moved the throttle forward smoothly.

It was not a good takeoff and his grin faded. In the climb the tachometer went awry. One moment he had 2,450 RPMs, the next it faded to zero. What the hell was going on? He reduced power by guess, leveled off at 1,500 feet, and looked around the area. By chance, he found himself over his old bomber base. Look at the B-17s on the ground, he thought, all lined up for strafing. He checked his gunsight—then it, too, went out. What kind of hex flight was this?

He soon found how differently the '51 trimmed from an AT-6; every time he changed altitude he had to roll in right or left rudder. Climbing higher, he decided to do some aerobatics. He tried a roll, but stalled out and, he wrote later, "almost spun in." He decided it was time to look at Bassing-bourn again.

Greasing his fighter in at the 91st airfield was a weird experience. He wasn't sitting passively watching Green or Newton land a lumbering Fort any longer; he was actually dusting around the sky in a P-51 all by himself!

At Bassingbourn Operations, he found a few people he knew, had a cup of coffee, watched a Fort line up for takeoff. He didn't stay long. He wanted to get back in the saddle of his personal flying horse.

During takeoff his canopy flapped wildly and finally blew off, clattering against the fuselage on its downward plunge, so he blithely flew home in the breeze and made the kind of landing you're just glad to walk away from.

Well, Stiles, he thought, not too auspicious a first flight, but if they don't ground me forthwith, I'll do better tomorrow.

He *was* better the following day, putting his Mustang through the paces. After his third flight, he wrote home:

> Today I went up to 10,000 and tried a couple of rolls and they weren't bad. I figured I was beginning to be a hotrock. I did a halfway sort of loop then split-s-ed out of a half roll from 8,000. I was hitting about 450 when I got around it and I was moaning down towards the ground at a terrific rate. Coming in, my engine cut out. Just after landing the plugs loaded up.

The 339th Fighter Group, part of the Eighth Air Force, had not been in England long before Bert Stiles joined them. The unit arrived in England in March 1944 and began its operations by flying a sweep on April 30. Just before Bert became operational with them, on September 11, its Mustangs tangled with more than 100 German fighters which had formed to attack U.S. bombers. In the air battle which followed, fifteen enemy planes were downed with an American loss of five Mustangs. The Group was rapidly winning a name for itself.

Bert was assigned to the 505th Fighter Squadron, said to be the top squadron in the group. He felt fortunate to be in the flight led by Jim Starnes. Captain Starnes was the leading ace of the group, with seven kills in the air and more on the ground. Bert liked him because, as he wrote to Rosemary, "He isn't a hot rock like a lot of these jokers, he is just sure and really good." They flew together to the North Sea and shot up a few waves and boxes on the water. When Bert fired his machine guns, he thought his plane was standing still.

He practiced flying formation off Starnes' wing for a while, then mock-fought some P-47s. Later, by himself, he buzzed some lethargic seals on a sandbar, then moaned in on a freighter and nearly clipped off an aerial. He told Billy Behrend that night that he'd forgotten how crazy wonderful it was to fly.

Bert had sent *Serenade to the Big Bird* to Maxwell Aley in New York. He hadn't heard anything yet. It would probably never be accepted, he figured.

Bert kept up a good-natured pursuit of Jeanne, a Red Cross girl from his old bomber base. They dated often and enjoyed a lot of laughs. Now that he was a fighter jockey, he told her she'd find him even more daring and romantic. She agreed.

He put some thoughts on girls in a letter to Rosemary:

> I have the hellish way of always getting serious with any doll I'm with these days. It just seems impossible to take it easy and flick it out with the light touch. I guess it's time to make some mad love before the world ends.

> I think it would be wonderful having a child…to see it work out of formlessness and soft horror into something alive…something that is you and someone else you have known in the night…and it is all the rest of the world, too.

> I used to think that if I lived in a war and was lucky enough not to be killed I would know a lot more about the world and the people in it. But a war doesn't do that to you. I don't know anything about suffering or torture. I've been pretty close to death, I guess…and in the air, Bo, death is so cold and impersonal.

Flying a Mustang was everything Bert had imagined it to be. If he still didn't believe in killing, he didn't let it deter him from enjoying his present role. In a final flight before clearing for his first combat patrol, he shot up a sunken barge, played hide and seek with thick clouds, buzzed his old co-pilot's house in Bassingbourn. Was he ready for combat? Damn right.

On October 15, two months after he had flown his last mission in a B-17, he wrote to his parents:

> And so tomorrow if the wind is right and the clouds don't move in, I'll go back to the war and fly alongside the 17s and try to keep all harm from them...So I'm back in it, and it is time for you to put in the words again to whomever you put them to; and it is time for me to take it easy and cool.

Closet weather kept the group on the ground for three days but October 19 was clear and windy. Five groups of Fortresses needed escort. The big board had the name "Stiles, B" scratched in chalk with some seventeen others, so he flew aloft that day, into combat, for the first time in a fighter.

"109s at 11 o'clock low—let's go get 'em," his flight leader Starnes called. Heart pounding, Bert followed Starnes down, dropping his extra gas tanks, looking for the foe. He wrote to Kay Bisenius later that he "probably scared all the people in some little German mountain town—but found no Germans."

He nearly froze—his heater was defective and his oxygen mask wasn't working right.

Climbing through clouds, they topped out at 20,000 feet. Bert's oxygen gave out completely. He found a hole and headed down fast, then called Starnes and told him he needed to turn his nose homeward. The flight leader gave him a heading of 280 degrees and sent him off to England.

On his own, flying in and out of clouds, he let down slowly and watched his gas gauges. His left gauge was hovering on zero. What had happened? His next thought was to look for a soft place to land when he had to parachute. Through the clouds he could see a field. But where was he? Was this Belgium? Or France? Anyway, he had to go in.

The landing wasn't bad, considering the emergency. I'll just pick up some gas, he thought, and go on home. But on the ground he looked for the Nissen hut he had spotted from the air. Where was it? In *that* grove of trees? Or *that* one?

He taxied across grass for what he later termed ten miles or so, and finally found the hut. He was at an RAF base in eastern France.

As he clambered out of his plane, he noticed oil all over the cowling. An RAF mechanic was looking at him with interest. He asked the mechanic if he would pull the cowling.

The engine was nearly drowned in oil. Besides an oil leak, he had also lost most of his hydraulic fluid. The mechanic told him he was lucky to get in at all.

"Can your crew work on my ship?" Bert asked.

"Not just today, Yank. Got some of our own needs tinkering. Can you wait half a fortnight?"

Bert went over to get some chow and see what alternatives there were. A short airman spotted him and came over to chat.

"That you came in just now? In a Mustang?"

Bert grinned. "Yeah, sure was. You American?"

"As American as Kansas. A Yank in the RCAF. Now, how can I make your life rosy and sweet? Need some help?"

Bert told him of his beat-up airplane. They talked for a while and learned they had both been to Chicago and Hollywood. The RCAF pilot worked out food and a bed for Bert. The bed was in a tent. But how, Bert asked, was he to get back to England?

"That's the *easy* part, Stiles. I'll fly you back first thing tomorrow."

"Hey, that's great. What kind of plane do you fly?"

"Mosquito."

"Hey—a *Mosquito?* A great plane, I hear."

"Like it? Well you can *fly* it tomorrow if you'd like."

Lying on a narrow cot in his tent that night, Bert thought over his first combat mission: heater went out, oxygen failed, oil leak, got lost while taxiing, brakes went out, now sleeping in a tent in France. Was *this* a typical mission?

Bert telephoned his base operations from the RAF fighter base where he had been dropped by the Mosquito pilot. His Operations, sounding surprised to hear from him, promised to send an AT-6 to ferry him back to Fowlmere. Bert was himself surprised that they had him listed as "Missing in Action." Gosh, he thought, all I did was go down for some gas.

What an unusual way the Air Corps took to reward a new pilot. They loaned him Starnes' beautiful P-51 because the Captain was going on leave to the States. And this after leaving his own broken plane in France? So Stiles took over Tar Heel, a proven tight ship with numerous kills to its credit. But, because the plane needed some work and the weather was closing in, Operations almost insisted Bert take two or three days off.

It was his opportunity. He headed back to Furze Down where he had emotional reunions with Kattie Regan and Sir Charles MacGregor. He relived the past, flirting and swapping quips with Kattie and pulling in graylings with Sir Charles. He wrote home from there:

> After I finish up in fighters I think I'll get assigned here as Adjutant which I figure is a job designed for my caliber of performance.

Awaiting him at his base was a much-forwarded letter from Mrs. Annie Field, whom Bert had idolized when he was a sixteen-year-old Junior ranger. Annie informed him she was going to have a second baby in January. The letter and picture made Bert's day all over again.

He also heard from Rosemary and responded immediately:

> Just got back and there were *two* letters from you—it is just fate and luck and wonderful. You seem sort of foggy and knocked out and sad and frustrated and half-laughing at yourself—only not feeling like laughing too much because it is a sort-of-mixed-up-horrible-but-could-be-wonderful-if-only-one-damn-thing-would-come-through world.

> So it is a funny kind of night…and everyone is dying of weariness. If you ever do get in the Red Cross ask them to put you in the Rest Home Division—that is probably the best deal in the world.

The 339th Group sent up four Mustangs to a flight, four flights to a squadron, three squadrons to the group. The normal group complement was thus forty-eight P-51s. The lead squadron flew above and out in front of the bombers, with one squadron on the right, another to the left. The routine was to fly past the Forts or Liberators, make a 180-degree turn, and keep circling until the gasoline gave out.

Billy Behrend had offered his opinion on the Mustang to Bert a few nights earlier: "She's as honest as the day is long and hasn't a mean bone in her beautiful body." After about thirty hours of flight, Bert not only agreed but added a few comments next time they shared a beer: "The general flight characteristics are beautiful. Tar Heel makes me look much better than my level of skill." Both pilots had heard veteran fighter pilots swear their faith in the ability of the Mustang to make them feel like the hunter and not the hunted. The fine record of kills versus losses of the P-51 was difficult *not* to admire.

Bert was sorry that Jim Starnes had left for a thirty-day "rest and relaxation" leave in the States—he liked the flight leader and knew he could learn much about combat flying from the veteran. But he was happy to borrow—albeit temporarily—Starnes' crackerjack plane Tar Heel. He told Jim he would write to him at his stateside address in Wilmington, North Carolina, to let him know how his plane was doing.

Bert Stiles didn't have the opportunity to fire his guns in anger until his fourth mission on October 28. At 30,000 feet, while flying straight and level with outside temperature at 45 degrees below zero, he heard Lt. Daniell calling. Daniell was leading the element in a flight led by Chester Malarz. A bandit was coming in at six o'clock—directly behind their flight.

Bert pulled his Mustang into a tight turn—and an ME-410 slid under his wing. He thought, how come I'm not *dead?* He could have tapped the German pilot on the head. The enemy was black and had two engines and a single tail. Lt. Palmer, flying opposite wing, took after the ME but the German pilot had split-S'd for the clouds below. The element leader, Lt. Daniell, did a lazy turn to the right and Bert waited for him to break but he didn't. The moment for action had passed quickly.

Bert wrote home that night:

> The Blue Lady was there—my luck held again—he was close enough
> to hit me with a baseball bat. The system is you watch the other guy's
> tail, he watches yours. Nobody watched mine except the Lady to-
> day...funny war.

Bert wrote to Jim Starnes in North Carolina informing his flight leader he was thinking of having Tar Heel's crew chief, Sgt. Gabe Cutri, reverse the seat in his P-51 so he could "cover my own tail." He also asked Starnes to hurry back so he could accompany the flight leader on one of his "Lone Wolf" missions. Starnes had been successful in scoring kills while separated from the remainder of the squadron. While casually put, Bert was dead serious about the suggestion.

On November 1 they slept in. Attendance was required at 10:00 hours for an orientation lecture called "Why we Fight." Of course it was old hat; this sort of thing had been going on since the first week of cadets. But Bert listened—and wrote to his mother about it:

So I listened and sometimes wanted to say something—but I didn't. They are a little late. The time for that was 1935 and 1937 and 1940, and the place for it was 1245 South York and Byers Junior High School and South High School. It is pretty academic and a bit hopeless to be talking about it now.

To everything there is a season, and a time to every purpose under heaven…a time to weep, and a time to laugh; a time to mourn and a time to dance…a time to love and a time to hate…a time of war and a time of peace. That is from *Ecclesiastes* and it is cool and true. Maybe someday soon it will be the time of peace again…and a time for love…. There is love and then there is death…and there is peace. It is like being a little kid again and then growing old in an hour, and then being thrown in the middle. And there are no answers.

On Monday, November 6, he wrote that he had cast an absentee ballot for President Roosevelt, but that he had some misgivings about him. However, he ended the letter:

I expect when tomorrow night comes, probably the boss will still be boss.

Two letters on November 10 gave him great pleasure: a British magazine, *The Field,* printed two short pieces he had written on combat, and *Air Force Magazine* accepted an article. A day later, a third letter came. Maxwell Aley wrote that he would give his beautiful white setter Barry to Bert—as soon as the latter returned from the war. Bert was deeply touched.

On Armistice Day, November 11, Bert led his element for the first time. It was an uneventful flight, but Bert wrote home that he "flew very terrible today."

His letter to Rosemary that night was filled with poignancy:

Maybe there isn't much time…but sometimes there is forever and you slide along through the air coming home and England is out there, a low coast looming up sweet in the haze…. And here am I—in a lovely silver lady—sliding along at 275—going home.

I can't see how any of the past is going to fit into anything. You get the feeling here you are close to big things…and if you ever get a chance to go down a stretch of days without any death in them you will know how to live it up good. You've got to handle it true or it is going to go to hell in a bad way….

They are playing *Sweet and Lovely*…and it is a sad night and there is everything in the night…every wish, every dream, every half-hoped prayer and there is the promise of death…for somebody tomorrow...for some of these kids...it makes it so damned ugly that I don't see how it could ever straighten out...this war is all the hell and all the horror and all the hate in the minds of all the people.

Gordon Beach, Bert's former ball gunner, had visited B.W. and Elizabeth Stiles in Denver. His parents wrote that they liked the shy flyer. Bert wrote back that Beach was "just about the finest guy who ever lived in a ball turret."

He flew his tenth mission on November 18 and strafed a small town just across the Rhine. He also found a moving train in his sights, along with an old mine and some warehouses. "We just flew over the tops of spruces," he wrote home, "and moaned down in and squeezed the triggers and tried to keep from running into each other. It was a very tense little shooting match."

Their fighter group lost two planes that day.

He also wrote:

There is a rabbit who lives on the field and sometimes I chase him around in my airplane just to give him some exercise.

And once again he penned some deep thoughts to Rosemary:

With you and me, Bo, it never added up, did it? And it'll never be good like that again. It'll have to be new and different if it is going to be anything at all. I seem to be losing touch with everything I ever had...and the future isn't very clear...and there is always the gentle thought that there may be not be any future....

On Tuesday, November 21, Thanksgiving Week, he flew another strafing mission. Returning at dusk, he was too tired to approach his typewriter. But the following morning, a day of ominous clouds and no flying, he recorded the experience in a letter to his parents in Denver:

The Lady is still flying on my wing every day. Yesterday we went down through the clouds at about 3,000 feet into a town and they opened up everything at us. So we went back up through the clouds— and almost rammed into the Luftwaffe. There were at least forty planes in three big gaggles. We tagged into one group and were closing on them when these other jokers swung into position. So we turned and tacked onto *them*. Then a third outfit tagged onto *us*, and I saw those old 20 millimeters bursting around us.

I did three of the fastest, sloppiest rolls into the nearest cloud and threw everything to the firewall, and stayed in that cloud going about 400, headed for home. And after awhile I came out of the clouds and flew right on top of them into Belgium, really moaning...I landed in Belgium for a deep breath or two and some chow, and came on home.

Three from our squadron got it...all those good guys gone...so this is an empty barracks tonight. Tomorrow is Thanksgiving and I hope it rains like mad. Serenade, my parents...

Earlier, after landing, he had checked in at Operations to see if Billy Behrend had returned. Billy was in a different squadron and had gone strafing in another sector. He hadn't returned. Bert shed his flight clothes, had two shots of bourbon and went up to the control tower to wait for him.

Come on back, Billy, he thought. You shouldn't be one of those who crashes and burns and is forgotten forever in the minds of men and maids. Come on back...

Bert watched each Mustang enter the pattern, lower wheels and flaps, and come in on final approach. No Billy. Goddamn it, Behrend, get your butt back to base. That's an order.

And then there he was, making a perfect landing, taxiing in with alacrity. Bert took the tower stairs three at a time and was out at Billy's plane while the pilot was still talking with his crew chief.

They sat in the de-briefing room, shot glasses in hand.

"I thought you were a goner, Bill."

"Not me, Bert. Got a wife ordered me back safe. And Billie, too." Behrend had named his P-51 after his infant daughter, Billie.

They talked about Behrend's detached service coming up. He would be ferrying 51s and other fighter aircraft back and forth between the Continent and England. It would be a twenty-day stint.

"I'll miss you, Billy. Who's going to keep me safe and happy in these infernal machines?"

"You're doing just fine, Bert."

"Listen, tell me something, friend. Are you scared up there?"

Bill Behrend looked across the table and settled a level gaze at Stiles. "Damn right I am. Anyone who says they aren't is a colossal liar."

"Well, I won't lie. I'm scared, too. Most of the time. I saw Rogers go in today. Billy—I think he flew right into the ground."

"A quick death is a good one, some philosopher said."

Bert studied his friend. "No death is a good one. Death is forever. It only happens once. And it should be given the dignity it deserves."

Billy gulped his shot. "Let's not talk about death. Against regulations. Let's go huntin' strawberries again."

Thanksgiving Dinner featured real turkey, mashed potatoes, and canned cranberry sauce. There had been no mission. After the special dinner, Bert sat on his bed and wrote to his old friend and sometime sweetheart Kay Bisenius. Earlier, he had written to her about meeting Kattie Regan, recounting their adventures together. Now, he was much more serious:

> This is a rugged life and I'm not sure I'm cut out for it. But I can't complain—I always wanted P-51s and now I have them. I just can't get over the beauty of the plane—it has a sort of Godlike beauty, eternal and mystical.
>
> I almost had it a couple of times and I've got to get on the ball...and soon. With my Lady up there in my corner, perhaps I'll make it...and perhaps I won't. From high in the blue, Kay, the world appears a better place—no woes, no dirt, no homeless, no killing wars. When I come back, I'll tell you about it....

Still not written-out, still thinking of old friends, Bert wrote a few lines to Rosemary:

> There is no sense talking about anything that is further than ten hours away...because, Bo, the war is down in the short rows now and these SOBs are throwing everything in the book...we are going down on the deck practically every day...and every day we go down some good guy gets it. So it is Thanksgiving, cool and deep in the mud of England. It is a day to give thanks. It is sort of queer and beautiful to be alive.

The following day there was still no flying—the weather had closed in again. After lazing around the base, bored, he turned once again to his personal therapy: a letter home. There was something he needed to tell his mother:

> Mom, your honesty and integrity is something that has always amazed me...it seems so easy for you, so routine. What I know is that it gives me a shockproof base that plenty of guys don't have. The way I figure it, if I did half as straight a job here as you do...as you have been doing for as long as I could sit up and eat on my own, then I'd be doing better than I am. So take it easy, and I'm glad you're there to come home to....

On Sunday, November 26, Bert and thirty-two other pilots from the 339th Fighter Group were assigned for escort duty to Hanover. They were to accompany several groups of B-17s.

Bert was flying Tar Heel and leading the second element with a call sign of White Three. Captain Archie Tower was leading the squadron. .

Since taking over Jim Starnes' plane, Bert had gotten to know and like Gabriel Cutri. The Sergeant was the crew chief for Tar Heel and knew the Mustang inside out. Starnes had thought so highly of Cutri that before he left for the States, he had asked the chief whether he thought it was okay to loan out Tar Heel for a month—to a Lieutenant Stiles.

As he usually did, Bert stopped for a chat with Cutri to ask if the Chief had any comments about his airplane. Sergeant Cutri mentioned a few things—little things—but Bert didn't appear to be paying much attention. Cutri thought he looked tired and preoccupied.

"Lieutenant Stiles," he said, suddenly. "you look like you could use a rest. Why don't you stand down today?" Gabe Cutri was never one to mince words.

Bert looked at him curiously. "Funny you should say that, Gabe," he said. "I had that same thought this morning myself—as I stood in front of the mirror."

"You know, Lieutenant, I have the authority to pull this plane off flying status. Maybe I should do just that."

The two men looked hard at each other for several seconds.

"You said the airplane's all right," Bert said, finally. "So forget it, Gabe. The plane's ready...and so am I. Now, I'm going *flying*, Chief!".

Their squadron climbed through scattered clouds, across the North Sea, overflying portions of France and Belgium—into the heart of industrial Germany.

After his squadron had completed the rendezvous with the Fortress group, Bert, as an element leader, began a throttle reduction. Even at 210 miles per hour they were still overtaking the B-17s. As they cruised past, Bert stared at the cockpit of the lead Fortress.

"Hello there, Big Friend," he said aloud. "There but for the grace of God go I—" He smiled as he moved past fast. "May your own Lady of the Skies fly with you today."

They flew well past the Fortresses, swung a tight turn, and bore down on them again, this time from the front. What a great feeling flying is, Bert thought: seeing the world from a P-51, the finest ship aflying. He was swept with nostalgic memories of days—of years—roaming and dreaming, gazing starward, seeking out his Blue Lady. *Oh, God, what a wonderful thing life is…to live and breathe and seek and wonder and love and—*

"Bandits at eleven o'clock high," Bert's headset, turned up high, blasted his eardrums. "Here they come—FWs—a million of them." His squadron leader, Captain Tower, was already in a climbing turn. "Go get 'em on your own—and good hunting!"

Bert rammed his throttle forward, banked steeply to the right and went into a climbing turn. He looked around rather wildly to see where the action was. Almost immediately he spotted a gaggle of FWs bearing down on the B-17s and saw that their noses were blinking fire. The Fortresses were throwing everything they had at the Germans and Bert felt a flash of pride in his former boxcar mates. Then he went after them.

Mixing with a diving flight of 190s, he let go a burst of fire as one of them came briefly within his line of fire. He could see no hit. An instant later, he heard and felt a drumming behind him—he thought it sounded like pebbles raining hard on a beer barrel he was hiding under. Hey, he thought, guess I've collected a few holes.

A moment later, Bert saw his chance. One of the Focke-Wulfs was departing the scene, in a steep dive. Bert took after him, full tilt. With the Mustang's superior speed and maneuverability he picked up a piece of his tail. The German fighter began a bank to the right and Bert let him have a full burst.

He watched the FW take some hits, and, with amazement, saw the fighter wobble, smoke, then belch fire, and finally go streaming off in a nearly vertical dive.

"Who—ee-ee-ee," he yelled aloud and snapped a salute to the stricken German pilot. "That was really *something*," he shouted. "So *that's* what it's like to shoot down a plane." Then as he pushed his Mustang into a steep dive, following his enemy down, his mood switched suddenly: the poor son-of-a-bitch, he thought, probably about twenty years old, dead or dying now, and I did it to him. What a lousy war.

Fascinated, he watched his enemy, in a vertical dive now, disappear into some thin clouds. He pushed his own plane into a steeper dive: he *had* to see him go in. It was like watching the climax of *Dawn Patrol*, he thought wildly, at the old Washington Park Theater. He *couldn't* leave now.

Still in a dive, trying to pick up his foe's plane, he knew he must be getting relatively low: he could clearly see the green hills of the Third Reich, and a river, and a town off there to the right. Keeping his eyes moving widely, he finally caught sight of the German plane again, streaming fire. Even as he watched, fascinated, it plowed into the ground in a flash of fire and smoke. My enemy is dead, Bert thought, with a strange mixture of triumph and unutterable sadness, long live my enemy.

Instinctively and abruptly, he hauled back on the stick. But with instantly dawning horror, he realized he had allowed himself to get dangerously close to the ground. God, the ground was right on top of him! God...

He only had a moment left, and he knew it, and he accepted it. His thoughts raced: Oh, God, is this how life ends? Is this *it*? But now—I'll meet *You* and love *You*...

And Blue Lady: this is the way it was meant to be, isn't it? You *knew* I would die in the skies I loved so much.... So now I'll meet *you* and join *you* and love *you* and fly away with you into the blue...forever...

And—Mom and Dad...I wanted to be a good son and I *was* part of the time...but I wasn't at times...I'm sorry, I'm sorry...I love you, love you both, so much. And goodbye May and Beth—and Rosemary and Kay and Sleepy and Sam and Green and June and Beach and Sharpe and Kattie and Billy—and all the others I've loved—goodbye...and Serenade...

> With death I will gather all the particles that have become me—and will ease me out into the blue finally—perhaps—to meet my God. I see no reason why a man cannot conceive his very own eternity; and mine, I hope and pray, will be out in the blue. I will be in motion—millions of miles in a long dive—then float—adrift. Eternity will be the gaining of that realm of beauty—the capturing of the thrill of that beauty, that I find up there in the sky....

To a Fallen Friend

(Dedicated to the memory of Bert Stiles)

The Almighty looked down and saw you fall
No longer will you answer the flight line call
Nor hear the mighty Mustang engine roar
Or see the blood and feel the hate of war
You ventured forth on a noble quest
To challenge the Luftwaffe's very best.

The sky was filled with bursting flak
Followed by the fatal Messerschmitt attack
They came spurting fire out of the sun
You were their target, your life was done.
War with its glory, war with its shame,
Wrote your last chapter in smoke and in flame

You flew your final mission without regret
A mission most mortal men will soon forget
But rest in peace you will receive your due,
For the eternal skies are always blue.
Yes, await God's call, again to fly
With an angel squadron in the heavenly sky.

Richard T. Pressey, First Lieutenant
401st Squadron, 91st Bomb Group
Bassingbourn, England, 1944

Epilogue

28 February 1945
Telegram: Washington, D.C.
To Bert W. Stiles—1245 South York St., Denver, Colo

REPORT NOW RECEIVED FROM THE GERMAN GOVERNMENT THROUGH
THE INTERNATIONAL RED CROSS STATES YOUR SON FIRST LIEUTENANT
BERT STILES WHO WAS PREVIOUSLY REPORTED MISSING IN ACTION WAS
KILLED IN ACTION ON TWENTY SIX NOVEMBER IN EUROPEAN AREA THE
SECRETARY OF WAR EXTENDS HIS DEEP SYMPATHY CONFIRMING LETTER
FOLLOWS

J. A. ULIO THE ADJUTANT GENERAL

Bert Stiles was laid to rest in the U.S. military cemetery at Neuville-en-condroz, Belgium. His parents, Elizabeth and Bert W. Stiles, visited him there in the mid 1950s.

Photographic Credits

1. Elizabeth Leffingwell
2. Elizabeth Leffingwell
3. Elizabeth Leffingwell
4. Elizabeth Leffingwell
5. Elizabeth Leffingwell
6. Robert Floyd Cooper
7. Elizabeth Leffingwell
8. Elizabeth Leffingwell
9. Robert Floyd Cooper
10. Robert Floyd Cooper
11. Rosemary Prindle
12. Roland Dickison
13. Steve Simer
14. Kay Beimford
15. Kay Beimford
16. Kay Beimford
17. Dan Bauer
18. Dan Bauer
19. Mike Minnich
20. Dan Bauer
21. Mike Minnich
22. Dan Bauer
23. Sumner Morris
24. John Green
25. Dan Bauer
26. Kathleen Burgy
27. Dan Bauer
28. Robert Floyd Cooper
29. Dan Bauer
30. Mike Minnich
31. Colorado College
32. Jim Fletcher
33. Jim Fletcher
34. Robert Floyd Cooper
35. Robert Floyd Cooper

Selected List of Unpublished Short Stories

"A Co-Pilot's Education" (Education)
"First Mission" (First hand account)
"Portrait of a Guy With Blood on His Hands" (Bombers)
"Portrait of the World From 20,000 Feet" (Bombers)
"Serenade to an Air Medal" (Bombers)
"The Cowboy Goes to Town" (Fiction)
"Dancing Lady" (Fiction—laid in England)
"Dear Mrs. Lefty" (Letter to a friend's mother)
"Death Stands By" (Rangers)
"I'm looking for a Girl" (Fiction)
"It Happened in Pre-Flight" (Flight training)
"Check Pilot" (Flight training)
"Kit Carson the Second" (Bert's father)
"Little Boy Blue" (Skiing)
"A Luck Charm Goes to College" (Rockies and college)
"Maybe This Is It" (Spitfire pilot)
"Moon Boy" (A doctor with the RAF)
"Moonstar Jones" (Mountains; college)
"Somebody Got Left" (Baseball)
"Murder Rides the Ski-ways" (Ghosts on the ski runs)
"On Getting in the Mood" (On moods for writing)
"Portrait of a Commando" (Piccadilly commandos)
"Portrait of a Lonely One" (Pilot on leave in London)
"Portrait of a Sad Sack" (Flight training)
"The Quintessence of Sport" (Sports and skiing)
"Return of Pegasus" (Fantasy)
"River and I and the Fish" (Fishing in England)
"Shining Armor" (Fraternity story)
"Someday I'll be Back" (Boy/girl in Hollywood)
"Education As I See It" (Progressive education)
"Sun Valley Susan" (Romance, skiing)
"To the People Below" (Pilots' ode to the Germans)
"Water Monster" (Adventure in Rockies)
"Wildcatter" (Adventure)
"By This I Live" (Bert's personal philosophy)